Eco-Efficiency, Regulation and Sustainable Business

ESRI STUDIES SERIES ON THE ENVIRONMENT

In April 2000 the Japanese government launched a series of comprehensive, interdisciplinary and international research projects called the 'Millennium Projects' and as part of this initiative the Economic and Social Research Institute (ESRI) of the Cabinet Office of Japan initiated a two year project entitled 'A Study on Sustainable Economic and Social Structures in the 21st Century', which focuses on ageing and environmental problems in the Japanese and international context.

The *ESRI Studies Series on the Environment* provides a forum for the publication of a limited number of books, which are the result of this collaboration, on four main issues: research on solid waste management; the analysis of waste recycling and the conversation of resources and energy; research on the compatibility of environmental protection and macroeconomic policy and the analysis of problems related to climate change. The series is invaluable to students and scholars of environment and ecology as well as consultants and practitioners involved in environmental policymaking.

Titles in the series include:

Firms, Governments and Climate Policy
Incentive-based Policies for Long-term Climate Change
Edited by Carlo Carraro and Christian Egenhofer

Eco-Efficiency, Regulation and Sustainable Business
Towards a Governance Structure for Sustainable Development
Edited by Raimund Bleischwitz and Peter Hennicke

Eco-Efficiency, Regulation and Sustainable Business

Towards a Governance Structure for Sustainable Development

Edited by

Raimund Bleischwitz

Wuppertal Institute for Climate, Environment and Energy, Germany

Peter Hennicke

Wuppertal Institute for Climate, Environment and Energy, Germany

ESRI STUDIES SERIES ON THE ENVIRONMENT

Edward Elgar

Cheltenham, UK • Northampton, MA, USA

Published by
Edward Elgar Publishing Limited
Glensanda House
Montpellier Parade
Cheltenham
Glos GL50 1UA
UK

Edward Elgar Publishing, Inc.
136 West Street
Suite 202
Northampton
Massachusetts 01060
USA

A catalogue record for this book
is available from the British Library

Library of Congress Cataloguing in Publication Data

Eco-efficiency, regulation, and sustainable business : towards a governance structure for sustainable development/edited by Raimund Bleischwitz, Peter Hennicke.
p. cm.—(ESRI studies series on the environment)
1. Sustainable development. 2. Industrial laws and legislation. 3. Environmental policy. 4. Industrial management—Environmental aspects. I. Bleischwitz, Raimund. II. Hennicke, Peter. III. Series

HC79.E5E2163 2004
338.9'27—dc22 2003062356

ISBN 1 84376 687 6

Typeset by Cambrian Typesetters, Frimley, Surrey
Printed and bound in Great Britain by MPG Books Ltd, Bodmin, Cornwall

Contents

Figures

Tables

Boxes

Contributors

Dirk Assmann, formerly Senior Fellow at the Energy Division of Wuppertal Institute, Wuppertal, now at Deutsche Gesellschaft für Technische Zusammenarbeit (GTZ), Eschborn, Germany

Peter Bartelmus, former Director of the Material Flows and Structural Change Division at the Wuppertal Institute, Germany, now retired and living in New York

Raimund Bleischwitz, Head of the Material Flows and Resource Management Research Group at the Wuppertal Institute, Germany and Professor at the Toyota Chair for Industry and Sustainability at the College of Europe, Bruges, Belgium

Stefan Bringezu, Head of the Material Flows and Resource Management Research Group at the Wuppertal Institute, Germany

Manfred Fischedick, Head of the Future Energy and Mobility Structures Research Group at the Wuppertal Institute, Germany

Justus von Geibler, Fellow at the Sustainable Production and Consumption Research Group at the Wuppertal Institute, Germany

Thomas Hanke, Senior Fellow at the Future Energy and Mobility Structures Research Group at the Wuppertal Institute, Germany

Peter Hennicke, President of Wuppertal Institute and Professor of Economics at Wuppertal University, Germany

Michael Kuhndt, Director of Triple-Innova (Consulting), Wuppertal, Associated Fellow at the Wuppertal Institute, Germany and Fellow at the United Nation's Environmental Programme

Sylvia Lorek, former Senior Fellow at Wuppertal Institute, now Vice-President of the Sustainable Europe Research Institute, Vienna, Austria

Rainer Lucas, Senior Fellow at the Material Flows and Resource Management Research Group at the Wuppertal Institute, Germany

Stephan Moll, Senior Fellow at the Material Flows and Resource Management Research Group at the Wuppertal Institute, Germany

Sebastian Nowak, formerly Assistant Fellow at Factor Four Research Desk at the Wuppertal Institute, Germany, now Coordinator for International Relations at the Sapporo International Communication Plaza Foundation, Sapporo, Japan

Eberhard K. Seifert, Senior Fellow at the Wuppertal Institute, Germany

Stefan Thomas, Head of the Energy, Transport and Climate Policy Research Group at the Wuppertal Institute, Germany

Holger Wallbaum, Director of Triple-Innova (Consulting), Wuppertal and Associated Fellow at the Wuppertal Institute, Germany

Ernst U. von Weizsäcker, Member of German Parliament, Head of Committee on the Environment, former President of Wuppertal Institute

Foreword

Ernst U. von Weizsäcker and Peter Hennicke

Ever since mankind pursued wealth, nature was supposed to support this pursuit. Today's focus is still on the creation of goods and services that satisfy human needs, but our view of the environment has changed dramatically. Most societies have become increasingly conscious of the manifold environmental problems caused by human impact. Not long ago, environmental policies mainly consisted of reducing the damages environmental pollution had already caused. Policies focused on problems related to the deposition of garbage, not on the reduction on the garbage-producing side.

With the Earth Summits in Rio de Janeiro (1992) and Johannesburg (2002), people became aware of the necessity to tackle these environmental issues at their roots. While many of the industrialized countries meanwhile were able to overcome their traditional 'end-of-pipe' environmental problems, there is still need to further promote 'front-of-pipe' solutions. Environmental policies are no longer regarded as contradicting economic growth, but are to be brought into harmony with economic goals. Sustainable development means that future generations can benefit from natural resources in the same way as society does today. It has to be the motto for all fields of future policies.

Though the term 'sustainable development' is nowadays being used in many fields, it has yet to be implemented in practical action schemes and valuable methods of measurement. Concrete policies are necessary to turn ecological consciousness into effective ecology-oriented action that ultimately may lead to a wealth-creating recycling-oriented society with lowered resource use.

Germany and Japan share like experiences in the field of economic growth and related environmental issues. The enormous postwar economic growth in the 1950s, 1960s and 1970s brought with it heavy burdens for both countries' environments. It was not before confronting a broad range of environmental concerns (air pollution, deposition of waste, acid rain and so on) that both countries became aware of the environment's fragility. Questions of sustained energy supply arose, and societies realized the scarcity of natural resources. Here and there, the implementation of laws on the protection of environment, as well as other supporting legislations and governmental institutions, came into play fairly soon. Beginning in the 1970s and 1980s, respectively, Japan and Germany steadily established themselves as forerunners in the field of environmental protection. Before long, a legislative framework was built up in both countries in response to increased environmental pressures and a growing public consciousness of related concerns.

With a suffering global economy that is now putting heavy pressure on Germany and Japan, people certainly have become more aware of the instability of wealth. These issues are undoubtedly important future tasks, but they should also be regarded as an opportunity for fostering environmental policies, which do not necessarily contradict further environmental growth. On the contrary, Wuppertal Institute believes in the compatibility of creating real wealth and easing environmental pressure. Here, the concept of eco-efficiency comes into play. This concept addresses the challenge of achieving a sustainable development with benefits on behalf of the ecology as well as the economy. Since it allows environmental protection measures from a market-oriented point of view, it can also mean a gain for enterprises. Eco-efficiency, standing for a better management of the economy with less environmental pressure, therefore represents a promising sustainability approach. It is tested with good success in many firms and products.

In this context, concepts like 'Factor Four' and 'Factor Ten' integrate the normative dimension into eco-efficiency concepts. Having been awarded the prestigious Takeda World Environment Award in 2001 for the 'Factor 4/10' concepts, along with the underlying concept regarding material flows, Wuppertal Institute feels honoured and confirmed even more in the appropriateness of its policy approach and will continue to make every effort to develop further policy concepts.

While eco-efficiency is regarded in Europe as a quite ambitious concept, Japanese pioneers have begun to challenge their European counterparts. Numerous researchers, such as Ryoichi Yamamoto and Hiroshi Komiyama, are developing fascinating visions of the future. Taking into account Germany's and Japan's shared experiences in the fields of economic growth and connected environmental concerns, they should, as two of the world's leading industrialized countries, continue to spearhead the process of ecological modernization.

Many issues, mostly caused by the different sociocultural backgrounds involved, justify in-depth research on sustainability-related policies. Questions include the conditions for technology dissemination and ecological modernization, as well as the role of the state government enabling business and society while safeguarding a frame for stabilization. In this connection, Wuppertal Institute regards the study also as a means of scientific communication, with possible merits both for Germany and for Japan, as well as other nations with an interest in eco-efficiency concepts. Being aware of the difficulties that go along with Europe-based scenarios and their applicability to Japanese sustainability policies, we believe that, by communicating these issues at an international level, we take a useful step towards fostering the horizontal diffusion of different policy concepts, even though their individual approaches might remain imperfect.

It is an honour for Wuppertal Institute to be enabled by the Japanese government to disseminate its findings on environmental policy concepts, not only to European researchers, but to Japan and a wider international audience as well. In this context, the Millennium Collaboration Projects offer an outstanding opportunity to extend the international collaboration on environmental issues and questions related to sustainable development. Germany and Japan have so far been at the forefront of formulating environmental policies: the collaboration projects raise these discussions to a new level that will surely benefit from the synergies provided by the exchange of researchers and opinions across national borders.

Preface

The world at the beginning of the 21st century must place the highest priority on constructing a sustainable socioeconomic system that can cope with the rapid ageing of populations in developed countries and with the limited environmental resources available in both developed and developing countries. At first glance, the problems of ageing and the environment may seem to be quite separate issues. However, they have a common feature: they both deal with intergenerational problems. The essence of the ageing problem is how to find effective ways for a smaller working generation to support a larger, ageing generation. The crux of the environmental problem is to find a feasible way to leave environmental resources to future generations. Moreover, in terms of consumption, slower population growth may slow consumption and help environmental problems. On the other hand, a rapidly ageing society may use more energy-intensive technology to compensate for the inevitable labour shortage, and deteriorate the natural environment by doing so.

Today, these concerns are highly applicable in Japan. The pressure created by the rapid ageing of the Japanese population is becoming acute; Japan must construct a sustainable society that does not create intergenerational inequity or deteriorate the public welfare. At the same time, Japan cannot deplete its environmental resources and energy, which would leave future generations with an unbearably heavy burden.

The government of Japan has recognized the vital importance of both problems. To explore and implement solutions for this difficult task, in April 2000 former Prime Minister Keizo Obuchi launched several comprehensive and interdisciplinary research projects that he called the 'Millennium Project'. As a part of these projects, the Economic and Social Research Institute (ESRI), Cabinet Office, Government of Japan, initiated a two-year project entitled 'A Study on Sustainable Economic and Social Structure in the 21st Century' in April 2000. While the Millennium Project covers a wide range of topics and a wide range of disciplines such as natural science and technological innovation, the project conducted by ESRI places major emphasis on social science. While taking into account technological innovation and feasibility, it focuses on ageing and environmental problems. It aims to design a desirable socioeconomic structure under the pressure of an ageing population and environmental constraints by identifying the necessary policy tools to attain stable and sustainable growth.

This project is being implemented with close collaboration among Japanese as well as foreign scholars and research institutes. Besides Japanese scholars and institutes, foreign participants have been involved from, among other countries, the USA, the UK, Norway, Austria, Italy, Australia, Korea and Thailand. In all, there are ten countries and 30 working groups.

In this project, ESRI explores optimal solutions to problems in social science terms. After taking into account the political and social constraints we face, and after alignment and coordination with the results of the studies, it sketches an ideal design and examines the possible direction of future research. This project came to an end in March 2002. It resolved many theoretical and empirical issues, but has created new debates. Twice a year, all the participants in the project, along with invited others, meet to discuss the results of the research. Regrettably, it has not been possible to reproduce the fruitful discussion in the present volume.

Overall, the papers presented in the project were extremely challenging, and covered a wide range of topics. In the near future we strongly hope we will have a chance to discuss the research once more from a common standpoint. The result of this research is published by Edward Elgar Publishing Ltd as part of an ESRI study series, available to policy makers, academics and business people with a keen interest in these subjects. The series on environmental problems covers climate change, sources of energy and technology, and environmental and employment policy. Unfortunately, because of space limitations, we regret that we are able to publish only selected papers from the total research effort. The research papers to be published were selected by the Editorial Board members. We would like to acknowledge the ceaseless efforts of the members of ESRI throughout the project period, especially those of the Department of Administration Affairs. Last but not least, we would like to thank Dymphna Evans from Edward Elgar Publishing.

Yutaka Kosai, President, ESRI

Introduction

This book covers Wuppertal Institute's findings on applied eco-efficiency concepts throughout Europe, with particular emphasis on Europe-based policies on material flows and energy. These findings are based on research, conducted from June 2000 until January 2002, in the context of the collaboration projects initiated by the Economic and Social Research Institute (ESRI), Mitsubishi Research Institute (MRI) and Nomura Research Institute (NRI). This book also contains conclusions regarding any application of the discussed concepts to Japanese sustainable development policies.

Since the beginning of the collaboration projects, four conferences have been held in Japan (Osaka, September 2000, Tokyo, March and September 2001, February 2002). The Wuppertal Institute (WI) itself has gained valuable experience through participating in these conferences. In addition, WI has convened small workshops in Wuppertal for selected experts with knowledge of Japanese policies. We consider these workshops essential for our research.

The publication of the revised and updated edition of our final report (in January 2002) is an additional reward and quite a good opportunity to disseminate Wuppertal Institute's policy analysis to a broader public. It covers a broad review of eco-efficiency concepts as they are in effect in several European countries, including Germany.

At this point we would like once more to thank cordially the Economic and Social Research Institute (ESRI), Mitsubishi Research Institute (MRI) and Nomura Research Institute (NRI) for entrusting WI with this study.

We are greatly indebted to all those who were engaged in the discussion of this book, and who, through their comments as well as constructive criticism, certainly contributed to its successful emergence. Since an uncountable number of people have been involved, we are able to name but a few of them: Otto Linher (European Commission), Jan Dirk Seiler (WI visiting researcher at IGES, Kobe), Hiroko Kudo (Waseda University), Georg Schmidt (German Embassy, Tokyo), Leo Schrattenholzer (IIASA), Hans Vos (EEA), Nobukazu Hayashi (chairman of the Duesseldorf-based consulting group M.I.K.), Uwe Kerkmann (chairman of the German–Japanese Economic Council), Nicole Zingsheim (Bonn University), Daijo Tsunoda (German Environment Industry Office, Tokyo), Atsushi Inaba (Tokyo), Morio Kuninori (Development Bank of Japan), Kazuaki Iwata (City of Kitakyushu), Yuchi Moriguchi (National Institute for Environmental Studies, Tokyo), Kazuo Matsushita (Institute for

Global Environmental Strategies, Tokyo), Karl Baeuerle (Managing Director, IKOS), Robert Horres (Bonn University), Werner Pascha (Duisburg University) and Wilhelm Meemken (Ecos Consult, Osnabrueck). Jackie Sairawan and Dorothea Frinker did excellent language editing and formatting work. Sebastian Nowak was most valuable in providing additional Japanese skills as well as in coordination tasks, together with Bettina Bahn-Walkowiak, for WI's study group. Last but not least, our thanks go to Carlo Carraro, Frank Convery and Christian Egenhofer.

Raimund Bleischwitz
Peter Hennicke

1. Translating sustainable development into practice: a 'patchwork' of some new concepts and an introduction to material flows analysis

Peter Bartelmus, Stephan Moll, Stefan Bringezu, Sebastian Nowak and Raimund Bleischwitz

This chapter introduces briefly the paradigm of sustainable development. With sustainable development, new concepts going beyond traditional 'pollution prevention' policies and 'end-of-pipe' measures were introduced during the early 1990s. Those concepts widely overlap each other, partly still under development and still have to be fully integrated into policy, markets and society. The 'patchwork' of concepts (which is also presented in this chapter) is to be seen in conjunction with industrial transformation as a whole. It is the main thesis of the book that these emerging concepts have consequences for both policy makers and business makers. They bring along a new kind of technological progress, which requires a new thinking about incentives from a regulatory perspective. This is mainly because the new technological progress is closely related to markets and business opportunities, not only to negative externalities. In proving the thesis, the book will lay down these new concepts and analyse technological progress and regulatory policies in the following chapters.

1.1 CONCEPTS FOR SUSTAINABLE DEVELOPMENT: AN OVERVIEW

Sustainable Development

The term 'sustainable development' was introduced by the so-called Brundtland Commission, a working group chaired by the former Norwegian Head of State, Gro Harlem Brundland, which prepared the UNCSD conference in Rio de Janeiro. According to the definition of the Brundtland report (WCED, 1987: 43), sustainable development is a 'development that meets the needs of the present without compromising the ability of future generations to meet their own needs'.

The paradigmatic term significantly covers all the Rio documents adopted by the world community. Since 1992, sustainable development has been laying the basis for a new leitmotiv in environmental policies and beyond. Two major conceptual elements can be associated with sustainable development (Sachs *et al.*, 1998: 9–11). The first is *the four pillars of sustainable development*. Sustainable development clearly goes beyond traditional environmental policy. It entails recognition that environmental problems cannot be considered in isolation from economic, social and also institutional aspects, since these are inextricably interlinked. The holistic approach is to reconcile economic, social, environmental and institutional development. The second major element is the *equity and global perspective*. Sustainable development encompasses normative implications, in particular the intragenerational equity between developed and developing countries and the intergenerational equity between present and future generations. By this, it also emphasizes the global perspective. Everyone has the same right to an intact global environment. This sheds light on the current per capita resource use pattern of developed or industrialized economies, which are not transferable to developing economies. Current consumption and production patterns in industrialized economies are not appropriate to serve as a global model.

The definition of sustainable development and sustainability, respectively, is rather loose and open. The Brundtland definition, for instance, fails to specify what human needs are, omits to clarify the time frame for the analysis of future generations' needs and does not even mention the environment as the current key concern in sustainability (Bartelmus *et al.*, 2000). There is no consensus about or clear perception of *the* 'sustainable model' (one might also see it as a modified comeback of the ideal of 'human rights'). Concrete translation into action clearly depends on societal discursive processes about the meaning of sustainable development, and the meaning might be changing as a result of sociocultural value changes. In our view, sustainable development is the equitable growth of current and future world population's *welfare* respecting the natural (physical) carrying capacities of the Earth.

Maybe one of the most significant features which makes a difference to traditional environmental policies is that of acknowledging the need for a structural change of economic activities, that is, sustainable production and consumption patterns. Environmental policy no longer means repairing the damages of economic activities; rather, it means changing economic activities so as to avoid environmental damages. 'Progress towards sustainability and improved environmental quality will come mostly from better economic policies, as influenced by environmental objectives' (European Environment Agency (EEA), 1999: 4). Therefore the European Union and its member states have committed themselves to integrating environmental concerns and sustainability into all their policies. The precautionary principle is a rational basis for these efforts.

In spite of its vague definition, at least for the ecological dimension of sustainable development, four basic rules for sustainability have been developed and widely accepted (Enquête Kommission, 1997: 16; Sachs *et al.*, 1998: 12–13):

1. The depletion rates of renewable resources should not exceed their renewal rates. This is tantamount to the demand to preserve the ecology's efficiency, that is (at least) to safeguard the ecological real capital as defined in terms of its functions.
2. Consumption of non-renewable resources should be limited to levels at which they can be replaced by physically or functionally equivalent renewable resources or at which consumption can be offset by increasing the productivity of renewable or non-renewable resources.
3. Disposal of substances into the environment should be oriented towards the maximum absorption capacity of environmental media, taking into consideration all their functions, not least their 'hidden' and more sensitive regulating functions.
4. There must be a balanced ratio between the time scale of man-made outputs to, or interventions in, the environment and the time scale of the natural processes which are relevant for the reaction capacity of the environment.

A fifth rule can be added which addresses human health (Bleischwitz and Weizsäcker, 2000: 11): damages and irresponsible risks to human health resulting from human activities are to be avoided.

However, these principles are still faced with some basic methodological limitations, one of which is the uncertainty and limited knowledge about interrelationships of anthropogenic and natural material flows. There are a number of concepts and strategies, introduced briefly in the following sections, which are trying to make sustainable development clearer and more operational. They can also be seen as attempts to meet the challenge of moving towards a transformation of current production and consumption patterns.

Environmental space: carrying capacity

The conceptual carrying capacity term expresses the fact that the global ecosystem has its physical limits and implies that human activities should respect these. Carrying capacity refers to the limited ability of ecosystems (the

Earth) to bear environmental load without significant damage (the threshold is the *critical load*). A parallel concept exists for humans or biota: thresholds of harm.

In practice, it may be impossible to define the carrying capacities of some ecosystems (such as the Earth's atmosphere or regional water systems), but it is certainly impossible to define a global carrying capacity, one for the Earth as a whole. A common argument is that policy makers can hardly wait until there are scientifically defined carrying capacities.

The concept of environmental space 'reflects that, at any given point in time, there are limits to the amount of environmental pressure that the Earth's ecosystem can handle without irreversible damage to these systems or to life support processes that they enable' (Hille, 1998). 'Environmental space similarly means the space available to *humanity as a whole* for utilisation of stocks and sinks' (Hille, 1998). In short, environmental space refers to 'the maximum amounts of natural resources that we can use sustainably and without violating global equity' (Hille, 1998).

The recognition and acknowledgment of global natural limits, carrying capacities, leads to the question of how this limited global environmental space is to be allocated between regions and generations. With relation to the normative paradigm of sustainable development, the answer is to aim for an equal distribution in time and space (see Figure 1.1). To summarize, the per capita environmental space of Japan is for most of the variables above the global reference value (with the exception of N-fertilizer and timber use). Depending on the variable, the reduction factor required to achieve the global reference value varies between factor 1.7 and 17.9. For CO_2 emissions and energy supply, the Japanese per capita status quo is in the same order of magnitude as Europe and significantly below the US levels. For some non-renewable materials (cement, iron, aluminium, copper) it is higher than the US levels.

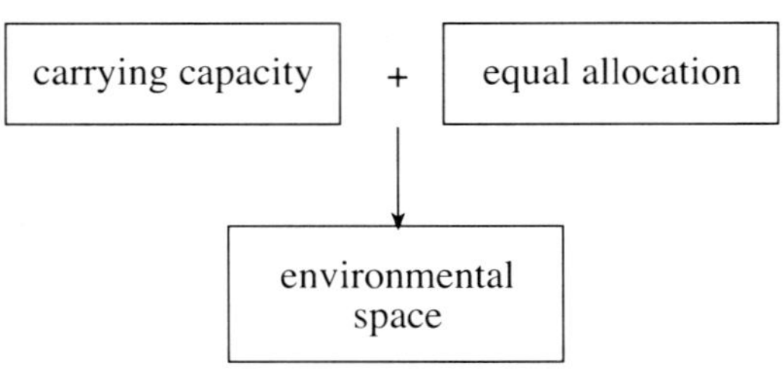

Figure 1.1 Carrying capacity, equal allocation, environmental space

BOX 1.1 ENVIRONMENTAL SPACE

The global amount of environmental space has been quantified for some major resources. Assuming a fair, that is, equal, distribution world-wide, this global environmental space can be translated to a per capita share (simply by dividing the global environmental space of a given resource by the world population). By multiplying again this per capita share by a nation's population one tentatively arrives at the environmental space share of a nation. The global per capita environmental space for several pollutants and resources (CO_2, energy, raw materials) is shown in the second column of the following table. Some preliminary estimates for Japan, Europe and the USA are also given in columns 3–5.

Several pollutants and resources (raw materials, land use, water use)	Global per capita environmental space	Japan	Europe	United States
CO_2 emissions (tonnes per capita)	1.7 *	9.8	8.2	21.2
Primary energy supply (GJ per capita):	60 *	171	159	340
Fossil	25 *	137	126	295
Nuclear	0 *	28	25	27
Renewable	35 *	6	8	17
Non-renewable materials (kg per capita):				
Cement	80 *	677	303–736	288
Iron	36 *	645	16–6414	187
Aluminium	1.2 *	17	19	11
Chlorine	3.2 **	–	7–46	4
Copper	0.75 **	11.1	9.2	8.1
Lead	0.39 **	3.0	5.3	3.9
Nitrogen fertilizer	5.5 **	3.8	25.9	42.3
Phosphorous fertilizer	2.6 **	4.5	9.2	14.8
Timber use (m^3 per capita)	0.56 *	0.28	0.77	1.81

Notes:
* See J.H. Spangenberg (ed.) (1996), 'Towards Sustainable Europe: A Study from the Wuppertal Institute for Friends of the Earth Europe', 2nd revised version, Wuppertal, p.12.
** See J.H. Spangenberg (1995), Ein zukunftsfähiges Europa – Towards Sustainable Europe', Wuppertal Papers no. 42.

Sources:
EEA/Eurostat (1998), Europe's Environment: Statistical Compendium for the Second Assessment, Luxembourg: European Communities, International Energy Agency/OECD (1999), Energy Balances of OECD Countries 1996–1997, Paris: United Nations (1994), Industrial Commodity Statistics Yearbook Production and Consumption Statistics, New York: UN: pp. 931–2. Metallgesellschaften AG/World Bureau of Metal Statistics (1994), Metal Statistics 1983–1993, Frankfurt; FAO, http://apps.fao.org.
CO_2, 1995, EEA (1998); Primary energy supply, 1997, IEA (1999); Cement, 1991, apparent consumption, UN (1994); Iron, 1992, production, UN (1994); Aluminium, 1993, consumption, Metallgesellschaft AG (1994); chlorine, 1991, apparent consumption, UN (1994); copper, 1993, consumption, Metallgesellschaft AG (1994); Lead, 1993, consumption, Metallgesellschaft AG (1994); nitrogen fertilizer, 1998, consumption (FAO); phosphorous fertilizer, 1998, consumption (FAO); Timber-use (in m^3); 1998, consumption (FAO).

Industrial metabolism

Industrial metabolism is an analytical concept based on the physical laws of thermodynamics, particularly the conservation of matter and energy (Ayres, 1989; Ayres and Simonis, 1994). The concept is based on an environment–society model (see Figure 1.2) where the latter is embedded in the former and connected with the surrounding environment via material and energy flows (Georgescu-Roegen, 1971; Daly, 1991, 1996; Strassert, 1993).

An industrial, societal or economic system can be characterized by its physical metabolism: the extraction of raw materials, their transformation into economic goods and services and the final release of those materials back to the environment. All of those material transformation processes are fuelled by energy. Quantity and quality of the material and energy throughput, the industrial metabolism, is subject to discussion on how to manage the material and energy flows in a sustainable way.

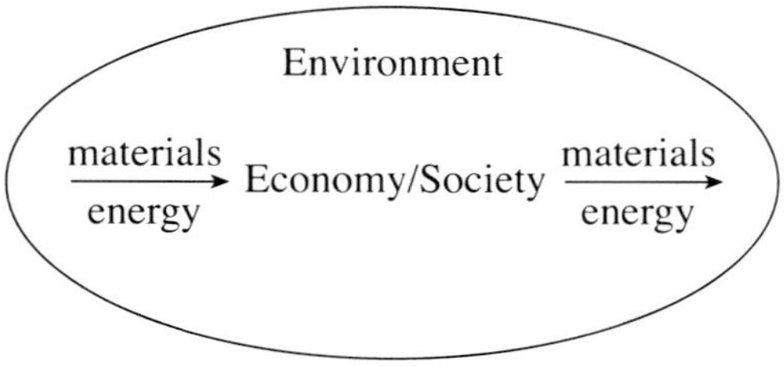

Source: Adapted from Allenby (1999).

Figure 1.2 Industrial metabolism

Industrial ecology

Industrial ecology is closely related to the previously introduced industrial metabolism. It aims at being an objective scientific discipline rather than a normative concept. However, stated to be the 'science of sustainability', it certainly also encompasses normative elements. Industrial ecology mainly pursues a reconciled coevolution of natural and industrial (human) systems based on widely objective information about the physical performance of both systems and their interrelations. It is defined as follows (see Graedel and Allenby, 1995; Allenby, 1999).

Industrial ecology is the means by which humanity can deliberately and rationally approach and maintain a desirable carrying capacity, given continued economic, cultural and technological evolution. The concept requires that an industrial system be viewed not in isolation from its surrounding systems, but in concert with them. It is a systems view in which one seeks to optimize the total materials cycle from virgin materials, to finished material, to component, to product, to obsolete product, and to ultimate disposal. Factors to be optimized include resources, energy and capital.

The concept of industrial ecology can be illustrated by considering three different models of systems with regard to their material and energy regimes (Allenby, 1999, see also Figure 1.3). Type I characterizes a linear system where virgin materials enter the system, are used once and are then disposed of as waste. The more complex Type II system has developed internal cycling loops, and internal reuse of materials can become quite significant.

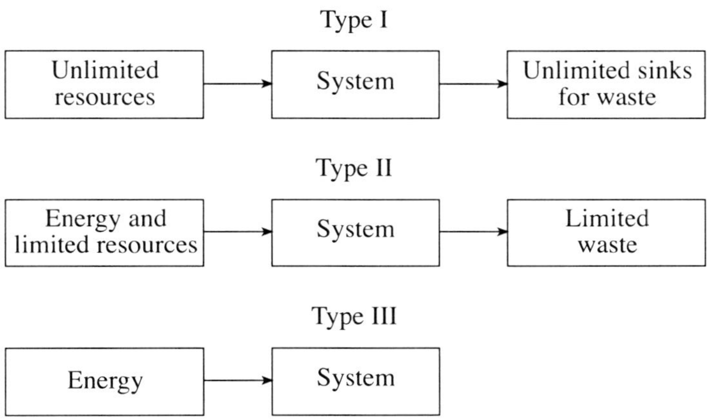

Source: Adapted from Allenby (1999).

Figure 1.3 Industrial ecology

Accordingly, flows of material into, and waste out of, the system are diminished. The Type III system is one in which full material cyclicity has been achieved and only energy input is needed.

The Natural Step

The Natural Step (TNS) is another promising concept for realizing sustainable development.[1] In addition to concepts such as 'zero emissions', this concept has also become popular in Japan. The Natural Step is an international non-profit non-governmental organization (NGO) with offices in different countries (for example Sweden, New Zealand and Japan) that was established to foster the dialogue between scientists and decision makers in business and public policy. Main objectives of TNS are the following:

- to identify overarching principle levels of strategic planning towards sustainable development that can be agreed upon;
- to develop a framework, based upon such principles, for planning that can serve as a shared mental model, or language, for sustainable development;
- to support the implementation of the framework in various kinds of firms and organizations; and
- to study the actual results of this implementation.

To transfer these findings into a concrete decision-making scheme, TNS set up The Natural Step Framework (TNSF). Its specific design allows qualitative problem analysis and community building, as well as the development of investment programmes in business corporations and municipalities. The primary focus is on a comprehensive definition of the targets to be reached. Resulting from this target setting, TNS therefore has developed a framework of complementary, non-overlapping conditions for ecological sustainability (dematerialization, substitutions of material) and social sustainability (for example the health aspect of pollutions) also referred to as the four system conditions.

The actions necessary to move society in the direction of sustainability should be fostered through a set of principles for the process. Since ecological sustainability has to be brought in parallel with improvements in social and economic performance, investments should be selected by a number of essential principles, among which backcasting methodologies form a major element. These methodologies describe the starting point for strategic planning, which is an envisioned and well-defined successful future outcome of the planning. The strategic processes and action schemes that are necessary to realize sustainability are then designed on the basis of this outcome. It therefore seems important to limit the influence of today's trends (customers' preferences) to aspects such as the pace and the initial scale of the transition, not the direction.

This essential planning methodology is especially being used when the system is complex and when current trends, actions and planning are part of the problem. Although often omitted in previous sustainability efforts, it is important to have such an informed vision of one's goal in order to deal strategically with potential trade-offs from different decisions. Nevertheless one may conclude that this tool should be complemented by methodologies of forecasting, that is the recognition of current problems and trends in planning and their various costs and benefits.

Additionally, other aspects of the model depend on tools developed by others, including more quantitative assessments, such as of the objective of meeting the above-mentioned system conditions, but also on tools to monitor the transition (for example performance indicators or management tools like ISO 14001).

Dematerialization and detoxification

Referring to sustainable development and the concept of industrial metabolism, the strategy of dematerialization aims at reducing quantitatively the material throughput of economic systems (Hinterberger and Schmidt-Bleek, 1999). The precautionary rationale is that reducing the material throughput automatically reduces the material outputs (releases of pollutants, wastes and so on) as well as resource extractions harmful to the environment.

Dematerialization implies a more efficient use of the natural resources fed into the economic system through, for instance, improved re-use and recycling of materials. It thus seems superior to any known waste strategy. Dematerialization is the complementary strategy to detoxification, which focuses on the quality of the industrial metabolism, that is on material flows harmful to the environment. The detoxification strategy refers to the mitigation and the releases of critical substances to the environment by pollution control.

Eco-efficiency, resource productivity and Factor X

The concepts or strategies of eco-efficiency, resource productivity and Factor X are closely interlinked. They express the idea of getting more service or welfare from less nature. Whereas eco-efficiency relates to natural resources in a broad sense (natural resource inputs and all kind of output such as emissions and wastes), the term 'resource productivity' relates more narrowly to resource inputs only (land, energy, materials). 'Factor X' stands for both Factor 4 (introduced by Weizsäcker *et al.*, 1997) and Factor 10 (introduced by Schmidt-Bleek, 1994). Factors 4 and 10 are also used as strategic goals.

Factor 4 means the concept of doubling wealth while halving the resource consumption which results in a quadruplication of resource efficiency. It is connected with the names of Weizsäcker, Lovins and Lovins and the Club of Rome who developed this idea in the book *Factor 4* first published in 1995. The Factor 10 concept dates from Schmidt-Bleek (1994) who argues that even a tenfold increase of resource efficiency is technically feasible. Factor X concepts all refer to the idea of decoupling wealth from resource use.

Eco-efficiency has been defined as 'a concept and *strategy* enabling sufficient de-linking of the "*use of nature*" from economic activity needed to meet human needs (*welfare*) to allow it to remain within carrying capacities; and to permit equitable access and use of the environment[2] by current and future generations' (emphasis in original) (EEA, 1999: 4). Eco-efficiency, hence, aims at a development allowing an increase of welfare for all whilst the use of nature is decreasing. This has also been called 'de-linking welfare from use of nature'. Eco-efficiency is perceived as an indispensable strategy towards sustainability: 'It is in this light that the objective of sustainability, so far as industrialized countries are concerned, can be reformulated as the capability of creating human welfare with an ever diminishing amount of natural resources' (Sachs, 1999: 176).

Bleischwitz (2002b) explores the cognitive and institutional dimensions of eco-efficiency. In a formal way, eco-efficiency is a ratio. It can be monitored through two generic indicators: eco-intensity and its inverse, eco-productivity (see Box 1.2). On a conceptual level, the term 'resource productivity' is commonly used synonymously with 'eco-efficiency'. In a formal way, it represents an eco-productivity ratio using primary raw material inputs indicators to operationalize 'use of nature'.

The term 'productivity' is rather used by economists, since productivity is a commonly and well-established concept in economic theories and analyses (for example labour productivity, capital productivity, see Bleischwitz, 2001). The term 'intensity' tends to be preferred by (environmental and energy) engineers.

According to Bringezu (1997a: 81) and Ayres and Ayres (2002:8) there are four basic strategies for raising the productivity of material resources:

1. *Service* orientation is the function or service which is to be provided, rather than a certain type of hardware. For instance, bright rooms with convenient temperature are required rather than certain bulbs or radiators; or cool compartments for kitchens rather than refrigerators; these functions can be provided by technologically different means (for example highly energy-efficient buildings plus adequate lighting and heating systems, or a resource-efficient cooling chamber). The functional

BOX 1.2 THE TWO GENERIC ECO-EFFICIENCY RATIOS

Eco-intensity is an indicator for the use of nature (materials + energy + pollution) per unit of welfare output. The sustainable objective is to decrease the eco-intensity over time in order to achieve delinking, so that this ratio decreases in the 'right' direction.

$$\text{use of nature} = \frac{\text{use of nature}}{\text{welfare}} \times \text{welfare}$$

Eco-productivity is an indicator for the welfare output (for example value added) per unit of use of nature (materials + energy + pollution). This ratio increases in the 'right' direction.

$$\text{welfare} = \frac{\text{welfare}}{\text{use of nature}} \times \text{use of nature}$$

orientation provides engineers and designers with more options for resource-efficient design.

2. *Reduction of resource requirements from cradle to grave*: focusing only on the dematerialization of a certain product (such as lightweight cars) may lead to counterproductive effects when other processes in the production chain require more primary materials or energy.
3. *Shift to renewable energy*: a stepwise but continuous shift to renewable energy resources is a precondition for sustainability; renewable energy sources should be preferred with high materials resource efficiency.
4. *Repair, re-use, remanufacturing and recycling*: reducing the need for virgin materials and, indirectly, all of the environmental damage and energy consumption associated with the extraction and processing of virgin materials, including their toxic by-products.

The concept or strategy of eco-efficiency attracted particular attention in the business sector (see Chapter 2). It was the Business Council for Sustainable Development which introduced the concept for the first time (BCSD, 1993; WBCSD, 1998) and contributed to its wide dissemination world-wide. On the macro level, it is closely related to the 'De-linking' issue (see below).

De-linking welfare/GDP from use of nature

As already mentioned in the previous section, eco-efficiency at the level of national economies means de-linking of 'welfare' and 'use of nature' over time. This de-linking can be monitored by looking at the co-development of welfare indicators and selected environmental indicators (representing use of nature).

A few words should be said on welfare indicators and the relation between welfare and economic development. Commonly, the Gross Domestic Product (GDP) is the indicator used as a surrogate for measures of welfare or well-being. The GDP in a narrow sense, however, is a measure of the level and value of all economic activities within a national economy in one year. Hence, GDP is not a real indicator for welfare or well-being and has often been criticized. The development and establishment of an appropriate measure for welfare or well-being has still not been solved, though some alternative indicators have been introduced, such as the Index of Sustainable Economic Welfare (ISEW) (Jackson and Marks, 1999) or the Human Development Index, HDI (UNDP, 1997). Some studies on such alternative welfare measures have observed a 'de-linking of welfare from economic growth' (for example Jackson and Marks), implying that in spite of economic growth there is no increase in 'well-being'.

Owing to the lack of an appropriate measure for welfare, the GDP is commonly used to monitor the de-linking of welfare and use of nature – though, correctly speaking, one would have to decompose this relationship into two distinct components: the 'welfare intensity of GDP' and 'nature productivity' (see Figure 1.4).

Until the mid-1970s, the growth of GDP in industrialized economies was closely linked to the use of nature: using natural sources like energy and raw materials but also using nature as a sink for emissions, waste and so on. Since the 1980s, the use of nature has been more or less constant whilst welfare in terms of GDP has been growing. This has been called 'relative de-linking'. Normatively, however, an *absolute* reduction of use of nature is needed in industrialized economies, since the per capita use of nature in these economies is at an unsustainable level. An absolute reduction of use of nature while economy or welfare is growing has been called 'absolute de-linking'.

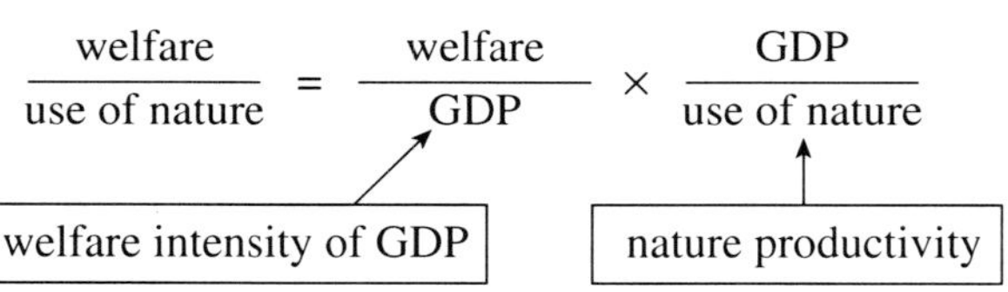

Figure 1.4 Welfare intensity of GDP and nature productivity

BOX 1.3 DE-LINKING OF GDP AND SOME ENVIRONMENTAL INDICATORS IN JAPAN

In Japan only some of the environmental indicators have de-linked absolutely from economic growth in terms of GDP, namely waste and SO_x emissions. Other environmental pressures have been kept fairly constant (NO_x and VOC emissions) or have been increasing slightly (CO_2 and direct material inputs). This can be called relative de-linking since their growth rates kept significantly below economic growth.

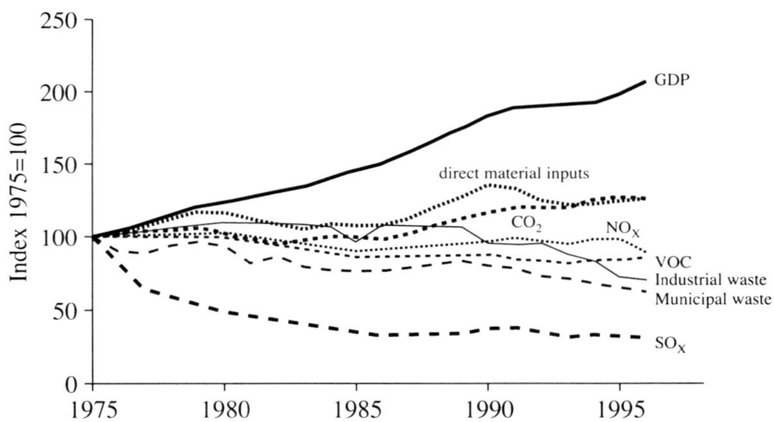

Source: Matthews et al. (2000).

For the time being, it is not clear whether the use of nature in industrialized economies may rise again with further economic growth ('re-linking', 'rebound-effect', N-curve).

Zero emissions

The zero emissions approach, as promoted by its main advocate Pauli (1998) and the Zero Emissions Research Institute (ZERI), overlaps to a certain extent with the previously discussed concepts of eco-efficiency, resource productivity and Factor X. It also promotes achieving 'more with less' nature and assumes industries following a more resource-productive technology path leading to increased competitiveness. The principal idea is to save resources through industrial processes producing no wastes or emissions at all. Any industrial output forms input for other industrial processes. This idea of a comprehensive material-cycling economy is derived from the 'eco-system's way of using materials' (see http://www.zeri.org).

The zero emissions concept is a business-oriented approach representing a shift in industry away from linear models, in which wastes are considered the norm, to integrated systems in which everything has its use. It heralds the start of the next industrial revolution in which industry mimics nature's sustainable cycles, and humanity, rather than expecting the Earth to produce more, learns to do more with what the Earth produces. Zero emissions envisages all industrial inputs being used in the final products or converted into value-added inputs for other industries or processes. In this way, industries will reorganize themselves into 'clusters' such that each industry's wastes/by-products are fully matched by others' input requirements, and the integrated whole produces no waste of any kind.

The theoretical concept is corroborated by examples for the cascading use of biowaste. Non-organic abiotic waste, however, constitutes the major component of all outflows of industrial economies. In addition, some flows such as the hidden flows of mining may not be recycled to a reasonable extent in the future either (for example with overburden in minerals mining). For those waste flows other strategies have to be pursued.

Conclusions

To summarize, the following conclusions might be drawn from the patchwork of concepts introduced above. In general, all concepts and strategies introduced correspond to the paradigm shift from a more narrow environmental policy approach towards a more integrated sustainable development approach. Accordingly, the considerable overlaps between the particular concepts do not make it easy to differentiate between them distinctly, and they are sometimes confused or are used synonymously. A strong normative element seems to be embodied in more or less all concepts: the insight that industrialized societies have to reduce absolutely their use of global natural resources. Within all concepts, a shift towards the application of the precautionary principle is observable.

The role of (state) governments is gradually diminishing compared to the former pollution control and prevention approach. Nevertheless, an increasingly new role of the state is to 'facilitate' institutional changes. On the other hand, the role of business, consumers and the civil society is gaining more and more focus, opening 'new arenas' of environmental policies. In line with the rising economic focus, the business sector is seen as an increasingly proactive player by envisaging 'win–win' constellations between economy and environment. This also emphasizes the importance of changed production patterns

BOX 1.4 ZERI METHODOLOGY

1. Total throughput: a review of the industry identifies opportunities to minimize inputs and maximize outputs. The target is full use of inputs, that is total throughput. If this cannot be achieved, the next step of the methodology is applied.
2. Output–input models: an inventory is made of all 'wastes', that is, outputs not consumed in the final product or its process of manufacture. An active search is then initiated to identify industries which could use the outputs, or modified versions of them, as inputs.
3. Industrial clusters: the output–input models are used to determine potential candidates for clustering. The next step is to identify optimal clusters in terms of size and number of participating industries.
4. Breakthrough technologies: in cases where present engineering know-how, product and process technologies are not yet able to secure effective and economical coupling of outputs and inputs, research into breakthrough technologies or system designs is initiated.
5. Industrial policy: identification of clusters and isolation of the breakthroughs required must be accompanied by the design of appropriate government policies. As sectors with no previous tradition of working together are combined, collaborative efforts involving policy makers, industry representatives and academia are launched.
6. The global information economy: the rapid spread of the Internet opens up an additional information channel for ZERI design dialogues. We can now publish our existing models online and invite the world to critique and improve them through a global dialogue about zero emissions – which is the ultimate function of this website.

Source: http://www.zeri.org.

within the context of a sustainable development: changes which are primarily up to the business actors to implement.

Although all concepts by and large acknowledge the necessity of fundamental and structural changes, none of them presents a 'master plan'. Moreover, a tendency to acknowledge uncertainties, limited knowledge and imperfection of purely technical solutions (trial and error) can be observed as well as strategies to consider 'knowledge of the unknown'. An overall guardrail policy seems to open up which defines a sustainability corridor; beyond the guardrails natural resource use is definitely non-sustainable and degrees of freedom for decision decline sharply in the future; a policy framework may provide adequate orientation and incentives to lead the economic actors towards and along the corridor and the actors may apply key strategies such as resource efficiency to keep on the sustainability track.

1.2 THE RATIONALE OF DEMATERIALIZATION

As outlined above, dematerialization, the absolute reduction of man-made material flows by, for example, a Factor 10, constitutes one strategic objective for an industrial transformation and hence one means of making sustainable development more concrete. Dematerialization addresses economic activities and the structure of national economies. Normatively, like the other concepts introduced, it is based on the insight that the current production and consumption pattern, that is, per capita material and energy throughput, in developed economies is not applicable on a global level. Also, as already mentioned, dematerialization is a complementary strategy to the detoxification approach which has evolved under the 'pollution prevention and control' paradigm.

The following sections will provide a more thorough insight into the rationale of the dematerialization concept and strategy as developed by the Wuppertal Institute. It will explain arguments for systematically focusing on material flows in general and on material inputs in particular. It will also present some economic reasons for a dematerialization strategy and will discuss strengths and weaknesses of the concept.

'Matter Matters Too!'

Using the concepts of industrial metabolism and industrial ecology, it is useful to have a look at the physical performance of human, and in particular economic, activities, both in a quantitative and a qualitative way. 'Since all industrial processes involve extracting natural resources from the earth, transforming them into goods and services, and leaving behind wastes of all kind, it is the material cycle – the flow of materials from nature to the economy and back – that is fundamental to both the economy and ecology' (Sachs, 1999: 176). Nature serves as a production factor for humans' economic activities, both in terms of natural resources (materials, energy, land) and in terms of nature's carrying capacities to absorb residuals from economic activities.

Since the famous Club of Rome report, 'Limits of Growth' (Meadows,

1972) it has become evident that the absorption capacities are the limiting factors rather than the exhaustion of natural resources. The latter constitutes an economic problem whereas the level of emissions to air and water and the flows of waste back to the natural system are seemingly coming closer to the limited carrying capacities boundaries, as in the case of global climate change. However, in addition considerable negative effects on local to regional ecosystems are connected to the raw materials extraction process itself (for example, liquid mining of minerals, reduced groundwater tables, emissions from extraction and land use change).

Any material input into the technosphere will sooner or later become material output. In other words, there is a causal link between inputs and outputs due to the law of conservation of matter. A (quantitative) reduction of material inputs also constitutes a strategic means to diminish quantitatively the material output flows back to nature and, by this, traditional environmental problems. That is why in general it makes sense to consider the total material throughput associated with human activities. In this context, it is interesting to note that the major part of material flows never enters the economy in the form of objects, but remains degraded or wasted somewhere alongside the life cycle of a given product (so-called 'hidden flows' or 'ecological rucksacks').

Although the total metabolism is considered, particular material flows are also recorded and addressed separately within the dematerialization approach. This allows for relating particular material flows of the total metabolism to particular environmental problems without losing the overall context. As a simplification, we can distinguish the following broad classifications of material flows:

- resource extraction (by agriculture, forestry, fishery, mining and quarrying, basic industries) associated with the direct problem of resource depletion and environmental impacts related to the extraction processes themselves, such as erosion, fragmentation of landscape and ecosystems, emissions to air, soil and water;
- transformation of resources to goods by industry (producers) and use of goods by private households (consumers), both associated with the release of residuals back to nature; that is, the traditional subjects of environmental policies (waste, emissions).

Another question is why focus quantitatively on material flows? There is some evidence that the pure amount of materials moved by industrialized economies is a problem per se which needs to be addressed. This seems of value, in particular, when comparing the per capita material throughput of developed countries with those of developing countries and relating this to the globally available environmental space. In order to underline the importance

$$\text{Total environmental pressure} = f\left(\frac{\text{specific impact (s)}}{\text{unit of flow volume}} \times \text{volume}\right)$$

Figure 1.5 Decomposition of material flow-related total environmental pressure

of the volume aspect of material flows, the overall environmental pressure induced by the material throughput can be analytically decomposed into a qualitative and a quantitative component (see also Bringezu, 2000a): on the one hand we have specific environmental impacts of one unit of a selected material (input and output) flow, and on the other the overall volume effect (see Figure 1.5).

Two basic questions are connected to those generic components. The first question, related to the specific impact of a selected material flow, is how to indicate the specific environmental pressure caused by material flows. First of all, this selected material flow has to have been evaluated as 'harmful'; that is, this has to be known already. Environmental policy has evaluated certain themes to be of prior importance (global warming, acidification and so on). These could also be related to selected material flows (for example, fossil energy carriers, CO_2, SO_2, NO_x). Manifold scientific efforts have been undertaken to gain knowledge about the property of certain materials and specific substances in order to derive data for the specific impact assessment per unit of material flow. It is evident that this kind of scientific information cannot be generated for all potential 'harmful' material flows owing to the complexity of global ecosystems and the multitude of potential human disturbances.

Information on specific environmental impacts per material flow unit has sometimes to be used for weightings. In that case, a specific problem is the aggregation of the different impact potentials of the different flows (such as global warming and eutrophication potentials) in order to obtain a sufficient overview of the total environmental pressure. It seems that only personal or societal weighing can solve this problem.

The second question, related to the pure volume of unspecific material flows, is how to indicate the environmental pressure of material flows in a generic way, if it is not (yet) known specifically, or if it is not related to specific substances. This situation seems to be the usual case rather than the exception. For most of the toxic, nutritional, mechanical, structural and physiochemical effects associated with material flows, a standardized method for a reproducible quantification does not exist. The impacts may result from subtracting materials from the environment (for example, drainage of mines) or from adding something to nature. Some impacts are rather non-specific with respect to the chemical nature of the materials (as with the devastation of landscape and the mechanical destruction of organisms due to the extraction or the harvesting of renewable raw materials). Moreover, from a scientific point of view, it is generally impossible to foresee all possible impacts of human-induced material flows that may be of relevance in the future.

Thus, in most cases, information is only available about the volume and the classification of the material flows themselves, and the question may also be formulated: does the accounting of material flow volumes yield any information about the environmental pressure of those flows? Indeed, any material flow induced by man changes the environment in a more or less unpredictable manner. Therefore any quantitative flow account will indicate the actual situation of environmental pressure. Irrespective of the unknown impacts per unit of flow, any flow account may be interpreted as that the pressure will increase with the amount of the accounted flow (unless specific knowledge is available to prove otherwise).

For these reasons, the dematerialization strategy aiming at the quantities of material input and output flows (that is, the entire throughput) constitutes one side of the coin. The other, complementary, side of the coin is the aforementioned detoxification strategy.

Reasons for an Input-oriented Policy Approach

This section will present some reasons for an input-oriented policy approach derived from the dematerialization strategy. 'Input orientation' stands for a general policy approach addressing industrial metabolism, mainly in a quantitative way, on the material input side of the technosphere. Again, it has to be seen as a complementary approach to the widely output-oriented traditional environmental policies established over recent decades.

Besides the effect that reducing material inputs implies also reducing outputs, focusing on the material input side has some particular advantages. One is that the control of material input 'gates' to the economy are lower in number than the often dispersed 'gates' of material outputs (such as emissions to water and air). Hence focusing on a limited number of economic activities on the material input side might be more effective in tackling the overall material input. There are only a few economic sectors which extract primary materials domestically, namely agriculture and forestry, mining and quarrying, energy and the construction sector.

There is, further, some evidence that input-oriented approaches might be more cost-efficient. 'Surrounding the industrial system with pollution control technologies is an enormously costly enterprise, and not even rich countries will be able to shoulder such an expense in the long run' (Sachs, 1999: 175). Saving material inputs in production processes even has a twofold economic benefit: reduced input costs and reduced waste treatment/disposal costs.

Input-oriented policy sets incentives for resource-saving technological progress, stimulating innovation and hence competitiveness. Traditional regulative environmental policies focusing on the reduction of selected output flows (that is, repairing damages of economic activities) only set incentives for 'end-of-pipe' technologies. They do not support ecological modernization of products and processes. Dematerialization, as a principle, allows for information management along the production chain. It aims at a physically optimized process chain (integrated product policy, IPP). This might also increase value added (that is, total quality management).

Dematerialization (reduction of material inputs) might offer more degrees of freedom to economic actors (producers and consumers) since it is based on a limited number of parameters. For instance, a material-input label, expressed in tonnes or kilograms, is easy to understand and communicate, both for the producer and for the consumer. It might also be more transparent than, for example, a complex ecobalance based on often unknown weighting schemes. Transaction costs to gain appropriate information on the way to 'save the environment' might be relatively lower compared to a complex 'end-of-pipe' approach, which is also linked to a relatively high administrative effort due to numerous technical regulations. In addition, output-oriented policy approaches may bear the risk of problem shifting owing to a narrow focus on selected output flows (for example, waste incineration shifts the problem from soil to air).

Also from an environmental perspective the input orientation might be more efficient: an input-oriented environmental policy addresses the causes of environmental problems and not the symptoms. Prevention is always superior to therapy. In this sense, it is more intelligent to avoid pollution right from the beginning, at the planning stage, rather than cleaning up at the end of the pipe. Input-oriented policy might allow analysing the ecological effects of human activities in a more comprehensive way: economically unused material inputs (such as mining overburden or erosion), with various environmental impacts, are also the focus of material input-oriented environmental policies.

Input-oriented policy might be more adequate to meet the uncertainty problem of limited knowledge about complex ecosystems: many potential effects of human activities on the complex natural system are hard to anticipate (for example, CO_2 used to be regarded as a harmless substance). Reducing the material inputs follows the precautionary principle, trying to avoid future impacts as yet unkown.

Finally, reducing material inputs means saving resources, which goes along with a lower dependency on raw material imports; that is, less dependency on supplying countries (such as OPEC) and highly fluctuating markets (such as oil prices).

Limitations of Dematerialization and Rematerialization

It is evident that a dematerialization strategy is not supposed to address every kind of environmental problem. For instance, it does not address specific environmental problems related to selected output flows (such as heavy metal dissipation). Neither will it directly address problems like biodiversity or risks associated with nuclear power generation. In addition, future research is needed on the qualitative and quantitative composition of a 'sustainable metabolism'. As mentioned earlier, the dematerialization strategy is not the ultimate policy means. It is complementary to the detoxification strategy and will have to be succeeded by a consistency and sufficiency strategy. However, for the time being, focusing on the quantitative level of current industrial metabolism should gain first priority.

The overall goal of dematerialization and the increase of resource efficiency can be achieved by various strategies. A general distinction may be drawn between *dematerialization* (in a strict sense), the avoidance of materials and energy use leading to the prevention of waste and emissions, and *rematerialization*, comprising the re-use, remanufacturing and recycling of waste.

Although a strict dematerialization strategy is certainly less oriented towards current technology than other approaches (such as the end-of-pipe approach), it is also faced with important technical limits. The provision of certain functions requires utilities, which demand a minimum of materials and energy use. Rematerialization may also have its limits. As a consequence of the second law of thermodynamics a perfect 'cycling economy' will not be feasible (see Box 1.5). A considerable part of the material throughput cannot be reduced by re-use and recycling. In particular, energy carriers can only be 'used' once. In this context, the role of renewable energy carriers has to be explored more systematically. This will require risk analysis and technical assessment.

Finally, the current economic markets are sending misleading signals for an overall dematerialization and resource efficiency strategy: since the environment is not priced, technological development (progress) is moving in the direction of saving labour on account of produced and natural capital (see also Chapter 3). This is certainly connected to the fact that dematerialization (in a wider sense) has still to be adopted by society as a leitmotiv for the decision making of all actors (producer, consumer, government). However, the dematerialization concept per se does not allow for setting targets or establishing specific societal or economic institutions. This is up to society, which can develop normatively certain targets. However, the broad dissemination of the basic ideas of dematerialization could stimulate such a process.

BOX 1.5 BASIC RULES AND LIMITATIONS FOR A 'CYCLING ECONOMY'

Hierarchy of strategies

Prolongation of product life: extending duration of product use (final end-user).
More efficient material use: optimizing production processes with regard to material use (producer).

Re-use of products: re-using a product for the same purpose for which it was originally produced (e.g. re-use of bottle/packaging or car engine); re-using a product for a purpose other than that for which it was originally produced (e.g. cans, boxes).

Mechanical recycling of materials: re-use of materials and products in earlier production process stages with partial or complete conveyance/dissolving or changing form/shape (e.g. glass).

Chemical recycling of materials: re-using materials in new production processes through transformation into new base materials or products, associated with a loss of material identity (e.g. recycling paper, plastic granulate).

Thermal and other energetic re-use of materials: incineration, fermentation.

Limitations of recycling

The problem of 'down-cycling': with each recycling loop, quality of material decreases; i.e. 'material entropy' increases (e.g. plastics, paper, steel).
In some cases, recycling induces too high costs.
Technological limits to recycling.
In some cases, life cycle-wide resource requirements (energy, materials) to produce secondary raw material might exceed those of the primary raw material.
Material flows that are in principle not suitable to be re-used or recycled – approximately 50 per cent of all material flows (e.g. energy carriers).
In principle, any mixing and watering down is hindering re-use and recycling.
Any use of materials will mix raw materials, which in the end leads to unfeasibility of recycling.
There is no 100 per cent re-use or recycling owing to entropy law (Georgescu-Roegen, 1971; Schmidt-Bleek, 1994: 163)

Source: Adapted from Schmidt-Bleek (1994).

1.3 MFA: A METHODOLOGY TO ANALYSE MATERIAL FLOWS

Policy Support through MFA

MFA stands for material flow accounting or material flow analysis. Broadly speaking, MFA refers to a number of methodologies providing information on industrial metabolism in order to identify major material (resource) flows which a policy of dematerialization can tackle. Similar to energy policies, where energy balances (that is, a harmonized statistical methodology) provide the basic information for policy making, MFA serves as an information basis for a policy of dematerialization. Such a policy of dematerialization would be a cross-cutting policy field embracing several issues, in particular waste prevention issues. So far, a 'policy of dematerialization' has not been established in Europe. However, the European Commission (Directorate General for the Environment) is in the process of defining such a policy field in the context of the development of the 6th Environmental Action Programme (6EAP). The recent draft of the 6EAP presents a future policy field entitled 'Sustainable Use of Natural Resources and Waste', one out of four priority areas within the 6EAP. The objective of this new priority area is 'to ensure the consumption of renewable and non-renewable resources does not exceed the carrying capacity of the environment. To achieve a de-coupling of resource use from economic growth through significantly improved resource efficiency, dematerialisation of the economy, and waste prevention' (European Commission 2001c).

What is MFA?

MFA describes national economies in a physical way, hence constituting a complement to monetary accounts such as the System of National Accounts (SNA). Conceptually, MFA is based on the concepts introduced in the previous sections. Basic methodological elements of MFA have been developed by the Wuppertal Institute (Bringezu, 1993, 1997a).

MFA refers to accounts in physical units (usually in terms of tonnes) comprising the extraction, production, transformation, consumption, recycling and disposal of materials, such as raw materials, base materials, products, manufactures, wastes and emissions to air or water.

MFA is conducted on different levels, from the (supra)national and regional down to the community and firm level. According to different subjects and various methods, MFA covers approaches such as substance flow analysis, product flow accounts, material balancing and bulk material flow accounts (see Bringezu, 2000b). MFA was conducted in a number of industrialized and developing countries. The accounts are part of official statistics in, for example, Austria, Denmark, Finland, Germany, Italy and Japan (for an overview, see Bringezu, 2002).

Two basic types of material flow related analyses may be distinguished according to the primary interest, although in practice a continuum of different approaches exists. Whereas type I analyses are often performed from a technical engineering perspective, type II analyses are directed more to the socioeconomic relationship.

Type Ia Substance flow analysis (SFA) has been used to determine the main entrance routes to the environment, the processes associated with these emissions, the stocks and flows within the industrial system as well as the trans-media flows, chemical, physical, biological transformations and resulting concentrations in the environment. Spaciotemporal distribution is of high concern in SFA. Results from these analyses are often used as inputs to further analyses for quantitatively assessing risks to substance-specific endpoints. A variety of studies has been conducted on heavy metals, nutrients, carbon and halogenated compounds.

Type Ib Selected bulk material flows have been studied, for various reasons. The resource extraction by mining and quarrying was studied to assess the geomorphic and hydrological impacts. The flow of biomass from human production was analysed to evaluate the pressure on species diversity. On the one hand, metals like aluminium, timber products like pulp and paper, and construction aggregates represent important base materials for industrial purposes. On the other hand, these flows – although per se rather harmless – may be linked with other flows significantly burdening the environment, for instance the 'red mud' problem with aluminium production and the energy-intensive production of aluminium. Base materials such as plastics have been subject to various studies on the potentials and environmental consequences of recycling and cascading use.

Type Ic When the environmental impact of certain products and services is the primary interest, it is normally addressed as life cycle assessment (LCA). In general, the system boundary of LCA ('cradle-to-grave') corresponds with the systems perspective of the anthroposphere, technosphere or physical economy.

Type IIa The primary interest may also lie in the metabolic performance of a firm or household, a sector or a region. In this case, there may be no or insufficient information about specific environmental problems. Often the main task is to evaluate the throughput of these entities in order to find the major problems, support priority setting, check the possibilities for improvement measures and provide tools for monitoring their effectiveness. Accounting for the physical throughput of a firm is an increasingly common feature, at least for bigger companies, as sometimes found in corporate environmental reporting. Materials accounts are used for environmental management. Attention is paid to eco-efficiency at the firm level. Flow analyses of materials have been applied for optimization within companies. However, the limited scope of firm accounts calls for complementary analyses with a wider systems perspective, either through LCA-type analyses for infrastructures and main products or by analyses of higher aggregates of production and consumption, that is analyses of total production sectors or entire national economies.

Type IIb When the primary interest is devoted to certain industrial sectors or fields of activity, MFA may be used to identify the most critical fluxes in terms of quality and/or quantity. For instance, different industrial sectors may be compared with regard to various inputs and outputs either from other sectors or from the environment. Certain sectors or activities, such as the construction sector, or activities such as nutrition, cleaning, dwelling and working, transport and communication, may be analysed in detail.

Type IIc A major field of MFA represents the analysis of the metabolism of cities, regions, and national or supranational economies. The accounting may be aimed at selected substances and materials or at total material input, output and throughput (see Table 1.1). Economy-wide MFA at the national level has attracted special attention (see below). The main interest lies in the overall characterization of the metabolic performance of the studied entities, in order to understand the volume, structure and quality of the throughput and to assess the status and trend with regard to sustainability.

The term 'MFA' usually refers to analyses of type Ia, Ib, IIb and IIc. Studies of type Ic are dealt with under the heading of LCA. Accounting of type IIa is mainly related to environmental management. There are also combinations of regional and product-oriented analyses. Nevertheless, all of these analyses use the accounting of material inputs and outputs of processes in a quantitative manner, and many of them apply a systems or chain perspective.

As mentioned above, aggregated economy-wide material flow balances (MFB) – one particular MFA method (type IIc) – represent the most consistent accounting scheme for measuring the metabolism of economies. They provide, similar to energy balances, the appropriate tool for measuring the entire metabolic performance of a national economy in terms of material flows. MFBs also serve as an accounting framework to derive selected aggregated indicators (see below). The next section will focus on methodology of economy-wide material flow balances, but first, it should be mentioned that further sectoral disaggregations of MFBs are also provided by so-called physical input–output tables. Physical input–output tables (PIOT) are widely compatible with the SNA and are also part of the physical modules of the UN System of Integrated Environmental and Economic Accounting, SEEA (United Nations, 1993). In addition to economy-wide MFB, PIOT also show the internal material flows within the economy: that is, flows from one economic sector to another. So far, PIOT are available, for example, for Germany (Stahmer *et al.*, 1998), Denmark (Gravgaard Pedersen, 1999) and Japan (Moriguchi *et al.*, 2000).

Table 1.1 Types of material flow-related analysis

Type of analysis	I			II		
	a	b	c	a	b	c
Objects of primary interest	Specific environmental problems related to certain impacts per unit of flow of			Problems of environmental concern related to the throughput of		
	Substances	Materials	Products	Firms	Sectors	Regions
	e.g. Cd, Cl, Pb, Zn, Hg, N, P, C, CO_2, CFC	e.g. wooden products, energy carriers, excavation, biomass, plastics	e.g. napkins, batteries, cars	e.g. single plants, medium and big companies	e.g. production sectors, chemical industry, construction	e.g. total or main throughput, mass flow balance, total material requirement
	within certain firms, sectors, regions			associated with substances, materials, products		

Source: Bringezu and Moriguchi (2002), after Bringezu and Kleijn (1997).

Focus on Economy-wide Material Flow Balances

Economy-wide MFB are comprehensive accounting schemes, presenting the entire metabolism of economies by means of aggregating material flows in a consistent manner. The general scheme of an MFB is illustrated in Figure 1.6. Basically, an MFB counts all material flows crossing the functional system boundary between 'environment' and 'economy'. On the material input side, they comprise domestic resource extractions including associated domestic 'hidden flows' (such as mining overburden), imports and, optionally, upstream foreign 'hidden flows' associated with imports. On the output side, they include domestic material releases to the domestic environment, domestic 'hidden flows' and exports. Economy-wide MFB further monitor the net material additions to domestic stock (buildings, infrastructure, durable consumer goods and so on) in order to balance material input and output flows. Several indicators (for example, TMR, DMI, TDO – see Figure 1.6), aggregating particular material streams, are derived from economy-wide MFB.

First steps towards a standardized statistical methodology for economy-wide material flow balances have been taken following the lead of the Statistical Office of the European Union (Eurostat): a methodological guide was developed by a task force in 2000. It is planned to develop this methodological guide

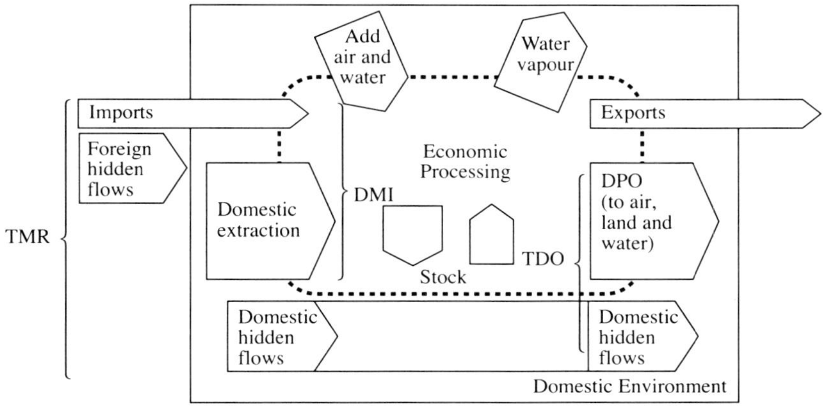

Note:
DMI: direct material inputs;
TDO: total domestic output to nature;
TMR: total material requirements;
DPO: domestic processed outputs to nature.

Source: Matthews *et al*., (2000).

Figure 1.6 Economy-wide material flows

further in the years ahead through testing by national statistical offices. The aggregated indicators DMI and TMR are supposed to be part of the EU set of 'Environmental Headline Indicators' (see below).

The main objectives of economy-wide material flow accounts and balances are (Eurostat, 2001):

- to provide insights into the overall structure and development of the physical metabolism of societies and economies;
- to derive a small set of highly aggregated indicators for resource use and resource productivity (and, more generally, eco-efficiency by relating resource use indicators to GDP and other economic and social indicators);
- to organize, structure and integrate available primary data and thus ensure consistency by linkage with national accounting and input–output tabulations;
- to react flexibly and quickly to new policy demands (related, for example, to specific material uses and their impacts) through quick adjustments of the databases;
- to facilitate analytical uses, in particular estimation of material and land use induced by imports (notably their 'hidden' flows), as well as decomposition analyses, modelling effects of technological, structural and final demand changes.

Similar to national accounts and energy statistics, the compilation of an MFB is based on different statistical sources. On the material input side, major statistical sources are industry and production statistics, statistics on foreign trade, agriculture and forestry and energy statistics. On the material output side, in addition, environmental statistics are used. All these statistics are recorded in physical units which, if required, can be converted into tonnes. Some elements of a MFB, material flows not subjected to official statistical sources, have to be estimated.

A set of indicators can be derived from economy-wide MFB (see Table 1.2) so as to provide an aggregate picture of the industrial metabolism. They refer, respectively, to materials, which are extracted domestically or imported and their hidden 'ecological rucksacks' (as for instance in the TMR indicator), to materials and substances which leave the economy (emissions and wastes) and to the net accumulation of materials in the economy. On the one hand, economy-wide material flow accounts provide a more comprehensive picture of the industrial metabolism than single indicators. On the other hand, they can be used to derive several parameters which, when taken in time series and for international comparison, provide certain aggregated information on the metabolic performance of national or regional economies. Indicators, derived from MFB, can be grouped into input indicators, output indicators, consumption,

Table 1.2 General accounting scheme for an economy-wide material flow balance with derived indicators

INPUTS (origin)	OUTPUTS (destination)
Domestic extraction (used)	*Emissions and wastes*
Fossil fuels (coal, oil)	Waste landfilled
Minerals (ores, gravel)	Emissions to air
Biomass (timber, cereals)	Emissions to water
Imports	*Dissipative use of products and dissipative losses*
	Dissipative use of products
	Dissipative losses
DMI – direct material inputs	**DPO – domestic processed output to nature**
Unused domestic extraction	*Disposal of unused materials domestically extracted*
from mining/quarrying	from mining/quarrying
biomass from harvest	biomass from harvest
soil excavation and dredging	soil excavation and dredging
TMI – total material input	**TDO – total domestic output to nature**
	Exports
	TMO – total material output
Indirect flows associated with imports	
TMR – total material requirements	*Net additions to stock*
	Infrastructures and buildings
	Other (machinery, durable goods, etc.)
	Indirect flows associated with exports

Note: Excludes water and air flows (unless contained in other materials).

Source: Eurostat (2001).

balance and efficiency indicators. The set of main indicators derivable from a complete material balance is briefly characterized below.

Input indicators

Direct material input (DMI) measures the input of used materials into the economy; that is, all materials which are of economic value and are used in production and consumption activities; DMI equals domestic extraction (used) plus imports. Materials which are extracted by economic activities but which do not normally serve as input for production or consumption activities (mining overburden and so on) have been termed 'hidden flows' or 'ecological rucksacks'.[3] They are not used for further processing and are usually without economic value. DMI plus unused domestic extraction adds up to Total Material Input (domestic).

Total material requirement (TMR)[4] includes, in addition to TMI, the upstream hidden material flows which are associated with imports and which predominantly burden the environment in other countries. It measures the total 'material base' of an economy, that is, the total primary resource requirements of the production activities. Adding these upstream flows converts imports into their 'primary resource extraction equivalent'.

Data for TMR and DMI (including composition, that is input structure of the industrial metabolism) have been provided for China (Chen and Qiao, 2000), Germany, the Netherlands, Japan, the USA (Adriaanse *et al.*, 1997), Poland (Mündl *et al.*, 1999), Finland (Juuitinen and Mäenpää, 1999, Muukkonen, 2000) and the European Union (Bringezu and Schütz, 2000). DMI is available for Sweden (Isacsson *et al.*, 2000). Work is in progress for Italy (de Marco *et al.*, 1999) and Amazonia. TMI has been accounted for Australia (Poldy and Foran, 1999).

Output indicators

Domestic processed output (DPO) represents the total mass of materials which have been used in the domestic economy before flowing into the environment. These flows occur at the processing, manufacturing, use and final disposal stages of the economic production–consumption chain. Exported materials are excluded because their wastes occur in other countries. Included in DPO are emissions to air from commercial energy combustion and other industrial processes, industrial and household wastes deposited in landfills, material loads in wastewater, materials dispersed into the environment as a result of product use (dissipative flows) and emissions from incineration plants. Material flows recycled in industry are not included in DPO.

Total domestic output (TDO) is the sum of DPO and disposal of unused materials domestically extracted. This indicator represents the total quantity of material outputs to the environment released into the domestic territory by economic activity. Direct material output (DMO), the sum of DPO and exports, represents the total quantity of direct material outputs leaving the economy after use either towards the environment or towards the rest of the world. Total Material Output (TMO) includes also exports and therefore measures the total of material that leaves the economy; TMO equals TDO plus exports.

Consumption indicators

Domestic material consumption (DMC) measures the total amount of material directly used in an economy, excluding hidden flows (for example, Isacsson *et al.*, 2000). DMC equals DMI minus exports. Total material consumption (TMC) measures the total primary material requirement associated with domestic consumption activities (Bringezu *et al.*, 1994). TMC equals TMR minus exports and their hidden flows.

Balance indicators
Net additions to stock (NAS) measures the physical growth rate of an economy. New materials are added to the economy's stock each year (gross additions) in buildings and other infrastructure, and materials incorporated into new durable goods such as cars, industrial machinery and household appliances, while old materials are removed from stock as buildings are demolished, and durable goods disposed of. NAS may be calculated indirectly as the balancing item between the annual flow of materials that enter the economy (DMI), plus air inputs (such as for oxidization processes), minus DPO, minus water vapour, minus exports. NAS may also be calculated directly as gross additions to stock, minus the material outputs of decommissioned building materials (as construction and demolition wastes) and disposed durable goods, minus materials recycled.

Physical trade balance (PTB) measures the physical trade surplus or deficit of an economy. PTB equals imports minus exports. Physical trade balances may also be defined including hidden flows associated with imports and exports (for example on the basis of TMC accounts).

Efficiency indicators
Services provided or economic performance (in terms of value added or GDP) may be related to either input or output indicators to provide efficiency measures. For instance, GDP per DMI indicates the direct materials productivity. GDP per TDO measures the economic performance in relation to material losses to the environment. Setting the value added in relation to the most important inputs and outputs provides information on the eco-efficiency of an economy. The interpretation of these relative measures should always consider the trends of the absolute parameters. The latter are usually also provided on a per capita basis to support international comparison.

1.4 MFB: A CONSISTENT INFORMATION FRAMEWORK INTEGRATING MOST ENVIRONMENTAL PRESSURES INFORMATION

Economy-wide material flow balances (MFB) comprise most of the environmental indicators associated with traditional environmental policy fields such as climate change (CO_2 emissions), acidification (emissions of SO_2, NO_x), waste (disposal to waste landfills), energy (domestic extraction and import of fossil energy carriers), eutrophication (N and P flows) and water quality (emissions to water).

Owing to the consistent and comparative presentation of material flows associated with several environmental problems, MFB allow priority flows to be evaluated. The specific pressure flows are often interlinked and specific solutions, aimed at selected substances, can lead to problem shifting instead of problem solving. All these interlinkages become visible through the MFB accounting framework.

The MFB accounting scheme also allows the relationship between resource inputs and waste/emission output flows to be investigated, showing that reduction of the resource inputs will contribute to the diminishing of certain emissions and a decrease in waste. But the extent to which the different targets may be combined into a functioning metabolism of the economy can only be determined by analytical cross-checks of the different inputs and outputs. Therefore the existing targets for selected material outputs (CO_2, SO_x, NO_x, waste and so on) should be combined in a consistent 'Target Material Flow Balance' (TargetMFB). The comparison of the actual MFB and the TargetMFB will generate a distance-to-target MFB. As a result, major material input and output flows can be classified as to their deviation from environmental objectives. Such analysis will facilitate the setting of priorities for material uses from an environmental perspective.

1.5 SOME EMPIRICAL FINDINGS: AN MFB COMPARISON OF GERMANY, JAPAN AND THE UNITED STATES

This section provides some main empirical findings on the 'Industrial Metabolism' of industrialized economies, namely Germany, Japan and the United States. These findings are mainly based on two international MFA studies recently performed following a harmonized methodological approach: 'Resource Flows: the material basis of industrial economies' (Adriaanse *et al.*, 1997) and 'The Weight of Nations: material outflows from industrial economies' (Matthews *et al.*, 2000).

The material throughput of industrial economies is dominated by water. However, water, as a renewable resource, might be disregarded in most of the industrialized countries because of its sufficient availability. In Germany, for instance, water throughput is about 600 000 tonnes per capita (Federal Statistical Office, 2000).

Summarized conclusions

Major contributions to the resource requirements of the Japanese economy are similar to those of other industrialized countries, although differences exist in volume, trend and detailed composition. For the Japanese economy, the following findings are especially important. Total resource requirements so far follow a gradually increasing trend in absolute terms. This indicates a growing pressure on the environment. Solid material requirements

BOX 1.6 THE LEVEL OF INDUSTRIAL METABOLISM IN INDUSTRIALIZED ECONOMIES, ITS DEVELOPMENT OVER TIME AND THE LINK WITH ECONOMIC GROWTH

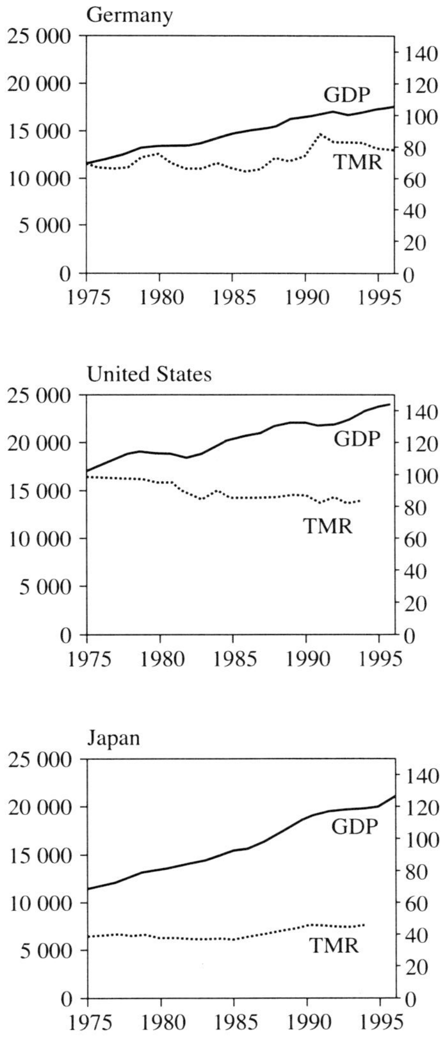

The metabolism of industrial economies measures, without water and air but including 'hidden flows', 40–90 metric tons (TMR) per capita per year. TMR of USA (84–100 tonnes per capita) is slightly higher than that of Germany (64–88 tonnes per capita). With 36–46 tonnes per capita, the Japanese TMR is at a significantly lower level.

Until the mid-1970s, material throughput was linked to economic growth. Since then, it has been de-linked from GDP in most industrialized economies. In the USA, TMR was absolutely de-linked, that is decreased in absolute terms. In Germany, it was fairly constant until reunification in 1990. After a steep rise in 1991, it has been constantly falling towards its 1980s levels.

Source: Adriaanse et al. (1997).

BOX 1.7 COMPOSITION OF TMR: DOMESTIC V. IMPORTED, HIDDEN V. NON-HIDDEN

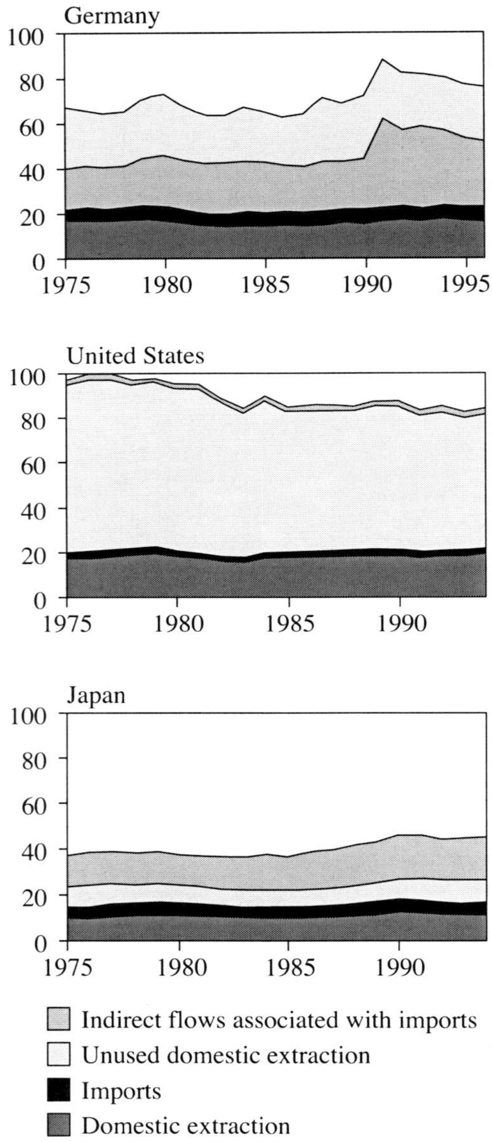

Imports are of different importance for the material basis of industrialized economies: whereas the United States is more or less independent and extracts most natural resources domestically, Japan is highly dependent on imports – particularly of energy carriers and metal ores.

German imports and associated indirect resource flows are comparable to the Japanese ones, although Germany has considerably more domestic extractions.

Accordingly, indirect resource flows associated with imports are less important in the USA.

Source: Adriaanse et al. (1997).

BOX 1.8 MAJOR COMPONENTS OF MATERIAL INPUTS

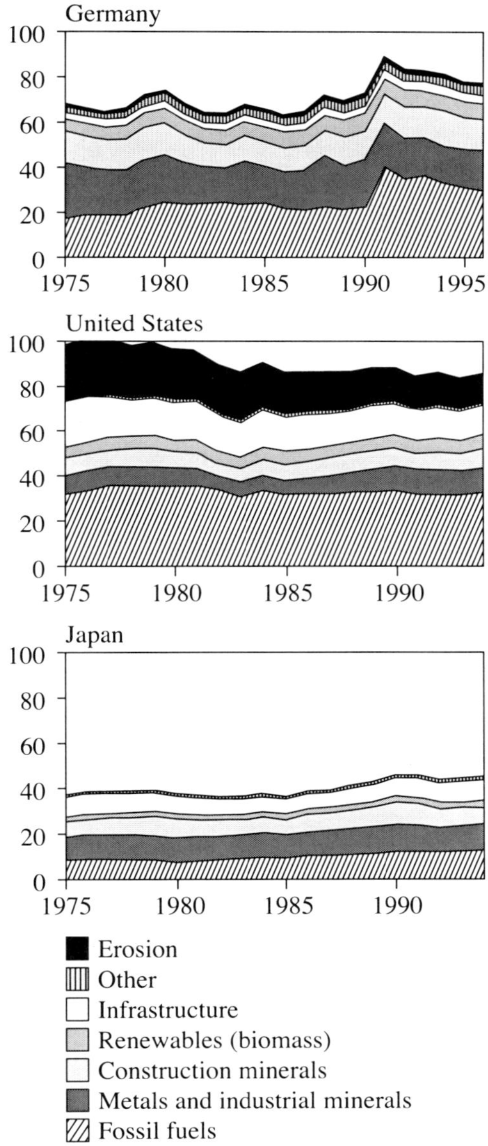

German material input is dominated by fossil fuels, metals, industrial minerals and construction minerals. Fossil fuels and metal minerals have high 'ecological rucksacks', that is, a high share of unused materials (for example, mining overburden). The US material inputs are dominated by fossil fuels, infrastructure excavation and erosion. The latter has been declining over the last decade.

The comparatively low resource inputs to the Japanese economy are dominated by metals and industrial minerals, fossil fuels, construction minerals and infrastructure excavations.

Source: Adriaanse et al. (1997).

BOX 1.9 OUTPUT FLOWS OF INDUSTRIALIZED ECONOMIES: COMPOSITION OF DOMESTIC PROCESSED OUTPUT (DPO) TO NATURE

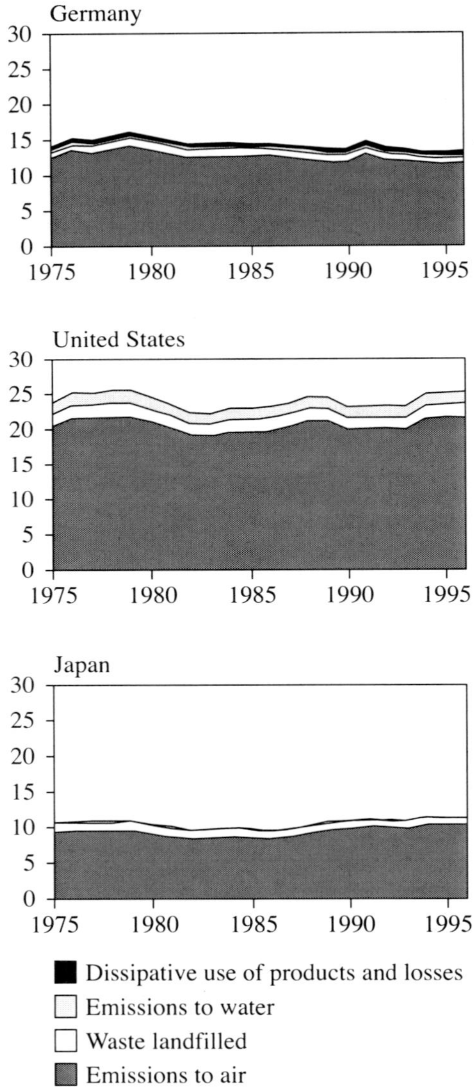

The atmosphere is by far the biggest dumping ground for the wastes and emissions of industrial economies. Output flows are dominated by the extraction and use of fossil energy resources: carbon dioxide accounts, on average, for 80 per cent by weight of material outflows (DPO). The difference in energy use patterns also explains the considerable differences between the industrial countries investigated (Germany, United States, Japan).

Quantities of solid wastes sent to landfills have stabilized or declined. Reductions have been achieved thanks to increased recycling efforts and greater use of incineration as a disposal option. The latter practice, however, has resulted in waste outputs being diverted from land to air, contributing further to atmospheric pollution – particularly climate change.

Source: Matthews et al. (2000).

BOX 1.10 NET ADDITIONS TO STOCK

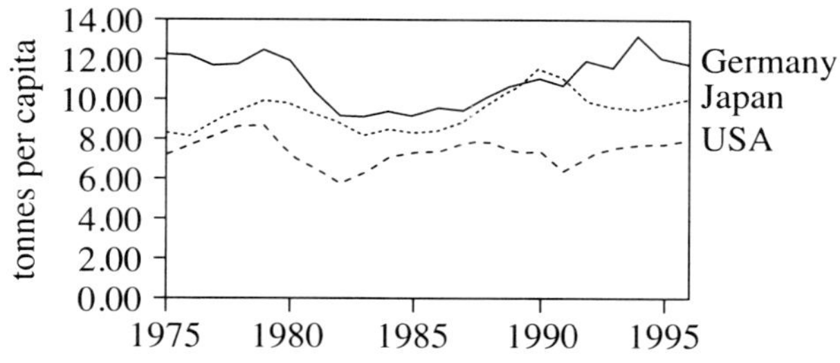

(excluding water and air) are dominated by abiotic, that is, non-renewable, material inputs. The relation of renewables to non-renewables is about 1:5 (only DMI). The replacement of abiotic materials by renewable biomass is clearly limited since arable land is limited. The extraction and transformation of fossil energy carriers (including their huge proportion of unused materials, that is 'hidden flows) constitute one major part of the material metabolism of industrialized economies. Material flows associated with energy transformation can only be used once; that is, they are immediately transformed into air emissions (in particular CO_2) and hence are lost for further re-use.

Extraction and transformation of minerals, in particular construction minerals and metals, constitute a further significant part. Minerals input is mainly used to produce capital and consumer goods. They all become wastes sooner or later. However, they constitute a potential stream for re-use and recycling. Another significant part is infrastructure excavation associated with considerable pressure on the local environment. The excavation of earth and soil contributes to landscape changes involving disruption of natural habitats and a loss of fertile ground for biomass production. The physical growth of the technosphere in the form of additional buildings and infrastructures aggravates the problem of limited natural, agricultural or forestry land. The associated expansion of built-up area leads to the devastation and degradation of the natural environment and the depletion of reproductive land.

NOTES

1. I am grateful for the inputs made by K.-H. Robért *et al.* (2002); see also: www.detnaturligasteget.se.

2. For example 'sources' of materials and energy; 'sinks' for wastes/pollution; 'services' of the environment, and as water and carbon cycling; and 'space' for economic activity and aesthetics.
3. Hidden flows (Adriaanse *et al.*, 1997) or rucksack flows (Schmidt-Bleek, 1994) comprise the primary resource requirement not entering the product itself; hidden flows of primary production equal unused domestic extraction; hidden flows of imports equal unused and used predominantly foreign extraction associated with the production and delivery of the imports.
4. In studies before Adriaanse *et al.* (1997), TMR had been termed as TMI (total material input) (Bringezu, 1997b).

2. Towards a new kind of technological progress

Raimund Bleischwitz

The challenge of sustainable development requires a comprehensive environmental policy taking into account scarcities of ecosystems and natural resources as well as economic and social conditions. Seen from environmental science, leading climatologists of the Intergovernmental Panel on Climate Change recommend a reduction in greenhouse gases by some 50 per cent by the middle of the 21st century. The process of the Framework Convention on Climate Change (FCCC) has led to the Kyoto Protocol starting with a moderate reduction in most industrialized countries. On the other hand, one can learn from the World Energy Council and other experts that the demand for energy and with it the emissions of CO_2 (a main cause of the greenhouse effect) are likely to double within the next few decades. The likely doubling of energy demand, together with the desired reduction in greenhouse gases, leads us to conclude that a gap as large as a factor of four at least will have to be closed.

A similar picture arises regarding the loss of biological diversity. Although the scientific debate about causes and effects is more complex than in other areas of environmental research, one reason for land conversion and habitat destruction can be seen in the gigantic flow of materials extracted and used by modern societies. On average statistically, each inhabitant in the European Union, the USA or Japan induces material flows of between some 46 (Japan) and 85 (USA, Germany) tonnes per year (Matthews *et al.*, 2000). Protecting the remaining biodiversity will require, inter alia, reducing the current amount of material flows transformed by the different economic sectors. This issue is further strengthened by land use changes and the overall concern with waste. A '3R' strategy of reduction, re-use and recycling has been adopted in the overwhelming majority of industrialized countries, stimulating the search for methodologies for managing material flows. Both factors of production, energy and materials, are gaining more and more attention on the development agenda.

From a global perspective, it has become obvious that any attempt of the developing world to emulate Western styles of industrialization would end up in a serious ecological crisis, most notably with regard to the greenhouse effect, the loss of biological diversity and clean water scarcity. Scientists are not suggesting that catastrophes will definitely happen during the next decades. But there is strong scientific evidence at the analytical level about the increasing likelihood of natural disasters (Bunde 2002), which challenge the adaptation flexibility of societies and their institutions. In addition, serious environmental impacts may increase international security conflicts. 'Resource wars' are likely to emerge, partly on a regional scale, partly on an international scale (Klare 2002). The Earth may become an inconvenient place to live in both industrialized and developing countries.

The present study suggests a total reduction in the use of energy and materials in order to tackle environmental problems. It may come as a surprise that the ensuing reflections will be discussed in terms of enabling innovations rather than commanding or restricting businesses. This is because change always refers to solving some problems which previously were thought of as being 'too difficult'. From this angle, a reduction of energy and materials means increasing resource productivity. Authors such as Weizsäcker *et al.*, (1997), Hawken *et al.* (2000) and Schmidt-Bleek[1] propose that economies will be able to increase their resource productivity by a factor of four or even ten (Figure 2.1) via the dynamics of eco-efficient economies. Yamamoto (2001) and Komiyama (2002) develop similar models about challenges ahead for the next decades. This is significant news for firms, policy makers and society!

In fact, this means a new kind of technological progress towards doubling wealth while halving resource use, halving kilowatt-hours, halving megatons,

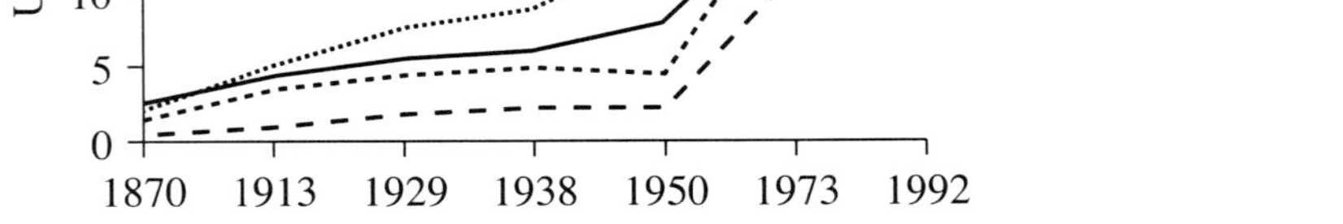

Note: Between 1870 and 1992, labour productivity in industrialized countries increased by a factor of 10 and even more. Why should an increase in resource productivity/eco-efficiency be less successful?

Source: Adapted from Maddison (1995).

Figure 2.1 A productivity increase by a factor of ten is possible

reducing waste and other emissions down to zero. The new direction would increase the market shares of products which meet the criteria of low or zero emissions, low waste, zero toxic dispersion and so on. Such a new kind of technical progress might become part of overall change as soon as business and politicians seriously start to integrate environmental concerns in their overall striving for added value. It will nevertheless lead *not* to a non-industrial service economy but rather to a service-driven industrial society with less production. Sooner or later, the coming age of resource productivity with low information prices and quality production may supersede the present age of labour productivity with low energy prices and mass production of goods.

The notion of productivity refers to other challenges to industrialized economies. Although sustainable development has become popular in recent years, overriding concerns of business managers and policy makers can be located in other realms. Technological change regarding information and communication, the globalization of financial and other markets as well as social concerns with unemployment, security systems and an ageing society have attracted at least similar attention. Taking these issues seriously will mean, for any sustainability strategy, minimizing negative impacts and maximizing economic and social welfare. Research is called upon to widen the scope of any narrow single issues and to develop methodologies for assessing and formulating comprehensive win–win strategies. Here the notion of productivity appears on the research agenda. Once again, a Factor Four strategy towards a new kind of technological progress means doing better in terms of wealth while reducing environmental pressure.

It is widely believed that productivity is somewhat like the engine that drives overall well-being. For business, increasing productivity means sinking costs for the factors of production and allows new products to be established. For employees, a better productivity performance leads to positive income effects, which also stimulates growth effects. The more productivity, the better for society – this sounds like a familiar message for policy makers and business people. But what kind of productivity is meant? Productivity may sound like a comprehensive and multidimensional concept, but it is usually restricted to labour productivity. And here the trouble begins. In the past, economic success due to labour productivity was overwhelming. Since the beginning of the industrial revolution in the 19th century, Western industrialized countries have witnessed a productivity growth by a factor of ten (UK) or even 40 (Japan), according to OECD researcher Maddison (1995). After a slowing down of average annual growth rates in the 1970s and 1980s, the 1990s saw a recovery, most notably in the US economy. Causes may be found in the micro-electronic revolution, 'lean production' efforts in manufacturing industry, productivity ambitions in the service sector and overall globalization.

Although the good times of the 'new economy' have been interrupted following the breakdown of the stock markets in spring 2000, labour productivity still offers a huge potential for further improvements in the economies of the European Union (EU), Asia and the United States.

But some of the related prospects may be questioned. Nobody will deny that focusing on labour productivity had its merits in former times of labour shortage and a clear direction of technological progress. Unfortunately, these prosperous times are over. In harsh times, with some 18 million people unemployed in the EU, rationalizing labour is not a wise strategy. Technical progress should be as labour-augmenting as possible – and not labour-saving. Human and social capital should be decoupled from rationalization of labour. From such a perspective, other types of innovation and other kinds of technological progress are desired. In the Wuppertal Institute's view, the traditional emphasis on labour productivity ought to be widened towards increasing eco-efficiency. The concept of multi-factor productivity ought to include the productivity of natural resources and material flows (Bleischwitz, 2001b). By still paying attention to increasing labour productivity while speeding up resource productivity, countries which have high levels of unemployment and which are faced with environmental problems should still prosper.

Economies can revitalize themselves by disseminating best practices, by stimulating innovation, by setting up new methods of efficient management and organization, and by investing in human and social capital. Though such a statement may sound like an economic textbook on new growth theory, the Wuppertal Institute study (this book) aims to demonstrate that sustainable development can be operationalized by strategies of eco-efficiency. Two propositions are advanced: firstly, environmental concerns lead to the emergence of new markets and business opportunities; secondly, regulation, if properly designed and incentive-oriented, although slow and imperfect, can be powerfully dynamic in the evolution of new technologies and eco-efficient services. A concept like Factor Four (or Ten), that is, increasing economic prosperity while reducing the use of natural resources, can be seen as a simple decision rule that makes people smart and provides orientation for business makers. Its merits, thus, can be located at the micro level of individual decision making in times of uncertainty. Seen from this angle, technological–economic change and sustainable development coincide to a greater degree than is usually expected.

2.1 THE ECO-EFFICIENCY REVOLUTION

Eco-efficiency means doing good business while improving the overall environmental performance of a firm or a product. The concept was introduced by the Business Council on Sustainable Development on the occasion of the Earth Summit in Rio in 1992 (Schmidheiny, 1992) and has been spread by its successor organization World Business Council for Sustainable Development (WBCSD) (2000), OECD (1998), Commission of the European Communities (CEC) (2001a), World Bank (2000), United Nations (1999), and various other organizations. Along with these efforts, five elements of eco-efficiency are seen as vital: emphasis on services, new perspective on human needs and life style quality, inclusion of the complete life cycle of a product, acknowledgment of limits to ecosystems' capacities, and continous improvement of the concept reflecting its dynamic character.

Eco-efficiency is certainly more than traditional efficiency improvements along 'business as usual' trajectories. It is hence no new word for the optimization of conventional management processes and no new slogan for better marketing of old-fashioned products. By and large, the concept of eco-efficiency assists companies in their quest for continuous improvement in minimizing their use of resources. Energy efficiency certainly is a cornerstone of that strategy because it has a clear focus on well-known factors of production (for example, fossil fuels) and most companies could already gain experience with energy efficiency strategies. Eco-efficiency encourages creative strategies of preventative management by integrating environmental considerations throughout the whole life cycle and promotes an active shift from a particular product to multi-use products and services. In doing so, it involves employees and creates tangible economic benefits.

The concept reflects a change in environmental management. Increasingly, the environment is being regarded as an opportunity for innovation, and not as a threat to a company. This shift is related to a parallel change in environmental policies from cleaning-up activities towards integrated and precautionary measures. Whereas cleaning-up and pollution control measures necessarily add additional costs to companies, the new approach allows for cost reduction and innovation. This is (still) beyond the usual ISO 14000 procedures. Measures aiming at recycling of waste and saving energy and other natural resources reduce existing costs within companies. In addition, new markets emerge that are triggered by both regulation and companies' self-interest. Companies actively enhancing eco-efficiency are able to improve their product design, procurement, manufacturing processes, product maintenance and customer relationships.

New and additional types of eco-efficient services appear: producers, broker agencies and specialized companies have to deal with re-using materials and product elements, and with operating heating and cooling systems generated by nearby sources. Financial services for high-quality goods offer opportunities for those reluctant to invest in high-priced goods (with lower running costs). Financial markets also pre-select supply options and may force producers to increase the lifetime of their goods. A third type of new service is related to information and communication. Companies and consumers have strong preferences for better information about eco-efficient innovations helping them to lower their costs. Any leasing and sharing of goods used only for a limited time is assisted by communication systems offered by small and medium-sized enterprises (SMEs) or larger companies.

The concept of eco-efficiency and its underlying philosophy of dematerialization open up new ways to look at the full system costs and the value associated with products or services. In most companies, inefficiencies in the form of incompletely utilized materials, undiscovered energy saving potentials and so on are obvious. Process control for natural resources often is relatively poor. These system costs have traditionally been overlooked by environmental management, which instead focused on pollution control. As a result of the new approach, companies can minimize or even save factor-related costs at a profit (Kuhndt and Liedtke, 1999; Porter and Linde, 2001: 37).

In addition to such a shift of internal attention, managers are rethinking the issue of quality. Eco-efficiency underpins a view of increasing the overall quality of production processes, products and services. Companies now unleash the power of innovation and quality management to eliminate what was previously accepted as necessary by-products. Process-related innovations occurring along the chain include replacement or re-use of production inputs, increases in process yields, careful monitoring and maintenance, and improvements in the product as a by-product of change. Product-related benefits result from safer and durable products high quality, new materials within products, and higher product resale. Additionally, elements of re-use, recyclability and durability are integrated, leading to better materials and a new product design.

2.2 CONSUMPTION AND SOCIAL CHANGE

Technologies and companies are not the only drivers of the new direction of technical progress. Resource productivity is strongly tied to consumer demand and societal values. Consumers are important for the demand for quality goods, energy-efficient appliances and their individual use. They might also practise new patterns of sharing goods, thus reducing the overall number of products produced. In this context, the factors of technology push and consumers' pull complement each other. Increasing services means also a better cooperation among producers and with consumers and their individual life styles. Moreover, the principle of durability extents the product life cycle and will certainly help to overcome the short-sightedness of many current economic processes. Against this background, eco-efficiency does not contradict sufficiency and a sustainable civilization, but is rather a supporting and coevolutionary activity. Experience and tradition might return as individual and societal values. Hence increasing resource productivity might facilitate new models of wealth based upon cooperation, learning, solidarity and prosperity in time (rather than in products). This idea is briefly touched on in the last chapter of the Wuppertal Institute's study on consumption as well as in its first interim report (Wuppertal Institute, 2001). Teramoto and Benton (2000) have outlined similar ideas for the Japanese industrial sector.

2.3 ECO-EFFICIENCY MEASUREMENT: MATERIALS MATTER

Measures of eco-efficiency integrate life cycle-wide material flows: resource exploitation, its transformation into various substances and products, and solid waste (see Figure 2.2). A rationale for integrating material flows into environmental management and policy basically follows three lines of argument:

- environmental impact of materials matters either directly from landscape alterations or land use change, or indirectly from solid waste or emissions resulting from both the extraction and use of materials;
- scarcity of natural resources is a case in point, in particular for non-renewable resources;
- only if material flows and energy inputs are measured can resource productivity gains be expected.

A methodology for measuring material flows as one ingredient of eco-efficiency has been developed and tested for some industrialized countries (Bringezu, 2002a; Matthews *et al.*, 2000) as well as at the company level (Kuhndt and Liedtke, 1999). Clearly, such a measurement methodology still deserves further research. It also has to be underlined that the methodology offered has its limitations as to that extent to which it covers overall environmental pressure (Hukkinen, 2001; Moffatt *et al.*, 2001). Nevertheless, material flows and the ensuing approach of 'dematerialization' evidently become an element, perhaps even a cornerstone, in sustainability strategies of companies and economies.

2.4 TOWARDS INNOVATION-INDUCING REGULATION

If profitable innovations follow from such a business concept, if improving resource productivity can offset compliance, production and transaction costs,

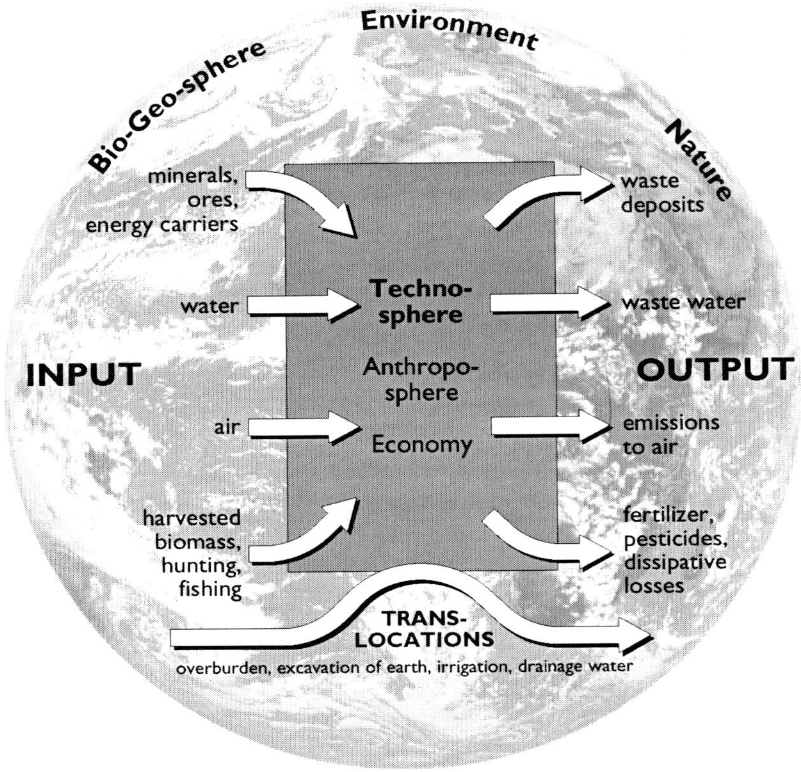

Note: Net materials addition to domestic stocks (stored in new buildings, infrastructures and so on) are relatively high, at 7–12 tonnes per capita a year. The physical growth of industrialized economies is of particular interest since it goes along with occupation of former natural, agricultural or forestry land. Since land is limited, there is some evidence that the physical stock cannot grow infinitely. In addition, those stocks constitute potential waste streams for the future.

Source: Bringezu (2002).

Figure 2.2 An illustration of material flows

the question arises whether regulation is necessary at all. Would companies not explore these fascinating opportunities and follow the path of new markets? That is like the notion of no big banknotes being left on the pavement because someone else will have already picked them up. Indeed, some pioneering companies pursue eco-efficiency without, or in advance of, any regulation. A few examples are given below. It may be expected that mechanisms of diffusion and imitation driven by competition work, but a general assumption that companies will pick up opportunities when they are faced with uncertainties, information deficits and unclear perspectives about trends would be too optimistic. In addition, eco-efficiency cannot ignore both negative and positive external costs associated with production patterns. Policies, therefore, have to address specific market failures in order to harness eco-efficiency.

A need for regulation favouring eco-efficiency arises for the following reasons (Porter and Linde, 2001: 44; Bleischwitz, 2003):

- to create attention that motivates companies to innovate;
- to overcome market failures such as external costs, the provision of public goods, information and adaptation deficits;
- to generate knowledge about likely resource inefficiencies and potential areas for improvements;
- to create and stabilize demand for environmental improvements;
- to level the playing field during transition periods between technological trajectories;
- to raise the likelihood of a new direction for technological progress;
- to retain political functions of stricter measures in cases where the environment continues to deteriorate or new negative external costs occur.

Given these insights, governance of eco-efficiency should primarily support business, and not restrict it. As Figure 2.3 shows, environmental policy and management have in fact always co-evolved. The current challenge of the

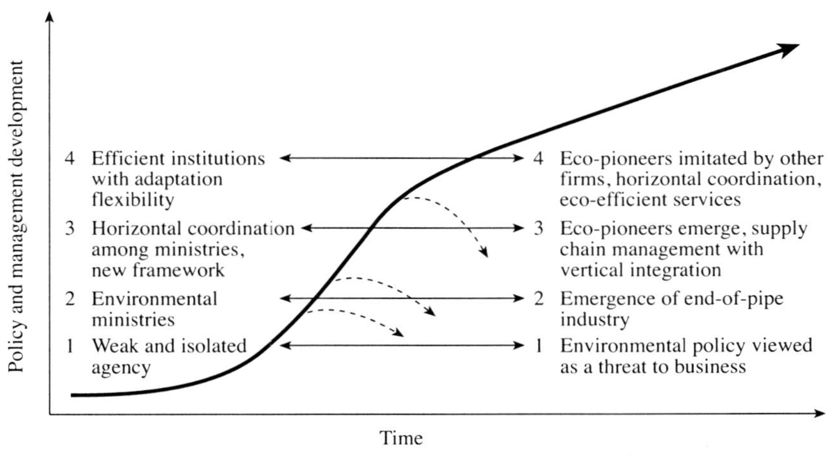

Source: Bleischwitz (2003: 117).

Figure 2.3 Emergence of policies between governments and business

policy cycle can be seen in moving from stage three to stage four towards flexible and horizontal coordination. The efforts for innovation-friendly regulation have not only been relaxed following the success of former pollution control policies, they too can draw upon mechanisms of self-regulation driven by competition and entrepreneurial spirit that are able to overcome some temporary market failures. Governments do not have to regulate minor deficits, but they will have to keep an eye on the speed and the direction of change, supported by increasing scientific evidence on environmental change and computer-based scenario analysis. Specific forms of regulation will have to be developed which foster the dissemination of innovations and the development of new products and services. Market introduction, technology transfer, institutional design as well as science and education policies will have to play their role. Criteria for choosing between different options may include (a) efficiency of instruments for different industries (for example SMEs) and the economy as a whole, (b) effectiveness regarding environmental targets, and (c) adaptation flexibility, which is useful to consider for unforeseeable events (see below).

Economic incentives are one eligible candidate for regulatory tools that allow companies and markets to emerge without those constraints that have been associated with command and control instruments. In addition, a critical employment situation suggests not drawing the largest share of fiscal revenues from labour while resource use remains essentially free of charge. In step with this line of argument, almost all EU member states have adopted some kind of eco-taxes since the late 1990s (Schlegelmilch, 1999; EEA, 2001). The predominant aim is a moderate but steady increase in energy or resource prices. Such an increase leads to further innovations and cumulative effects. If designed together with other tax reductions, the overall effects on international competitiveness do not seem to be insupportable. There is both increasing theoretical and empirical evidence from economics (Oates, 2001) that fiscal and regulatory competition resulting from unilateral action contributes to increasing economic efficiency and will not have dramatic effects. Ueta (1997) and Nakata and Lamont (2001) arrive at similar conclusions about the impact of carbon or energy taxes on Japan. OECD (2002: 3) thus recommends strengthening and extending the use of economic incentives for Japan in its recent environmental performance review.

But there is certainly no 'one-fits-all' instrument that tackles all the regulatory needs as identified above. Moreover, regulatory policies will differ because of specific national innovation systems (Nelson, 1993; Hill, 1995) and market conditions. Markets for energy and material flows, for instance, differ significantly with regard to the natural monopoly situation in the electricity sector and the inherent decentralization regarding materials. Differing conditions lead to case-by-case, market and country-specific analysis that prepares the ground for the diffusion of policies among jurisdictions. Our point here is that eco-efficiency requires some political support, but those specific regulatory features will differ from country to country.

As regards the employment situation, an eco-efficient technical progress will most likely be positive. One reason is simple and straightforward. New goods and services emerge which will improve competitiveness and employment. Besides these growth effects, the increasing attempts to enhance eco-efficiency will lower the pressure to rationalize labour alone. A push towards sustainability and resource productivity will stimulate learning processes and investments towards new technology paths. These new paths will partly consist of high-tech products. Recycling activities, for instance, can still enhance their labour productivity, but a significant additional share will be labour-intensive, resulting from repairing, remanufacturing and various other service activities. These activities normally require time-intensive manufacturing as well as communicative skills. Relatively low skills are required for processes like returning, dismantling, sorting, cleaning and repairing, as well as for some communication activities in the eco-efficient service sector. These low-skill activities will contribute to a labour-augmenting technical progress. In some cases (for example agriculture), human labour might even directly replace current energy and material-intensive processes.

While the direction of technological progress gradually changes, the employment threshold will stagnate or even come down. This would mark a break in current trends. Lowering the employment threshold would add substantial benefits to the employment situation, if the overall expectation for productivity is strong enough to stimulate further investments. What economies might aim at is a growth rate of resource productivity (R_p) higher than the overall growth rate (Y) which, in turn, would be higher than the average increase in labour productivity (L_p): $\Delta R_p > \Delta Y > \Delta L_p$, for example, $R_p = 5\%$ p.a., $Y = 2.5\%$ p.a., $L_p = 2\%$ p.a. It should be kept in mind that the idea of labour-augmenting technical progress would require special preconditions for experience-driven or low-skill jobs. Certainly the eco-efficiency revolution will stimulate new jobs in these areas for remanufacturing and certain services. One question, however, concerns the wage levels and their related labour costs. The standard argument about the necessity of low wages for these jobs is relatively convincing academically, but socially hard to accept. An ecological tax reform might provide some help as far as it allows for shifting from direct taxation (labour) to indirect taxation (energy/certain materials). Such a design lowers the overall costs for labour without diminishing the average wage level for individual employees. It can also be linked to an overall reform of social security systems, thus facilitating part-time jobs for the older generation. For a broad spectrum of low-skill jobs, the idea of a negative income tax (as proposed by Fritz Scharpf and others) seems to be reasonable and relatively easy to administer.

This book makes a plea for a new kind of technological progress. The Wuppertal Institute certainly admits the historical merits of labour productivity, but, looking ahead to the new millennium, a new paradigm for technological progress is needed if one wants to tackle successfully the challenges of environmental concerns, future technologies, unemployment and an ageing society. There are certainly many areas to be better explored from the research side. However, the general idea of increasing eco-efficiency looks very much like a reasonable one.

2.5 METHODOLOGICAL THOUGHTS REGARDING ANY APPLICATION OF ECO-EFFICIENCY CONCEPTS

This book endeavours eco-efficiency related European-based policies on material flows and energy with concluding views to any application within Japanese sustainable development policies. Such an exercise is ambitious and will remain imperfect. It is not possible to give a full overview of heterogeneous approaches within Europe, nor will any study be able to transfer concepts from one country to another without unforeseeable impacts or infringing upon sensitive issues. Horizontal diffusion is more than any transfer because it requires analysis of a different institutional context and of related actors. However, Europe has cautiously started to develop tools to deal with material flows and energy, which might be worth considering in similar Japanese debates. This book aims at contributing to a scientific communication among Japanese and European scholars. The splendid opportunity to collaborate in the projects under the aegis of the Economic and Social Research Institute (ESRI) and Nomura Research Institute (NRI) is gratefully acknowledged.

This book will move the subject one step further towards scientific communication with Japanese colleagues. It is recognized that Japanese debates on sustainable development are fundamentally connected to resources and waste and to the overall economic transformation of Japan as analysed by Boltho and Corbett (2000), Lazonick (1999) and others. Furthermore, the long-term issue of an ageing society is gaining some attention. These areas and their interconnections are truly challenging. The scarcity of resources and arable land, together with highly skilled employees and well-known industries of Japan might generally favour ideas of eco-efficiency, dematerialization and related services. Also, Japanese concepts of reduction, re-use and recycling ('3Rs') do not differ significantly from these ideas. Imura (1997), Wallace (1995), Watanabe (1999), Ren (2000) and the Clean Japan Center (2000) offer some insight into Japanese approaches to environmental policy making. Japanese policies have been summarized elsewhere (Bleischwitz, 2003).

The overall economic transformation of Japan and related political reforms may, however, lead to more severe questions. Can an economy revitalize itself while reducing emissions, waste and the use of natural resources? Based upon the European conclusions, the study may suggest here a 'Yes, it can', though many risks and uncertainties remain.

One thought on any application relates to long-term changes. History constantly recalls that in economics two types of change matter. On the one hand, there is continuing, incremental progress, partly routine and partly path-dependent improvements along existing trajectories. On the other hand, more fundamental changes occur, whether resulting from new basic technologies, Schumpeter entrepreneurs, new institutional features such as the deregulation of natural monopolies, or from societal changes. The study applies both types of change to the sustainability debate and innovative regulatory policies. It introduces tools for governance across multiple arenas. The arena of policy makers is at the heart of two chapters: emerging European regulatory approaches for material flows, energy, buildings, transport and target-oriented policies, in Chapter 3, and an enhanced information basis via improved statistics and data in Chapter 5. Nevertheless, addressing policy makers does not necessarily presuppose that this arena holds sufficient steering capacities for long-term changes. Governance across multiple arenas implies rather that business bears responsibility for the economy and for its various impacts on humans and nature. Analysing management tools for sustainable enterprises is a logical device following such a governance approach (Chapter 4). Here, SMEs may be of special relevance as they dominate in the numbers of employees while offering potential for productivity increase. Integrating business strategies refer to the second type of change: basic innovation towards a Factor Four (or more) must involve different businesses and will certainly lead to new markets that foster long-term change across all sections of society. New materials and new energy supply technologies (such as solar-based hydrogen fuels) are two examples for potential basic innovation with huge impacts over time.

It is important to note that technological and economic dynamics only stabilize when society, law and politics trigger them. Bubble economies are a good example of the way markets may break down if crucial 'soft' factors fall behind. Markets grow in any direction at any speed according to the law and other framework conditions (Metcalfe, 2001). For the sustainability debate and the proposed eco-efficient services, these features lead to the acknowledgment of the regulatory policies mentioned as well as consumption and life styles. There is, as this book claims, no general contradiction between economic efficiency and cultural sufficiency as they are mutually intertwined.

Such interdependence certainly differs from a possible interrelation as (cultural) ends and (economic) means, though economic policy rests upon the legitimacy of some non-economic goals. The objective lies in the identification of mutual lines between eco-efficiency, consumption and policies, not in any suggestion of a new culture!

These thoughts, as well as a distinction between policy analysis and normative statements, lead to the following conclusion on the methodological issue of application: it is not possible to export policy concepts like any other private good on the world market. As the great French philosopher Montesquieu noted, 'Laws should be so appropriate to the people for whom they are made that it is very unlikely that the laws of one nation can suit another.' Following that spirit, any research on a possible application of Europe-based concepts to Japanese policies as submitted by European researchers requires a stopping rule. Such a rule is drawn along the line of conclusions from the European perspective. This allows thorough analysis during the screening of potential concepts for a possible dissemination and related conclusions. It also may allow suggestions on additional research needs that may be of relevance to Japanese colleagues. As a final step, such an approach may lead to the emergence of mixed Japanese–European research teams, thereby helping to deter research from making normative statements and from touching sensitive internal affairs.

From a more theoretical point of view, these methodological remarks refer to country-specific transaction costs formed by national institutional structures, as analysed by Nelson (1993), North (1990), Dixit (2000) and, with a view to Japan, by Hill (1995). The approach chosen in this book follows a similar vein: any applicability of concepts depends on specific institutional features. Country-specific environmental capacities, as outlined by Jänicke (1997), are relevant on the policy maker's level. Business institutions, as outlined by Langlois and Robertson (1995), meet similar functions for the business level. Against this background, scientific policy analysis meets a very particular demand. It is the demand for enhancing information processing, including analysis on various specific constraints or capabilities that arise during evolutionary change. If sustainability research contributes to this end, it may fully serve its purpose.

NOTE

1. Ernst Ulrich von Weizsäcker and Friedrich Schmidt-Bleek, the founders of the Factor Four and Factor Ten concepts, were awarded the Japanese Takeda World Environment Award in 2001.

BOX 2.1 FACTOR FOUR BEST PRACTICES: LIGHT-EMITTING DIODES FOR GENERAL LIGHTING

Wuppertal Institute
Home

Science Centre
North Rhine-Westphalia
Institute of Work
and Technology

Institute for
Culture Studies
Wuppertal Institute for
Climate, Environment,
Energy

FACTOR FOUR - best practises

Light-emitting diodes

Light-emitting diodes for general lighting

A bright idea

Light-emitting diodes (LED) directly transform voltage into light in a process reversing that of solar cells. Different light-emitting materials produce light of different colours, and the relatively recent development of white-emitting compounds has opened up new possibilities. LEDs are increasingly used in general illumination in a range of uses extending from architectural lighting to traffic signals and automotive signal lighting.
More...

Source: Osram

Factor-four effects

- ! Low power requirement
- ! Low resource use
- ! Long lifespan
- High shock and vibration resistance
- Low heat generation
- No ultraviolet rays
- Small size
- Do not flicker
- Safe in use
- Respond quickly
- Low maintenance costs
- Attractive and flexible design

FACTOR FOUR welcome page

FACTOR FOUR best practises

FACTOR FOUR registration sheet

FACTOR FOUR publications

FACTOR FOUR ethics

FACTOR FOUR FAQ

Source: Wuppertal Institute 2003 (http://www.wupperinst.org/FactorFour/best-practises/led-short.html).

BOX 2.2 FACTOR FOUR BEST PRACTICES: CIRCULATING PUMPS FOR HEATING SYSTEMS

Wuppertal Institute Home

Science Centre North Rhine-Westphalia
Institute of Work and Technology
Institute for Culture Studies
Wuppertal Institute for Climate, Environment, Energy

FACTOR FOUR - best practises

Circulating pumps for heating systems

Circulating pumps for heating systems

More pumping power for less electric power

Conventional pumps in heating systems convert no more than an approximate 10 to 15 percent of electric power into pumping power. Improved circulating pumps now on the market achieve the same hydraulic pumping performance with 70 percent less power. Key innovations are highly energy-efficient permanent magnet motors, improved pumps and optimised controls. Better controls allow adjusting pump operation to different environments and demands and save additional energy. Today, circulating pumps optimised for various uses and performance requirements are available.
More...

Biral MC 10
Source: Biral GmbH

Factor-four effects

- **Saves energy**
- **Low emissions**
- **Reduces costs**
- **Low raw material consumption**
- **Growing markets**
- **Reduces dependence on foreign energy sources**
- **Competitive**
- **Secures and creates jobs**
- **Improves quality of life**

more information

Expert advice

FACTOR FOUR welcome page
FACTOR FOUR best practises
FACTOR FOUR registration sheet
FACTOR FOUR publications
FACTOR FOUR ethics
FACTOR FOUR FAQ

Source: As Box 2.1.

BOX 2.3 FACTOR FOUR BEST PRACTICES: DIRT-REPELLENT SURFACES WITH LOTUS EFFECT

Wuppertal Institute *Home*

Science Centre North Rhine-Westphalia
Institute of Work and Technology
Institute for Culture Studies
Wuppertal Institute for Climate, Environment, Energy

FACTOR FOUR - best practises

Lotus-effect

Dirt-repellent surfaces with lotus effect

Using nature as a model

Biologists at Bonn University discovered that the leaves of many plants not only repel water, but also dirt as water running off the surface takes dirt with it. The lotus or sacred water lily is a prime example. To use this effect, nano-technological methods were developed to apply extremely fine microstructured finishes to materials that imitate the surface of lotus leaves. So far, the lotus effect may be found in house paint, tiles, glass panes and plastic sheets. Roof tiles with lotus effect are at the development stage. Easy-to-clean surfaces in sanitary ceramics and flooring have qualities similar to the lotus effect. Since these surfaces do not feature an actual lotus effect, they cannot be called self-cleaning, but nevertheless offer comparable advantages.
More

Sacred lotus or waterlily
(Nelumbo nucifera)
(Source: Department of Botany at Bonn University)

Factor-four effects

- **Saves cleaning agents**
- **Easy to clean**
- **Durably attractive surfaces**
- **Saves water**
- **Low material consumption**
- **Long lifespan**
- **Less waste**
- **Lower costs**
- **Saves time**
- **Positive image**
- **Increased safety**

FACTOR FOUR *welcome page*
FACTOR FOUR *best practises*
FACTOR FOUR *registration sheet*
FACTOR FOUR *publications*
FACTOR FOUR *ethics*
FACTOR FOUR *FAQ*

Source: As Box 2.1.

3. Emerging regulatory policies for eco-efficiency

Raimund Bleischwitz, Stephan Moll, Stefan Bringezu, Dirk Assmann, Manfred Fischedick, Stefan Thomas, Holger Wallbaum and Rainer Lucas

3.1 INTRODUCTION

As outlined earlier, the eco-efficiency revolution is not going to happen unless the framework conditions for doing business are changed towards innovation-inducing regulation.[1] Eco-efficiency must become profitable. To an astonishing extent, however, eco-efficiency is already profitable now. Eco-pioneers and those companies undergoing eco-auditing procedures have discovered that they gain through innovations as well as through transparency of the link between materials and energy on the one hand and financial and knowledge flows on the other. It is nevertheless to be feared that the possibilities for resource productivity and a Factor Four (or Ten) will be limited if the present market conditions prevail.

Thus market deficits have to be addressed by regulatory policies. Economic incentives, such as eco-taxes or tradable permits, are eligible candidates for those policies that harness market forces to the business level. Sometimes, however, they fail to meet specific information deficits, adaptation problems, path dependencies or institutional inertia. A cross-cutting policy mix offers advantages that outperform single instruments. Research is required to choose from different policy designs and to select criteria that help policy makers in their decision. Three core criteria suggested in our study are the following:

- the *efficiency* of regulatory tools for different industries (for example SMEs) and the economy as a whole (internalization of external effects),
- the *effectiveness* regarding environmental targets, and
- the *adaptation flexibility*, which is useful to consider for necessary improvements and for unforeseeable events.

Considering these criteria leads to case-by-case and country-specific analysis and not to any 'one-fits-all' instrument for eco-efficiency. In this chapter we endeavour to present a careful selection of specific regulatory policies for eco-efficiency that have been formulated in response to those specific market deficits in Europe. Before analysing these case studies, some remarks on strength and weaknesses of established methodologies seem useful. It is proposed that the three criteria introduced above can be analysed partly via established methodologies of cost-effectiveness analysis and cost–benefit analysis. On the other hand, the study suggests taking efficiency as a dynamic concept and looking for adaptation flexibility as part of evolutionary change. This is why the two established methodologies might also have some shortfalls in analysing emerging regulatory policies.

Cost-effectiveness Analysis

By and large, cost-effectiveness analysis starts from a pre-determined goal and identifies those technical and policy options which achieve these goals at lowest cost. For each option, the costs as well as the level of reduction that can be achieved in using this option can be identified. This type of analysis is in principle relatively simple. However, in practice a number of analytical questions arise.

1. The costs can be gross costs, net costs to waste management companies, net costs to society, and so on.
2. They may be borne by producers (passed on to the consumer), utilities (included in the fees they charge), municipalities (recovered by taxes) and so on.
3. The system boundaries of the analysis need to be clearly defined.
4. The environmental benefits achieved by each option ought to be made comparable.

Our main conclusion for a departure from cost-effectiveness analysis refers to the assumption of pre-defined goals: a new kind of technological progress towards a Factor Four (or more) may be facilitated by formulating strategic goals (see below), but these goals can hardly be quantified prior to any analysis on regulatory tools. As long-term and strategic goals, they are different from prevailing environmental targets.

Cost–benefit Analysis

Compared to cost-effectiveness analysis, cost–benefit analysis (CBA) poses the question of which levels of targets should be envisaged for sustainability policies and/or whether a pre-defined policy is justified by its environmental benefits. This question is indeed much more difficult to answer since the environmental benefits of any measure are hard to estimate. The following questions may illustrate prevailing discussions about benefit valuation. How can research know how much clean air is worth? Can research put a price tag on a life saved and, if so, how? Is it ethical to put a price on the environment?

Although the questions are fundamental, the rationale in favour of related analysis is that every relevant policy decision puts an implicit value on the environment, whether wanted or not. To adopt any regulatory measure follows from policy makers' belief that the benefits outweigh the costs. This statement also holds for the 'doing nothing' option. The first question therefore is not whether to put a value on environment or not, but whether this is done consciously or not. Public budgets are limited, and so is people's willingness to spend additional money be it for cleaning up the environment or for preventive measures. Looking at least-cost options always is a wise strategy for policy makers. Therefore CBA mainly tells how much of their available income people are ready to spend for the protection and/or the production of a common good.

Quite a large number of methodological techniques can be applied to value environmental goods. Contingent valuation is based on asking citizens via questionnaires what their willingness to pay for certain options is. Hedonic pricing observes changes in, for example, housing prices around waste management installations. Clean-up costs use the value that policy makers attributed implicitly in an earlier decision to clean up pollution. All of these techniques (as well as other methods not mentioned here) have their own merits and none should be rejected in principle. Making an analysis of these methodologies, however, is beyond the scope of this study.

Worth underlining here, however, is a high degree of uncertainty: data on environmental impacts are incomplete, pollution pathways depend on both materials' and landscapes' conditions; local factors play an important role; many impacts do not occur immediately but many years and decades later. This needs to be taken into account in appropriate discount rates. Finally, the monetary valuation technique itself may imply a significant degree of uncertainty, in particular for impacts on soil and water. Similar uncertainties arise with regard to human dimensions: data on materials and energy used in societies differ and are incomplete (see Chapter 5). Local factors, too, play an important role regarding the absorptive capacities of societies. Impacts of innovation and innovation-inducing regulation do not occur immediately; they may also have undesired side-effects.

After this long list of uncertainties, the question may arise whether research can say anything at all on emerging regulatory tools for sustainable development. Though this question is well justified, policy analysis can refer to the following arguments. Firstly, the degree of uncertainties differs. Some conclusions can be drawn with a relatively high degree of certainty. Secondly, an ordinal ranking in the sense of doing better can be done via established methodologies of policy analysis. Finally, even if some factors remain uncertain and may have an important influence on the result, policy analysis can make the regulatory tools more transparent. In this way it leads to a better understanding and, thus, contributes to knowledge generation in the future.

As pointed out earlier, conclusions from policy analysis can never be used to determine an optimal policy. Policy analysis can, however, allow elimination of policy options which are disproportionately bad and the highlighting of those which are best practice at a certain stage of development. This does not imply that best practice cannot be improved, but rather that further policies ought to consider lessons in formulating and implementing these policies.

The following case studies have been the result of an internal screening process within the Wuppertal Institute (WI), which has also involved external experts (see introduction to this volume). The aim is to highlight a few 'good' examples, and not to present a full map of prevailing initiatives. The list of examples indeed might be longer. Given the focus of the study on eco-efficiency, however, the selection of emerging policies has to take into account that these policies are still at a relatively early stage. A list of 'eco-efficiency policies' would not be exhaustive. The following analysis has a strong descriptive element as it tries to inform about current policies. Any assessment about outcomes and impacts in society is, by nature, incomplete and must be considered as being undertaken during an early stage of policy development. Wherever possible, however, the study refers to results of empirical research.

3.2 RAW MATERIAL TAXES

Policy Context and Evolution

The materials flow through society starts with resource extraction, continues with production and use of products, comprises recycling and ends up with the final disposal in terms of waste and emissions. The ultimate objective of any policy which proximately aims at using materials as long as possible within the economy ('recycle-oriented society', Clean Japan Center, 2000) is reducing the output into the environment as well as the input from the environment (Schmidt-Bleek, 1994; Weizsäcker *et al.*, 1997; Bringezu, 2002b; Bartelmus, 2002; see also WI, 2001: chapter II). A major strategy towards this end is the increase of resource productivity and a dematerialization of the economy. A variety of policy measures can be used to steer the industrial metabolism towards a more sustainable volume and composition. Ideally a framework of integrated *sustainable resource management* (SRM) policies should be developed (see WI, 2001: chapter II.6).

So far, such an integrated policy framework has not been implemented in Europe. However, the European Commission is preparing a thematic strategy on the 'Sustainable Use of Natural Resources' in the context of the 6th Environmental Action Programme which will mark a first step towards such a policy framework (see CEC, 2001a) which in the end will have to be implemented at the level of individual member states of the European Union.

One may distinguish three 'anchor elements' from which integrated policy framework on SRM can be developed.

1. The well established but narrowly defined policy field of waste management could be successively extended to the 'front end' of the materials cycle as it is already expressed in the EU waste policy hierarchy (prevention of waste comes first, before recovery and management and final disposal of waste), that is, future waste policies will more and more tackle the issue of waste prevention which is identical with saving natural resources.
2. There are already some policy measures addressing the life cycle of products and aiming at a recycling economy (for example, producers responsibility or extended product responsibilities in the context of integrated product policy (IPP) and take-back systems such as the packaging directive).
3. Some new measures have been implemented to reduce the extraction of natural resources (for example construction minerals) to counteract increasing scarcity and promote nature conservation, waste reduction and increased resource efficiency.

Figure 3.1 illustrates at which stages of the materials cycle policy measures can be applied. Basically, three major leverage points can be distinguished with respect to the materials metabolism: the entry of primary resources, the product system (comprising production, consumption and recycling), and the exit of waste residuals. Starting with the extraction of raw materials, a first possibility is to put an environmental tax on natural resources in order to set an economic incentive to use natural resources more efficiently (1). A tax on the material input side subsequently affects all following processes. Further on in the materials cycle, policy measures might address the design of products produced and consumed (2) as, for example, by an integrated product policy (IPP) and extended producer responsibilities. This also includes recovery and recycling of waste materials that can be regulated by recycling quotas. The disposal of waste (landfills) and emissions (from incineration) can be tackled either by regulatory technical standards or by landfill taxes (3).

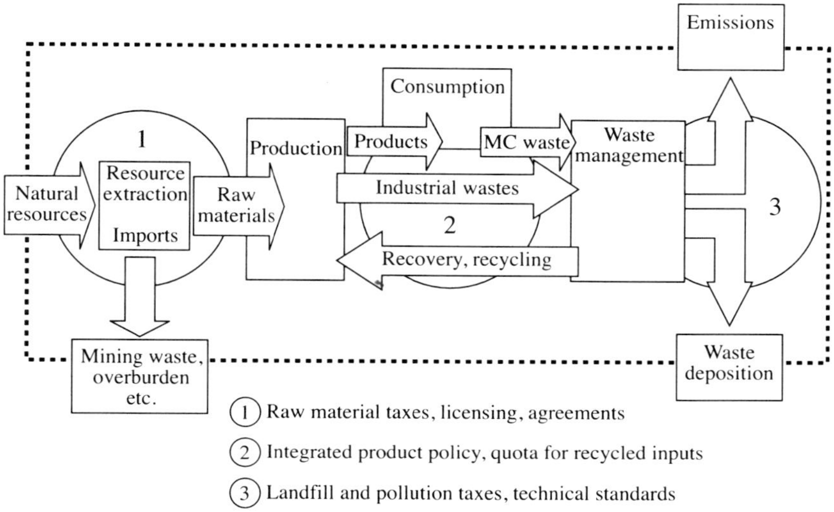

Source: Own compilation.

Figure 3.1 Materials cycle and possible policy levers

Policies aiming at only one of those three basic leverage points will probably fail. In the end, a 'balanced' policy mix will have to be designed comprising all three types of policy measures along the materials cycle, tailored to the resources, products and materials under consideration and also taking into account socioeconomic and country-specific aspects. In addition, adequate statistical systems monitoring the entire materials metabolism of an economy are required. In Europe, such statistical systems have been implemented in several countries and will be further implemented to provide policy makers with appropriate information (see opening section of Chapter 4).

From an administrative point of view, the question arises of where a comprehensive policy on 'sustainable use of resources and management of waste' (using the above mentioned policy instruments) could be implemented and integrated into existing resort policies. It seems that, in European administrations in particular, the 'waste units' will be in charge of the new policy field of sustainable management of resources and waste. For example, the European Commission Directorate General for the Environment (DG ENV) has restructured its organization whereby the former unit for 'Waste' was renamed 'Sustainable Resources – Consumption and Waste'. The mission statement of this new unit is 'to develop and implement policies designed to ensure sustainable management of natural resources and wastes – with particular emphasis on resource efficiency and lifecycle impact of products, consumption pattern, dematerialisation of the economy and waste prevention' (CEC, 2001b), indicating that solely end-of-pipe tackling of waste is not sufficient. However, recent experience indicates that it will still take some time for personnel who are trained to oversee management of waste to be able to cope with the new challenges of a widened system perspective.

Economic instruments ('getting the prices right') are going to play an increasing role in the future in order to increase the costs for natural resources relative to labour costs. Such an economic approach is supposed to offer a triple-win dividend: ecologically, it will lead to reduced use of natural resources and to securing a sustainable supply of particularly renewable resources; economically, it fosters competitiveness through generation of new innovative markets (in particular service sectors); socially, it contributes to secure employment through jobs in new innovative branches (CEC, 1993).

In the following sections the focus will therefore be on the presentation of raw material taxes as applied in a couple of EU member states, without giving them a predominant weight as compared to the other instruments. In general, raw material taxes establish an economic incentive to use virgin materials more efficiently. They also increase the price of primary raw materials relative to secondary raw materials, hence making recycling economically more attractive. Evidently, this incentive should approach the materials cycle at its very beginning in order to be effective along the whole chain.

All three European examples of raw material taxes presented below are addressing construction minerals in order to induce using those materials increasingly in cycles. Environmental pressures associated with the use of construction minerals are manifold. The raw material extraction itself has an impact on landscape and biodiversity and affects natural biogeochemical and water cycles. The subsequent construction of buildings and infrastructures (and the associated physical net growth of 'technosphere') goes along with land use increases, again affecting landscape and biodiversity, and occupying potential productive land for renewable resources. Finally, demolition and construction wastes constitute a major proportion of total waste generated.

Construction minerals are also one of the major resource flows required by the Japanese economy (see WI, 2001: chapter II.6). Domestic extraction of construction minerals represents almost 20 per cent of Japanese total resource requirements (around 8 tonnes per capita). Hence saving virgin construction minerals and using them increasingly in cycles may constitute one strategic building block for a 'recycle-oriented society'. Raw material taxation could significantly contribute towards this end.

Raw Material Taxes in Sweden, Denmark and the UK

In the European Union, three national raw material taxes are in force: in Sweden, Denmark, and the United Kingdom. The Netherlands is currently discussing the introduction of a resource tax as well. Another regional tax on aggregates is applied in Flanders/Belgium, but not presented here owing to lack of information (Ecotec, 2001).

As regards the effectiveness of these resource taxes, the first experiences are interesting. In Sweden the levy increased the price of gravel by about 10 per cent and led to a reduction of gravel in the same order of magnitude, corresponding to about 6 million tonnes. As intended by the government, the material was replaced by crushed rock. Therefore the tax contributed to the conservation of gravel, but only at the expense of an increased use of another natural resource and the associated environmental burden. Based on a much lower levy per tonne, the Danish raw materials tax did not halt the increase in the use of construction minerals that can be observed in Denmark since the mid-1990s. Obviously, the level of the tax was not sufficiently high to induce dematerialized modes of construction with a reduced demand for aggregates. However, the Danish landfill tax that is attached to the raw material tax significantly reduced deposition of construction and demolition waste. The level of the aggregate tax in the UK is significantly higher than in Denmark, and it will be interesting to monitor its effectiveness. Since it has been introduced quite recently (April 2002) it is too early to assess effectiveness.

Sweden: tax on natural gravel (aggregate tax)

Description In Sweden the tax on natural gravel (aggregate tax) was introduced in July 1996 to encourage conservation of natural gravel. The Geological Survey of Sweden (SGU) had calculated that Sweden would run out of natural gravel within 20 years in some 40 municipalities, assuming production at the 1996 level (Hellberg, 2001). The objective is to achieve proportions of 70/30 between the use of crushed rock and natural gravel. Originally, no deadline was set for that target. In 1998, use of natural gravel was 29.3 million tonnes, and the proportion between crushed rock and natural gravel was 55/45.

In autumn 1999, the Swedish National Board of Housing, Building and Planning proposed that consumption of natural gravel should not exceed 3 million tonnes per year by 2020. In 2000, the Swedish government refined its environmental objectives. As regards gravel extraction, the following interim target was set: by 2010, the extraction of gravel in the country will not exceed 12 million tonnes per year and the proportion of re-used materials will represent at least 15 per cent of the ballast used (Ministry of the Environment, 2000).

The tax base is natural gravel, which is naturally sorted earth materials consisting of sand, gravel, stone and rock. The tax rate is SEK5 (EUR0.58) per tonne. The forecasted revenue for the year 1999 was 100 million SEK (EUR 11.6 million). The tax revenue is used for the general budget.

Effectiveness and possible revisions When the tax of SEK5 per tonne of natural gravel was introduced in 1996, the price of natural gravel increased by about 11 per cent, and the proportion of natural gravel decreased by 10±5 percentage points. This effect has been measured for both 1997 and 1998. In absolute terms, a substitution amounting to 10 percentage points corresponds to about 5.6 million tonnes in 1997 and 6.6 million tonnes in 1998. Thus the tax has had an effect on the use of natural gravel and thereby contributed to its conservation. However, in total, the Swedish aggregate tax did not lead to a reduction of natural resources – it rather led to a substitution of materials. If it should become the political objective to reduce overall use of mineral resources, the tax scheme would have to be extended.

Denmark: Raw Materials Act (tax on waste and raw materials)

Description The Danish tax on waste and raw materials is regulated in the Raw Materials Act of 30 June 1997. The tax applies to the extraction and import of raw materials and to waste delivered to waste plants. Focus is laid on construction minerals on the input side and construction and demolition waste on the output side (Ecotec, 2001).

The purpose of the tax is to reduce resource use and to support the Danish waste hierarchy (1, prevention; 2, recovery and recycling; 3, incineration with CHP production; 4, other incineration; 5, final disposal). It is to ensure that exploitation of raw material deposits is based on the principles of sustainable development. The supply of raw materials to society will be ensured in the long term, and raw materials are to be used according to their quality; that is, materials of high quality will not be used where low-grade materials are available. Furthermore, waste products will be used to the greatest possible extent as a substitute for natural materials.

The tax applies to the extraction of raw materials and to waste delivered to a waste plant. Hazardous waste destined for incineration is exempted from the tax. Enterprises that extract and/or import raw materials are liable to the raw materials tax.

In order to reduce the use of natural resources and encourage re-use, a tax of DKK5 per m^3 (EUR0.67) is imposed on natural raw materials. The tax is levied after the following raw materials are commercially extracted (and permission is required as per the Law on Raw Materials), or commercially imported: stones, gravel, sand; clay, limestone, chalk; peat, top soil similar deposits. The full list of raw materials falling under the tax, together with conversion factors to cubic metres is attached to the implementing legislation (for example, 1 tonne gravel = 0.6m^3).

Tax exemptions exist for the following:

- raw materials extracted for coastal projects to protect beaches against erosive action,
- sea floor materials, which originate from maintenance and capital dredging projects and which are utilized as raw materials,
- residual products and waste products, which are extracted from already closed depots,
- top soil and mould, which are delivered without payment,
- raw materials commercially extracted or imported by a business, when the annual amount is less than 200m^3 of raw materials.

Waste tax rate is dependent on the waste plant it is delivered to. Tax rate for recovered waste is zero (Table 3.1). The tax rates have been steadily increasing in recent years without any announcement in advance (budget reasons). Facilities that deposit waste products from the combined production of heat and power (CHP) are exempted from the tax. Waste from heat and power production based on biomass is also excluded.

Since tax rates have been raised, revenues from the waste taxes have increased substantially over the years (Table 3.2). Though tax rate has been kept constant (DKK5 perm^3) revenues from the raw material tax have also been increasing, indicating an increased extraction and import of raw materials (see Figure 3.2).

Both revenues are used for the general budget: they are not earmarked.

Table 3.1 Waste taxes excluding sludge, 1996–98, DKK/ton (EUR/ton)

Waste type	1996	1997	1998
Waste for landfills	195 (26.1)	335 (44.9)	375 (50.3)
Incineration with complete or minimum (in the case of combined heat and power (CHP) plants) 10% power production	160 (21.4)	210 (28.1)	280 (37.5)
Other incineration	160 (21.4)	260 (34.8)	330 (44.2)
Recovered waste	0	0	0

Table 3.2 Revenue from the waste tax and the tax on raw materials 1996–99, million DKK (million EUR)

Year / Tax type	Waste tax	Raw materials tax
1996	601 (80.6)	135 (18.1)
1997	867 (116.2)	145 (19.4)
1998	889 (119.2)	157 (21.0)
1999	1150 (154.1)	160 (21.4)

Source: Finanslov for finansåret (1999) and Statsregnskab for finansåret (1998).

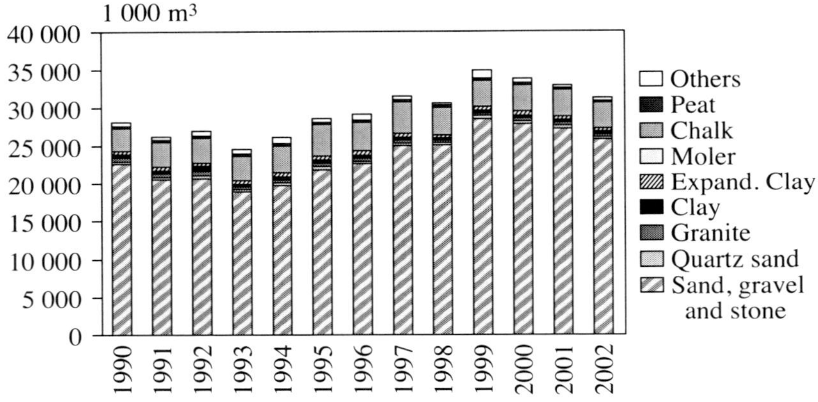

Source: Miljö and Energi Minesteriet (2000).

Figure 3.2 Extraction of raw materials, Denmark 1989–99

Effectiveness and possible revision The current structure of the combined raw material and landfill tax strongly encourages recycling and re-use, particularly of construction and demolition wastes, and provides a fairly strong incentive to minimize waste production. Recovery of the 3 to 3.5 million tonnes approximately of construction and demolition waste generated per annum increased significantly, from 10 to 90 per cent during the 1990s.

As Figure 3.3 illustrates, the raising of the waste tax from EUR5 to 17 tonne induced a recycling rate increase from 25 to nearly 80 per cent. Since then, the tax has been tripled, which has raised the recycling rate to about 90 per cent. However, the case indicates also that a tax of EUR17 seemed to be enough to reach a recycling rate of about 80 per cent and the effect of raising the tax above EUR17 has been minimal as regards construction and demolition waste. This,

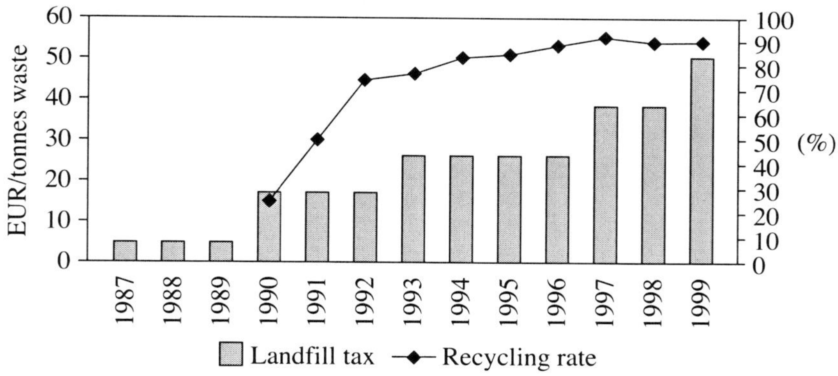

Source: European Environment Agency (2001).

Figure 3.3 Recycling rate for construction and demolition waste in Denmark compared to the waste tax rate

however, can be different in other countries, depending on the general waste regulation, the price difference between landfilling and alternative treatment forms, and on how accessible alternative treatment forms are (see EEA, 2001: 30).

Recycled construction and demolition waste accounts only for some 3 million tonnes per year, which is only about 10 per cent of the total input, which is about 25 to 35 million tonnes of construction minerals demanded per year. This shows that the potential to replace virgin raw materials is limited even if all the construction and demolition waste is to be recycled. Similar experiences have been met in Germany, where the recycling rate of construction and demolition waste has been increased thanks to a voluntary agreement.

UK: aggregates levy

Description The UK Aggregates Levy was introduced in April 2002 (Ecotec, 2001). It applies to sand, gravel and crushed rock subjected to commercial exploitation in the UK. This includes aggregate dredged from the seabed within UK territorial waters (the 12 mile limit). It is a one-stage, non-deductible specific tax charged at £1.60 (EUR2.53) per tonne.

The objective is to address, by taxation, the environmental costs associated with quarrying operations (noise, dust, visual intrusion, loss of amenity and damage to biodiversity) in line with the government's strategy of shifting the burden, over time, of taxation from 'goods' such as labour, to 'bads' such as environmental pollution and resource use. It further aims to reduce demand for virgin aggregate and encourage the use of recycled materials. To protect international competitiveness, the tax is levied on imports but exports will be exempted. Recycled aggregates also are not subject to the levy.

There is a comprehensive range of exemptions for other quarried or mined products such as coal, metal ores and industrial minerals. and for limestone used in the production of lime. Blocks of stone ('dimension stone') used for facing or repairing structures lie outside the scope of the levy. Aggregates used in prescribed industrial or agricultural processes are relieved, as will be exports of aggregate. Imports are taxed upon first sale or use in the UK.

Also, as a result of consultation, there are exemptions for the following:

- any aggregate necessarily arising from the dredging of marine navigation channels and inland waterways, road construction and building construction;
- the spoil or waste from, or other by-products of, any industrial combustion process or the smelting or refining of metals;
- offshore drill cuttings;
- excavation of highways for utility work.

Trader base is persons commercially exploiting aggregates in the UK (in most instances this will be the quarry operators) and imported aggregate on the basis of 'first sale or use in the UK'. The levy will raise around £380 (EUR601.9) million per year – all of which will be returned to business through a 0.1 per cent point cut in employer NICs (social security contributions) and a new Sustainability Fund aimed at delivering local environmental benefits to areas subject to the environmental costs of aggregates extraction.[2] There will be no net gain to the Exchequer from this reform. The government will be consulting on how the new Sustainability Fund can best be used to deliver local environmental benefits.

Effectiveness The UK aggregate tax has only been put in place recently. A best estimate of the impact of a £1.60 levy on the demand for primary aggregates would be a reduction of around 10 per cent, or approximately 25 million tonnes. These estimates are subject to a wide margin of error (Ecotec, 2001). Due to rather low price elasticities and the comparable high tax rate of £1.60, it can be expected that the UK model will have a more significant impact than the Danish and Swedish examples.

Conclusions on Raw Material Taxes and Possible Future Developments

The three taxation schemes on raw materials (construction minerals) presented above constitute first experiences with this instrument in Europe. Because of low price elasticities for construction minerals the effectiveness is strongly dependent on the level of the tax rate or relative price increase, respectively. The Danish case (EUR0.67 per m^3) seems to be too low to induce an absolute reduction in raw material use. The UK case (EUR2.53 per tonne) can be expected to have a more significant effect. The Swedish case does aim at a replacement of materials, not at an absolute reduction of aggregate construction minerals.

Low price elasticities are also due to a lack of technological innovations to provide more eco-efficient buildings and infrastructures. Therefore a raw material tax has to be accompanied by a technological development ('eco-efficiency revolution'). Other policy measures (such as R&D) that can be driven by sustainable enterprises (see Chapter 4) and information (see Chapter 5) could be considered towards this end. Only if alternative technologies are available to provide the same 'service' with fewer resources, will resource taxation be effective. At the same time, resource taxation would be an incentive for such a technological change.

It seems likely that the three examples will be fed into the discussion on a thematic strategy on the sustainable use of natural resources at the European Union level. They represent one instrument which addresses the source of major non-energetic material flows through the economy and thus contributes to a policy mix for a balanced management of the economic metabolism. The instrument of raw material taxation also supplements energy taxation.[3]

3.3 THE GERMAN RENEWABLE ENERGY SOURCES ACT: CREATING A DYNAMIC MARKET

Renewable energies in Germany are experiencing an upturn. That is particularly clear in power generation, where coverage increased from a good 4 per cent at the beginning of the 1990s to more than 7 per cent in 2000 (see Figure 3.4). For 2001, a share of more than 8 per cent is expected in power generation. The development is considerably supported by the surge of output gained from wind energy converters, while above all hydropower has been the dominant renewable energy source in Germany. Wind energy will presumably dislodge hydropower from its leading position in 2002. Less favourable are the conditions for renewables referring to the supply of primary energy. Here, there was an increase from 0.6 per cent at the beginning of the 1990s to 1.9 per cent in 2000.[4]

The Renewable Energy Sources Act ('Erneuerbare Energien Gesetz', EEG), which came into force on 1 April 2001, proves to be an important basis for power generation from renewable energies. In the interest of climate and environmental protection, which are equally important to supply reliability

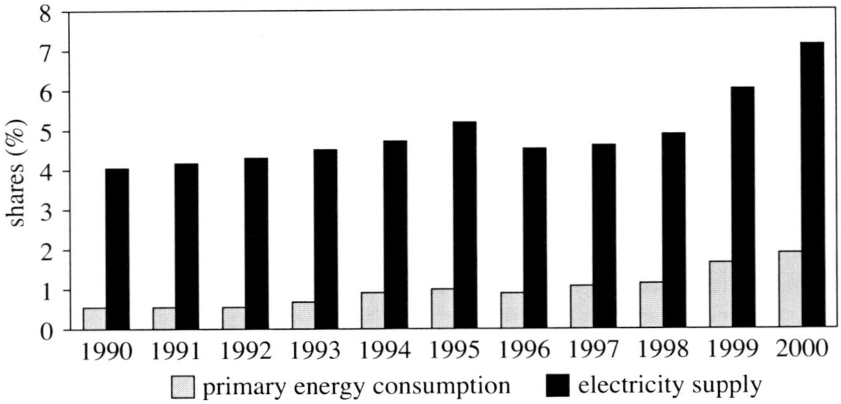

Source: Own compilation.

Figure 3.4 Development in use of renewable energies in Germany since the beginning of the 1990s

and cost efficiency in the energy sector in Germany, according to the amendment of the Power Industry Act in spring 1998, the aim of the Act is to support the extension of renewable energies. In addition, the Act should help to give important impetus to achieve the national and international aim of doubling the share of renewable energies by 2010. The central point of the Act is the regulation of purchasing and remuneration for power which is produced from renewable energies by energy supply companies that operate nets for public supply (system operators) that is, public budgets are not involved. Important features of the EEG are the following:

- integrating most of the renewable energy options by including water power, gas from sanitary landfills (dump gas), sewage gas, pit gas, solar radiant energy, geothermal and organic substances[5] as forms of renewable energy;
- greater incentives to extend the use of renewable energies by limiting the scope of validity[6] to more decentralized plants, that is, water power, sewage and dump gas stations as well as solar energy stations all reaching less than 5MW[7] and stations converting organic substances reaching a maximum of $20MW_{el}$;
- high degree of safety of investment and planning by fixed and technology specific remuneration for generating and feeding in electricity (for example 99Pf/kWh for power generation from solar energy and 20

Pf/kWhg for plants converting organic substances < 500 kW_{el}) over a fixed period of 20 years: remuneration is fixed in such a way that stations can be operated in good locations under economic conditions;
- incentives for a gradual (chronological) cost reduction of the plants through pre-fixed yearly sinking remuneration rates for plants erected in the individual year (the reduction comes for the first time into force for plants erected in 2002 by getting remuneration which is reduced by a certain percentage for the period of validity compared to plants erected in 2000 or 2001; with regard to power generation from radiant energy the reduction is, for example, 5 per cent per annum);
- development that is neutral with regard to competitiveness by implementing a nationwide compensation regulation, which imposes on system operators only expenses in proportion to the power consumption of the final consumers;
- specific regulations with regard to the assumption of costs for measures concerning the grid connection (system operators bear the costs up to the most economical connection within the net) and the grid upgrade (system operators bear these costs but can assert incidental costs within the context of the nationwide compensation regulation);
- possibility of reacting constantly to the actual market trend by ministries in charge regularly viewing the pre-fixed rates every two years and reporting to the German Bundestag.

The encountered regulations of the EEG revise some critical points which had been objected to by its successful predecessor, the Electricity Feed Act (StrEG). The StrEG came into force in 1991 and has already initiated an increasingly dynamic development in wind power together with the 250 MW support programme starting at the same time. This concerns above all the development that is neutral regarding competitiveness and thus the equal treatment of system operators[8] who provide different regions, the equality of power supply companies and private operators (excluded from the scope of validity are only plants more than 25 per cent of which belong to the federal state) and the safety of investment and planning which is higher because of the fixed remuneration rates.[9] In addition, the EEG tries to take the requirement into account to initiate self-organizing markets (instead of permanent subsidies) by pre-fixed remuneration rates that reduce in the course of time for the period of validity (for plants erected in the corresponding years).

Along with the criticism of the previous regulation, which among other things manifested itself in different actions of the power industry in national and European courts, the main impetus to the adjustment was given by the amendment of the 'Electricity and Gas Supply Act' (EnWG) and the resultant liberalization of the power market, which made legal regulations in conformity with the market necessary. Participants in politics, the energy sector and science argued persistently about the better plan. There was a range of several plans including the remuneration for feeding in electricity of the StrEG and also the EEG, the first priority being given to tender models and quota systems. Experience gained from the EEG agrees with the choice made because these instruments are by far the most efficient compared to many other implemented support models (such as tendering procedures) in Europe (see Table 3.3). The installed capacity per capita is much higher in countries with a long-time background of fixed price systems than in countries with tendering procedures, implemented for example in the UK in the mid-1990s with the Non-Fossil Fuel Obligation (NFFO). One problem of such procedures is that several winners of the yearly bidding competitions could not keep their promises because of a cancellation of installation plans.

The satisfactory experience gained by the EEG is also the reason why other countries (for example, Belgium, Greece) have implemented comparable regulations or are considering doing so. In this context it is very important that the EEG guarantees a constant basis for further development, particularly for young growth markets such as wind energy (see Figure 3.5). This stabilizes rational expectations for producers.

In addition, the main legal problems with regard to the EEG have meanwhile been sorted out. In the middle of 2001, the European Court of Justice in Luxembourg upheld the conformity of the EEG with regulations of the EU concerning allowance regulations. Since then the efforts to limit regulations of the EEG by the EU Commissioner for Competition have also stopped. Obviously, the EEG has additionally been established in the European context by the European Parliament through passing the guideline to support power generation from renewable energies on the electricity home market (EU, 2001). On the basis of the white paper, Renewable Energies of the European Union, of 1997, in which the EU aims to double the share of renewable energies by 2010, the guideline for the power market describes clear aims from now on. The share of power generation is to be increased EU-wide from 13.9 per cent in 1997 to around 22 per cent in 2010. The basis for realizing that goal are national aims which differ from country to country and which, along with the EU-wide aim, also derive from different demands recorded in the Kyoto Protocol (and the EU burden sharing which is based on the Protocol). For Germany, an increase from 4.5 per cent to 12.5 per cent is predetermined for the relevant period. The guideline gives the nations a free hand – in contrast to former views – to implement such support guidelines that suit specific requirements of the individual country (this is also explicitly true for feed-in regulations). In 2005, the effectiveness of individual national measures will be checked and, if necessary, on this basis an EU-wide coordinated support programme will be introduced. For national regulations which

Table 3.3 Comparison of efficiency of different models to support renewable energies in Europe

	Country	Installed capacity at the end of 2000 (MW)	Extension 2000 (MW)	Installed capacity per head (W/population)	Installed capacity per space (kW/km²)
Countries with fixed prices (Electricity Feed Act)	Germany	6.113	1.670	74.51	17.12
	Spain	2.481	939	63.02	4.92
	Denmark[1]	2.301	530	434.07	53.39
Countries with tendering procedures	Great Britain The Non-Fossil Fuel Obligation (NFFO)	406	62	6.88	1.67
	Ireland	93	20	25.1	1.32
	France	60	38	1.02	0.11

Note: [1]At present, Denmark is in the process of transition to a quota system.

Source: Gsänger (2001).

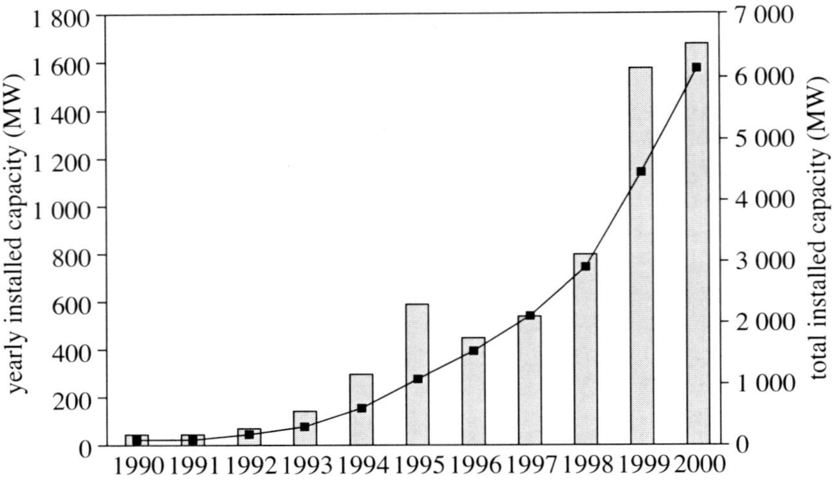

Source: Own compilation.

Figure 3.5 Dynamic development of wind energy in Germany since the beginning of the 1990s

are implemented by then, an adequate interim period (at least seven years) is granted. On the part of the EU there is a fidelity clause for the EEG until 2012.

Though the starting period of the EEG seems promising, some need for improvement still exists. This is especially important with regard to the following:

- improved hydro power stations that must be included in the scope of validity to exhaust potentials;
- prolonging the period in which special terms are granted to offshore wind power stations, owing to the fact that a final ecological sustainability study, done with care, has to be carried out beforehand;
- combining the scope of validity with specific requirements for the quality of a plant with regard to energy saving (minimum effectiveness) and encouraging an extension of the plants to cogeneration. This applies above all to organic substances, for which there was a planning boom for plants with a capacity of 20 MW_{el} after the implementation of the EEG. Owing to the size on the one hand and to the fact that these fuels only occur away from the consumers' location on the other, as a rule little or no heat use at all is planned for these plants. Over and above

that, the commitment to a single capacity leads to a concentration on technologies based on steam power, which are currently known and developed, while there is no impetus for innovative ideas (in particular biomass gasification).

Over and above that, it is clear that the aim of the federal government of doubling the share of renewable energies and even more additional aims such as those formulated by the Federal Ministry of the Environment (compared to the total of power generation a gradual increase in share of renewable energies of 10 per cent per decade to over 50 per cent in 2050), cannot be carried out without further supporting measures. Scenario analyses show that in reaching the aim of doubling there are assumed marginal costs of around Euro 2.2bn in 2010 compared to the assumed price of electricity supply (3 Eurocent/kWh). Compared to the autonomous extension of a development following business-as-usual methods, the marginal costs reduce to around Euro 1bn per year in 2010. Present experience shows that some means could be covered by private commitment of power consumers (see Chapter 4) and some parts may be raised by specific incentive programmes.

With the EEG, the 100 000 photovoltaic roofs programme, the launch programme of the federal government which was increased in 2002 to Euro 200mn (with special priority for heat supply from renewable energies) and the eco-tax in Germany, essential milestones have been set up in the area of power generation. In contrast, there still remains (above all because of decreasing state programmes) a substantial funding shortfall to cover the aim of doubling the heat supply. First, suggestions for instruments (such as a quota model for centralized heat plants) are being developed at the moment. To support renewable energies, a mix of measures has to be carried out if the aim of doubling is to be reached. In 2000, the entire support of renewable energies in Germany amounted to around Euro 1.2bn, with high shares of wind energy and bio-diesel (see Figure 3.6).[10] In the same year, the volume of investments induced amounted to around Euro 4bn (see Figure 3.7).

Only small parts of the support programmes of power generation have an effect on the federal budget. The main components are financed, not by tax, but through assessment systems by the customer. This applies in particular to the EEG. For consumers of electricity the current situation regarding renewable energies leads to additional costs of around 0.15 Eurocent/kWh; if the aim of doubling is achieved, these costs increase to around 0.4 Eurocent/kWh until 2010 (see Figure 3.8). For the period from 2000 until 2010, a volume of investments of around Euro 21bn is induced, with corresponding positive expectations for the labour market.[11]

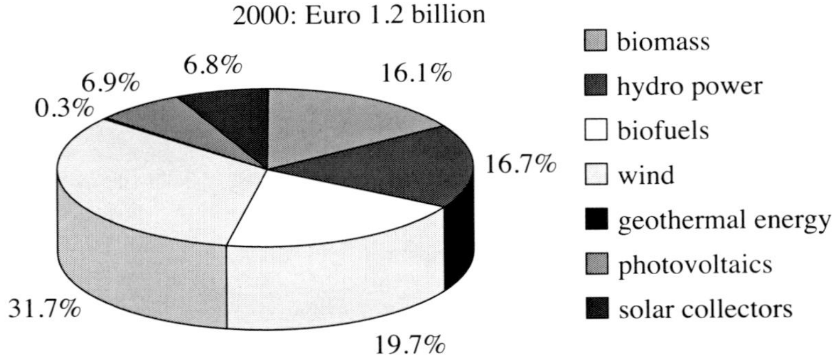

Source: Staiß (2001).

Figure 3.6 Public spending (government aid) in renewable energies in 2000, by technology

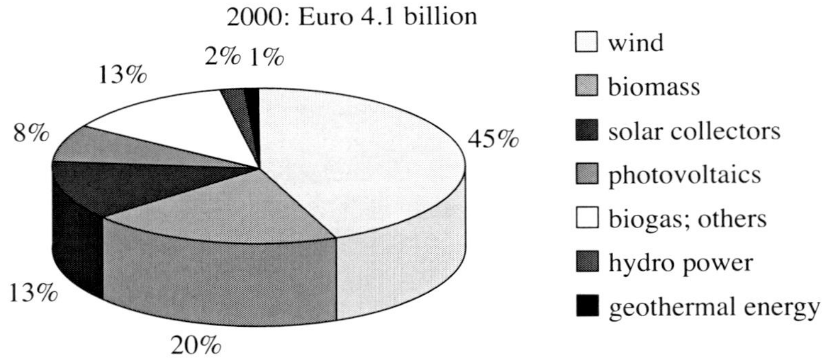

Source: Staiß (2001).

Figure 3.7 Induced volume of investments in 2000, by technology

3.4 POLICIES TO STIMULATE DEMAND-SIDE ENERGY SERVICES

Following the European Parliament and Council Directives 96/92/EC and 98/30/EC on common rules for the internal market in electricity and natural gas (IEM and IGM Directives), most EU member states have restructured and liberalized their markets for these grid-connected energies. It is expected that, over a number of years, more competition on the supply side of energy will

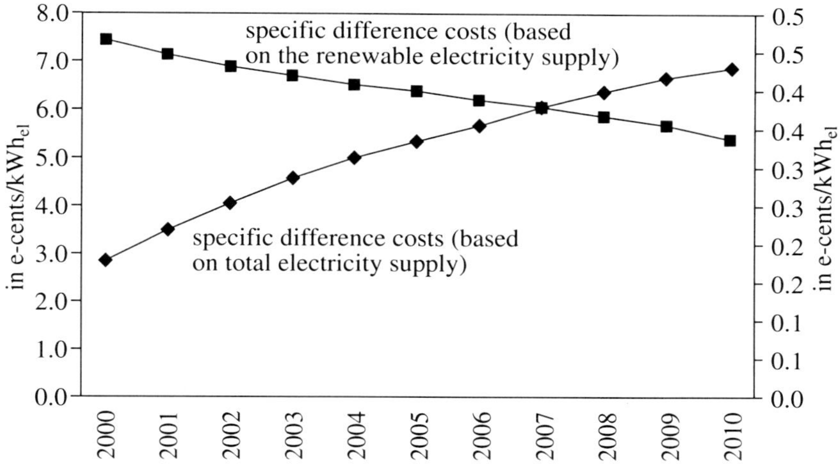

Figure 3.8 *Development of additional costs for German consumers of electricity by reaching the aim of doubling power generation*

have been introduced. On the other side, the harmonization of market conditions created by the IEM and IGM Directives does not extend to increased energy efficiency on the demand side, that is, in the final use of electricity and gas.

With the fact in mind that demand-side energy efficiency offers considerable potential for both economic and environmental improvement, a few European countries have introduced national activities and structures on integrated resource planning (IRP) or demand-side management (DSM) that could be a model for both the whole of Europe and other regions. One of the most interesting and advanced systems is represented by Denmark, and will be presented in the following. Before that, a short survey of important economic aspects will be presented.

What is the Basic Market: Energy or Energy Services?

The main target of restructuring the power and gas sector in the European Union, and elsewhere, is currently to capture economic efficiencies in energy supply resulting from direct competition of 'suppliers' of end-use energy and from price setting by market forces and distribution.

However, the cost-effective supply of end-use energy (for example gas, electricity) is only a necessary, not a sufficient, condition for an efficient allocation of resources. End-use energy is not the end product, but only an intermediate product. Final consumers in industry, private and public service and

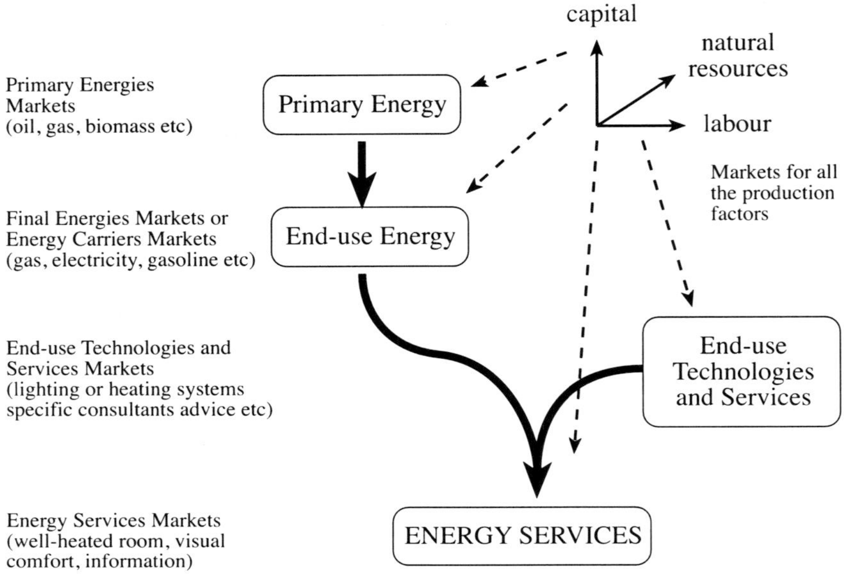

Source: Wuppertal Institute (2001).

Figure 3.9 The final product: energy services, provided by interdependent markets

the residential sector do not benefit directly from end-use energy, such as gas or electricity, but from genuine (physical) energy services, such as properly lit and heated rooms, 'hot pizza and cold beer'. Therefore these genuine energy services, not energy ('kilowatt hours'), have to be provided with as little damage as possible to health and the environment and at the least cost.[12]

Genuine energy services, like well-heated rooms, are produced by converting final energy using end-use technologies. This process can become more energy-efficient if energy efficiency technologies and services (such as an energy-efficient heating system, focused consulting) are used. End-use energy, and energy efficiency technologies and services, are themselves combinations of the factors of capital, labour (human capital, know-how, behaviour) and natural resources (see Figure 3.9).

It is not sufficient to limit market reforms to only a part of the market by stopping at end-use energy. This is a clear result of economic theory: only the optimization over all stages of the production process of genuine energy services, shown in Figure 3.10 (p. 82), leads to efficient allocation; that is, to a least-cost provision of genuine energy services.

The European Pioneers: the Example of Denmark

A number of European countries have introduced policies to stimulate the energy efficiency activities of energy companies and (private) energy service companies at the same time when liberalizing their electricity and gas markets. Among those countries are Denmark, Norway and the UK and, more recently, Belgium and Italy.

As the analysis of these DSM experiences has shown (Wuppertal Institute *et al.*, 2000), DSM has been most effective where a combination of the following has been created:

- an agreed, quantified target for energy savings,
- a regulatory framework which eliminates artificial incentives to increase sales when non-economic for customers and society,
- a channel or an allowance for raising funding, and
- a standardized and mandatory scheme for cost–benefit evaluation of the energy efficiency (EE-DSM).

Such combinations have been used, for example, in Denmark, the Netherlands and the USA. Sometimes the target is imposed (as in the UK or the USA); in other cases it is the result of negotiations (as in the Netherlands or in Denmark in the past). Furthermore, a policy package with the appropriate and needed legal and technical support mechanisms is useful in any circumstances. Since WI considers the Danish policy on DSM to be a comprehensive example, we will concentrate in this chapter on the policies and programmes that are in place in Denmark.

The Danish policy to stimulate the energy efficiency activities of energy companies and (private) energy service companies must be seen in the context of a comprehensive energy efficiency policy, including actions for all types of energy and all consumer groups. This policy was developed following the oil price crises of the 1970s, since Denmark at that time had no major energy resources of its own, and was largely dependent on oil. Since then, Danish energy policy has been developed in a consensus between policy, the energy industry, energy consumers and other stakeholders.

Stimulating demand-side management has been the most important instrument of Danish energy policy to encourage electricity savings. It is complemented by other policies on regulating the heat demand of buildings, advice on heat demand and labelling of buildings, a relatively high energy tax, and negotiated agreements with individual industrial companies to invest in measures to reduce their energy consumption. The companies can get a refund of their energy tax in return for the investments. This instrument achieves synergies with the DSM activities since the electricity companies are offering free energy audits to their industrial customers.

In the early 1990s, the Danish Energy Agency reached an agreement with the energy companies to implement DSM activities identified in an IRP process (obligatory since 1994). DSM costs are collected through the tariffs by electricity distribution/supply companies from all customers and on average amount to 0.05 cEUR/kWh, corresponding to about 1 per cent of the revenues. The administration of the funds, the programme design and the measurement and verification of the activities are done by the distribution network companies following guidelines from the Danish Energy Agency, which controls and evaluates the overall mechanism. With the new energy law implementing the liberalization of the energy markets, the DSM programmes are now an obligation on the unbundled distribution network companies. However, the IRP process has been abolished; it is generally recognized that 'traditional' electricity sector IRP is not possible any more owing to the IEM Directive. Still, the basic principles of assessing supply and demand-side options on an equal basis are supported widely. As for tariff regulation of the distribution business, as in the past it is formulated in such a way as to guarantee a fair and fixed level of return on investments for companies irrespective of sales variations; hence companies are not subject to artificial incentives to increase sales, nor do they suffer profit losses when undertaking DSM programmes which reduce energy consumption.

Amongst other reasons, this decision in favour of a continuation of DSM activities in the liberalized market was based on the fact that the results achieved and the expertise acquired prove that the energy companies are competent and committed to the task, and that it is thus natural to complete the market for energy with energy company DSM. Secondly, the separation by entity of distribution and supply is thought to minimize the potential problem of conflicting interests. Finally, a public service obligation on DSM combined with a cost-recovery mechanism represents a relatively robust and stable financing mechanism and also ensures a certain level of continuity and institutional capacity.

Around 700GWh/a of electricity was saved between 1994 and 1998 through energy companies' DSM activities, for example through free energy efficiency audits for industry and commerce, programmes promoting compact fluorescent lamps (CFLs), rebate programmes for Class A refrigerators and freezers (DEA/energy piano 2000). This saving compares to a total consumption of 32.4TWh/a. This success is based on agreements between utilities and government, the legal obligation to perform IRP, permission to fund DSM costs via the tariffs, and the 'no-profit-no-loss' principle of Danish electricity price regulation that allowed the utilities to recover any net lost revenues from the reduction in kWh sales. For 2000, further savings of over 160GWh/a had been planned, with an investment by the energy companies of about EUR20 mn, and EUR35 mn by the customers. The investment by the energy companies thus now equals about 0.06 Eurocent for each kWh sold (ELFOR og Sjaellandssamarbejdet, 1999). Danish experiences show that 0.5 to 1 per cent savings per year compared to the market trend appear feasible, with annual investments by the energy companies of 1 to 2 per cent of the revenues from the electricity business.

Further energy savings will be achieved in Denmark through the activities of the Electricity Savings Trust and from the agreements negotiated with industry in return for reductions in their energy tax. Since the Electricity Savings Trust (Figure 3.10) is financed from a special levy on the energy industry, and often cooperates with electricity companies in implementing the programmes, this system can be considered as part of the DSM policy as well.

The Electricity Savings Trust (EST) was created by the Ministry of Environment and Energy with the objective of reducing CO_2 emissions by 3 million tonnes by 2008, which corresponds to 8 per cent of today's emissions. The Trust's activities comprise conversion from electric heating to CHP or

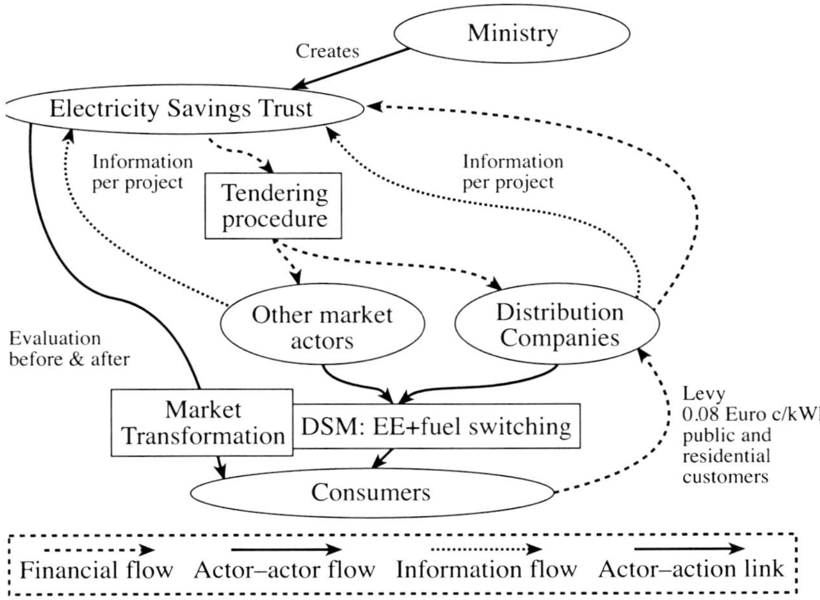

Source: Thomas *et al*. (2000).

Figure 3.10 The Danish Electricity Savings Trust and its context

natural gas, and other market transformation activities. It is a private independent entity with a board of eight members named by the Ministry of Environment and Energy representing NGOs, municipalities, industry, energy companies and energy conservation experts. The EST was created in 1997. In 1998, it was funded through a volume-based levy of 0.08 Eurocent/kWh, collected by distribution companies only from households and the public sector (an extension to the commercial sector and heating fuels is being discussed). The total amount is around EUR12 mn per year.

Private companies or electricity companies are invited to submit tenders to design and implement projects. The projects with the highest reduction in CO_2 emissions at the lowest cost are selected. The Danish example shows the most advanced European approach to EE-DSM. Nevertheless, there are a lot of improvement options, mainly with the focus on better coordination and cost-effectiveness.

EU Process on DSM

There is still a continuing discussion about whether and how to implement DSM at the European level. Following a recommendation from the European Commission's Energy Efficiency Action Plan (CEC, 2000) and from the European Climate Change Programme (CEC, 2001d), the European Commission is expected to launch a proposal for an EU Directive on Energy Services during the spring of 2003. This legislation is expected to set targets for the member states on energy savings to be achieved through creating a supportive framework for electricity and gas companies. This framework should allow the companies to realize and finance energy efficiency programmes and services without harming their competitive position in the liberalized EU electricity and gas markets.

Hence the EU would set the framework, but the implementation of DSM and the DSM programmes and services would still be the task of national policy. This adds to efforts to get the prices right via CO_2/energy taxes. Whereas the latter can be expected to have positive effects on a broad and long-term scale, DSM has comparative advantages to overcome specific information and adaptation deficits at the level of companies and consumers.

3.5 ECO-EFFICIENCY RELATED TO BUILDINGS

Housing as well as clothing and nutrition are elementary parts of a human being's basic needs. The WI (2001: 10) has illustrated the relevance of the energetic optimization of residential buildings as an opportunity for climate and resource protection as well as for the labour market in Germany. The importance of building renovation in Germany depends first of all on the high life expectancy of buildings and, secondly, on the constant climate conditions from north to south in the country, with a heating period lasting eight months (Wallbaum *et al.*, 1999). Consequently, the German government has identified building renovation as one of the most relevant subjects in the national climate protection programme.

Another important subject in the climate protection programme is the Energy Conservation Regulation (EnEV) that raises the energy standard in new buildings. This policy instrument seems to be well suited for the Japanese situation because of the high construction rate of new buildings, lower life expectancies of older buildings and the various climate conditions. Therefore, in this chapter we focus on one policy instrument that could foster the necessary structural change in the building sector. We also give a brief overview of the aims, the possibilities and obstacles in the introduction phase, as well as a statement on points to improve the policy instrument.

The New Energy Conservation Regulation in Germany

According to the Commission of the European Communities there is an estimated economic potential for energy efficiency improvement of more than 18 per cent over current energy consumption in the EU as a result of removing market barriers which prevent the satisfactory diffusion of energy-efficient technology and the efficient use of energy. For example, energy prices still do not accurately reflect energy costs including externalities: 'This potential is equivalent to over 160Mtoe, or 1900TWh, roughly the total final energy demand of Austria, Belgium, Denmark, Finland, Greece and the Netherlands combined' (CEC, 2000).

One measure to limit carbon dioxide emissions by improving energy efficiency of buildings in Germany is the proposed Energy Conservation Regulation 2002. The regulation is geared to a so-called 'primary energy approach' – in other words, the losses arising in the chain from energy extraction to energy use (accounting for around two-thirds of primary energy in the case of electricity) will be attributed to the end consumer as far as possible. This will ensure equal competition between fuels. This regulation came into force in February 2002. It follows the European harmonized standards and sets out a new basis for the calculation of heating and energy requirements. This new ordinance does not just apply to new buildings but also imposes an obligation to modernize building stock to meet the new requirement (BMVBW, 2001).

Referring to official sources, the Energy Conservation Regulation is designed to cut the energy demand of new buildings by around 20 to 30 per cent compared with current standards. Furthermore, the Regulation also envisages compulsory upgrading of existing buildings and extends more stringent requirements for structural measures. The regulation is designed to make a lasting contribution to energy saving in the building sector.

An Assessment of the Energy Conservation Regulation

A real step forward is the integrated view of the entire system, which means the building and heating system together. The introduction of a primary energy approach to rate the energetic quality of buildings is just as important as the integration of the hot water system. In comparison to the Heat Protection Regulation 1995, the new Energy Conservation Regulation 2002 includes also the power requirements of auxiliary systems, such as heat pumps. Another positive point concerns the demands for building insulation in the case of the rehabilitation of existing buildings.

Since 2002, the renewal of plaster on outer walls, with a *u*-value (heat transmission coefficient) > 0.9W/(m^2K), is acknowledged as an energetic optimization. A definition of a *u*-value is the quantity of heat which passes per unit of area and time through a partition of constant thickness from a fluid to another having a temperature difference of 1 kelvin. According to the new law, the retrofit of the top floor ceiling and the insulation of heating mains in existing buildings are also obligatory (see Table 3.4). Heat bridges and airproofness are further aspects that will be taken into account by the Energy Conservation Regulation.

Besides the improvements mentioned above, most experts share the opinion that the announced energy-saving potential of new buildings 'of around 30 per cent' could not be reached by the new regulations. It is obvious that a reduction in energy of 5 to 25 per cent on average could be reached, depending on the individual case. In particular, the low energy house standard (detached houses: ≤ 70kWh/m^2a; multiple dwellings: ≤ 70kWh/m^2a) will probably not be reached. The 'real' energetic values expected for typical detached houses are between 75 and 120kWh/m^2a and for multiple dwellings between 70 and 100kWh/m^2a (see Figure 3.11). Also a new approach to verify the implementation of the regulations is still missing. The chosen reference, 'usable building floor space', for the energy value in the new regulation is an artificial dimension and presents a lower energy value than actually occurs in reality. The reference 'living space' would have been more appropriate. Another negative point concerns the missing steps for a further tightening up of the Energy Conservation Regulation (dynamic component).

To sum up, it can be said that the new Energy Conservation Regulation offers a step forward, but does not cope satisfactorily with the long-term climate protection requirements in the building sector, whether for new buildings or for existing buildings. The intention to improve the energy efficiency

Table 3.4 Comparison of the minimum demands defined in the current Heat Protection Regulation 1995 and the Energy Conservation Regulation 2002

		Max. u-Value in $W/(m^2K)$	
		Current Heat Protection Regulation 1995	Draft of the Energy Conservation Regulation 2002
Outer walls:	renewal of facade	0.4	0.35
	interior renewal	0.5	0.45
Ceiling or roof:	steep roof	0.3	0.3
	flat roof	0.3	0.25
Cellar ceiling or ground floor:	renewal from cellar	0.5	0.4
	renewal from basement	0.5	0.5
Windows and doors:	renewal of the glazing	–	1.5*
	renewal incl. frame	1.8	1.7
	doors	–	2.9

Note: *u-value of the glazing

Source: Institute Wohnen und Umwelt (2001: 4).

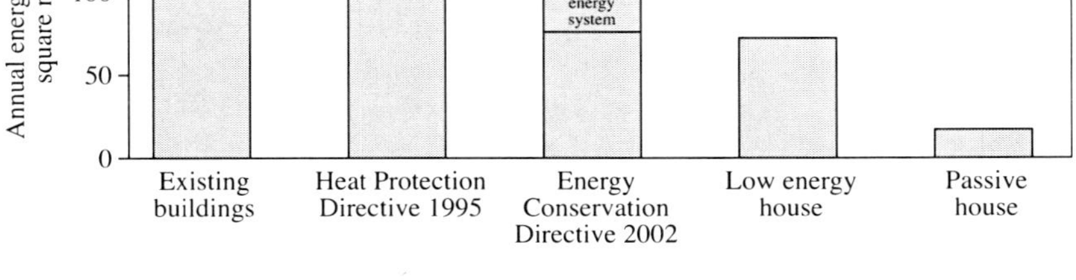

Source: Institut Wohnen and Umwelt (2001).

Figure 3.11 Energy demand for heating according to different heat protection standards (detached house)

of buildings and to combine the old Heat Protection Regulation and the Heating Systems Regulation can be considered a forward-looking strategy, but it seems that the necessary steps towards an active climate protection process in the building sector unfortunately fall short. In addition the Energy Conservation Regulation has to be seen as a purely energy-focused optimization instrument without setting environmentally advisable incentives regarding the reduction of material flows from a life cycle-wide perspective, through, for example, eco-efficient building materials and burden recycling.

From Energy-efficient Buildings to Sustainable Settlements

Apart from the mainly energy-focused debate on buildings in the 1980s and the early 1990s, the discussion later in the 1990s shifted more towards a whole life cycle respecting perspective (NRW decree, 1998). For example, at the international level the OECD's Sustainable Buildings Project was initiated in spring 1998 as a four-year project with the objective of providing guidance regarding the design of government policies addressing the environmental impact of the building sector. In this context a sustainable building policy strove to minimize the consumption of energy and resources in all phases, from its planning and construction through its operation, maintenance and renovation to its eventual demolition. It also aimed to minimize any possible damage to the natural environment, to improve the overall economic efficiency of buildings, such as costs of construction, operation, use, environment and health,[13] as well as non-monetary values and, last but not least, sociocultural aspects.

In Germany several actors, including politicians, NGOs and trade unions, have started initiatives to translate the normative concept of a sustainable development into action. Especially in the building sector, some respectable steps may be observed and these will be briefly presented in the following paragraphs.

Initiative for cost-favourable and quality-conscious construction

This new initiative is represented by a coalition of the Federal Ministry of Transport, Building and Housing, several associations and organizations, including the Federal Chamber of Architects, Trade Union for Building, Agriculture and the Environment, Association of Private Building Societies, Federal Association of the German Construction Industry and others.

The subscribers of the common statement support steps to tap all sustainable rationalization and innovation potentials in the planning and building process. They will also do their very best to enlarge information services and to broaden the information base. To offer an organizational platform for the initiative, the Federal Ministry of Transport, Building and Housing has founded a new centre of competence.[14] This centre should consolidate, assess, process and pass on all the information on the subject to make, more than in the past, all the knowledge usable to the actors involved – from communities through architects, consultants and planners to the initiator of a building project and craftsmen. Another particular task of the centre is the investigation of all materials available and the neutral information of the public. Apart from the points mentioned above, the centre will run different qualification and education workshops and further training programmes to promote the examples for cost-favourable and quality-conscious constructions.

Guideline for Sustainable Building

In January 2001, the Federal Ministry of Transport, Building and Housing presented the Guideline for Sustainable Building[15] (Federal Ministry of Transport, Building and Housing, 2001a). This guideline is a working aid and is intended to implement integrated principles for the sustainable planning, construction, operation, maintenance and use of federal landholdings and buildings. The guideline contains information, principles and benchmarks, such as the following:

- a checklist as the basis of the planning process, to ensure that all the criteria relevant to the subject of sustainability are given due consideration;
- the 'Planning Principles for the Design of Buildings and Landholdings', which is directed primarily towards architects who can use their design to exert a significant influence on the implementation of the principles of sustainability;
- requirements for health protection and comfort;
- a minimum standard for a sustainable approach to energy, water/sewage and waste to be achieved;
- an appendix, 'Design Principles for Outdoor Facilities' that presents important aspects which can be of significance in the design, construction, operation and eventual later demolition of building measures and outdoor facilities;
- a checklist to assess and benchmark independently the ecological, economic and sociocultural aspects of buildings and landholdings; and, finally,
- a model to draw up building certificates.

With this guideline, the Federal Ministry takes a courageous approach and sets a good example to private construction companies, education facilities, and so on, but it must be taken into consideration that the performance quality of this guideline depends on its motivational power and the generation of knowledge across different actors, as well as on the competences of the persons involved.

Nevertheless, the Federal Ministry has undertaken a far-sighted step that could probably also serve as a good basis for professional construction companies in the future. Similar to the EU directive on old vehicles, it is foreseeable that in the future also manufacturers of construction materials and construction companies will be entirely liable for collecting and recycling waste, just as car manufacturers today are responsible for the costs of collecting and recycling scrap cars, which owners are able to deliver to recycling centres free of charge. In this context the design phase of buildings will become more and more important to reduce the environmental impacts due to building infrastructure. In the national scientific debate the demand also to regard a building as a product and consequently to follow the rules of eco-design to reduce the ecological impact is not new (see Table 3.5). But in the future the ideas of modular buildings, like 'LEGO-Buildings',[16] will become more important also from an economic perspective.

The Socially Integrative City

In 1999, the German federal government and the Länder launched a joint programme, 'Districts With Special Development Needs – The Socially Integrative City'.[17] The project gives Germany an innovative approach to urban renewal policy. It is designed to pool resources (policies in the fields of employment, economy, ecology, social affairs, youth affairs, culture and urban development), to foster cooperation between all involved players and to mobilize the residents of a neighbourhood. 'The Socially Integrative City' is a complex and challenging programme. It was established to counteract the growing sociospatial disintegration in German cities and is based on model conceptions of urban 'social integration' and of a new 'civic society'.

The reorientation of urban development promotion introduced by the 'Socially Integrative City' programme is anchored in various reform initiatives that the federal government, Länder and municipalities have developed to solve the extremely complex problems they now face. This shift is due to the fact that it has become obvious that sectorial efforts to solve many policy problems are inadequate. The new approaches range from the Alliance for Employment to the tax reform, from the revamping of the welfare state to administrative reform, from Local Agenda 21 processes to crime prevention councils and the Healthy Cities Network. A peculiarity of the 'Socially Integrative City' programme is its encouragement of all levels of government as well as various neighbourhood players to cooperate and create interinstitutional and intersectorial structures to this end. Investment projects as well as initiatives which do not involve investment are to be dovetailed and merged

Table 3.5 Eco-efficiency strategies in the building sector

Level of product components	Level of product structure
Selection of materials with little environmental impact, e.g.: • environmentally compatible materials (small ecological rucksack; no human and eco-toxic substances), • renewable materials (if sustainably produced), • materials with low energy content, • recycled materials, • recyclable materials	Optimization of product techniques, e.g.: • alternative product processes, • more efficient energy use, • less product waste
Reduction of material inputs, e.g.: • reduction of the product weight, • reduction of the product volume	Optimization of the distribution systems, e.g.: • fewer, environmentally compatible and re-usable packages, • use of more energy-efficient transport systems, • choice of more energy-efficient logistics
	Reduction of environmental impacts during the use phase, e.g.: • more efficient energy use Energy from environmentally compatible sources
Shifting from product-oriented to service-oriented approaches • Mobility management, e.g. car sharing, removal services, caretaker services	

Source: Own representation by Wallbaum, based on Schmidt-Bleek and Tischner (1995).

into an efficient, high-impact policy 'for the citizens and by the citizens' in individual urban districts.

The German Länder nominated a total of 161 districts in 123 larger and smaller municipalities for the 1999 edition of the programme. During the year 2000 the numbers were increased to 210 districts in 137 municipalities. Two types of urban districts with particular development insufficiencies play leading roles: huge, densely populated housing estates built in the 1960s, 1970s and 1980s, and late 19th-century residential areas, primarily on the fringes of the inner city. In addition, each Land in the Federal Republic selected a model district for the programme. These 16 model districts will be accompanied by a procedure labelled 'on-site programme support'. This not only involves implementation and documentation, but also backs local activists with advice, information and 'logistical support'.

Reinforcement of civic participation and codetermination, such as establishment of neighbourhood management or similar organizational structures, is an integral part of the programme. This reorientation constitutes a major challenge for experts in town planning, urban development, youth services, social work, community affairs, labour administration, business promotion, culture and environmental protection. It requires a new perception of policy and administration, including the willingness to forgo a 'vested' authority to make decisions and design projects, to embrace less formal procedures, to get away from established, proven routines and to shape innovative concepts for integrative urban district development and put them into practice.

The overall benefit of the 'Socially Integrative City' programme should be more stability and improvement of life quality and living conditions in urban sub-communities. The new approach should also boost civic awareness and involvement in a larger number of residents. The success of the programme depends to a large extent on whether the programme is able to achieve the following:

- motivate residents, business and other players to take an active role in neighbourhood development and thus foster the evolution of sustainable, self-sufficient structures;
- develop cross-sectional and district-focused strategies without losing sight of the city-wide perspective;
- establish durable problem-oriented and locally relevant organization and management structures in municipal administration and in urban districts;
- understand integrative action, not as a generalist claim made by individual political and administrative bodies, but as a mandate to form partnerships and reach a consensus;
- design the programme as an open process and a mutual learning experience for players in all branches of government and in the local community.

In conclusion, it could be said that the energy dimension of eco-efficient buildings is already part of regulatory policies. Further progress from a low energy standard to a passive house standard can be expected. Beneath the minimization of the energy demanded in the heating period a further step towards an eco-efficient building is supported through the Renewable Energy Sources Act (EEG) (see section 3.3 above). The possible choice of more and more accepted and available renewable energy carriers and systems offers new opportunities for a higher energy and often simultaneously life cycle-wide material productivity.

Apart from this pure energy-oriented approach, material flows and other dimensions have started to be acknowledged and information-based tools represent the necessary starting point. Regarding the variety of actors, they will have to be approved step by step in the years ahead. Whether this will become part of EU legislation or whether competences at the national or local level are better suited to choose appropriate knowledge-creating institutions remains to be seen. A possible implementation of a resource taxation as shown in section 3.2 above would certainly stimulate this necessary change from an energetic to a resource-oriented focus to achieve the Factor 10 goal for Germany. As a result of such taxation for the building sector a shift from erecting new buildings to an energetic refurbishment of existing buildings could be assumed. Apart from this resource-saving effect, less land would be developed for new settlements and the related infrastructure. However, visual attractiveness of eco-efficient buildings serves as an additional benchmarking criterion and will support the dissemination of knowledge by professional groups.

3.6 END-OF-LIFE VEHICLES REGULATION IN GERMANY AND EUROPE

Introduction

For many years the motor industry has been taking environmental issues into account for the complete life cycle of their products.[18] In all stages of their lifetime – from design to use and disposal – products affect the environment. In Europe and Germany a more and more stringent environmental legislation has to be faced. Another important factor is the growing consciousness of customers and other stakeholders who, in their decision whether or not to purchase a product, are oriented towards the company's environmental activities or the product's impact on the environment.

Recycling, re-use and recovery are three important environmental challenges which have to be faced by the motor industry. In Germany, companies from different business sectors started from a common position in 1990 to create environmental or recycling policies to reach certain environmental targets. They are organized into a network called 'ARGE-altauto',[19] whose

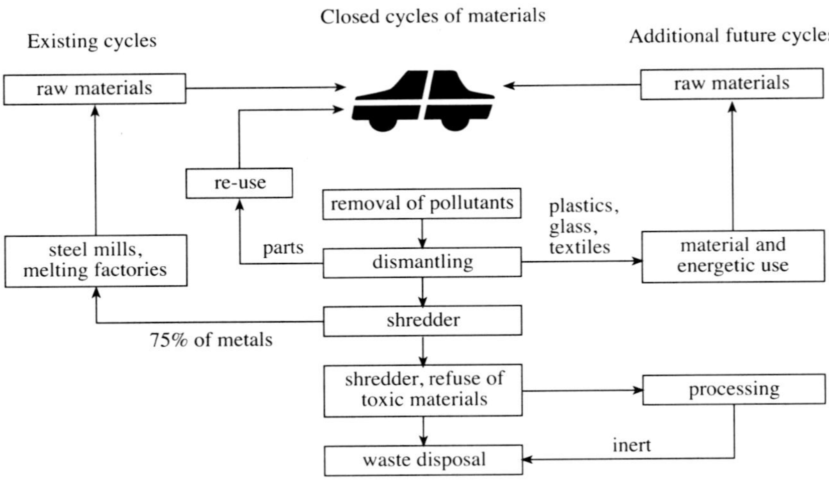

Figure 3.12 Material flows of ELV

main task is to fulfil the voluntary agreement on end-of-life vehicles (ELVs) in Germany, which was signed in 1998.

A nation-wide infrastructure of receiving stations and recycling plants for end-of-life vehicles was already in place when the ordinance came into force. Today, this network comprises approximately 1400 accredited recycling plants and some 15 000 accredited receiving stations to ensure environmentally friendly disposal and material flow cycles (Figure 3.12).

Owing to the disposal and material cycle problems of ELVs, similar activities can be found in Japan. The relevance of this issue mainly results from the large number of vehicles which have to be disposed of in Japan every year (Table 3.6). The number of registered cars in Japan amounts to 50 million, an estimated 4 million of which are disposed of in Japan each year. An estimated one million ELVs are exported.

In Japan a manifest system for ELVs was established in 1998 to ensure the proper handling of ELVs at the businesses that generate them. An analysis of the present situation came to a critical conclusion. As the MITI (Ministry of International Trade and Industry) points out, absence monitoring and spreadsheet systems makes the present manifest system incapable of ensuring proper handling and does not serve to monitor nation-wide recycling (JARI/JICA, 2000).

It can be stated that ELV regulation is a general problem of environmental regulation in industrialized countries. From this point of view, the present section tries to improve the understanding of the end-of-life vehicles regulation

Table 3.6 Number of end-of-life vehicles in Japan

Year	* Number of vehicles in use	Domestic sales	Number of ELVs
1990	57 697 669	7 777 493	
1991	59 914 623	7 524 759	5 307 805
1992	61 658 144	6 959 073	5 215 552
1993	63 262 534	6 467 279	4 862 889
1994	65 011 472	6 526 969	4 777 758
1995	66 853 500	6 865 034	5 023 006
1996	68 801 378	7 077 745	5 129 867
1997	70 003 297	6 725 026	5 523 107
1998	70 814 554	5 879 425	5 068 168
1999	71 722 762	5 861 216	4 953 008

Source: JARI (2000: 4).

in Germany and Europe. Spotlighting the situation in 2000, we would especially like to discuss the relationship between market-based activities and regulation by laws and directives. Our text focuses on the following topics:

- changing material proportions in end-of-life vehicles,
- characterization of evironmental issues and targets of German and European law,
- discussion of stakeholders' arguments,
- understanding of how to embed these aspects and positions into the decision-making process.

Basic Issues

For decades some 75 per cent by weight of an end-of-life vehicle (ELV) has been recycled. Hardly any other consumer product has a recycling rate as high as the motor car. Indeed, entire industries have developed around this task of vehicle recycling, currently focusing in particular on the process of returning metallic materials from ELVs to the materials loop. With the objective of achieving a quantitative reduction in the amount of ELV waste, the motor industry is focusing in particular on those residues which comprise approximately 25 per cent of the vehicle's weight and which currently go mainly to landfill sites. This portion of the vehicle is made up more or less equally of inorganic and organic substances (as shown in Figure 3.13). The organic substances are mainly polymer materials, followed by a small quantity of modified natural substances such

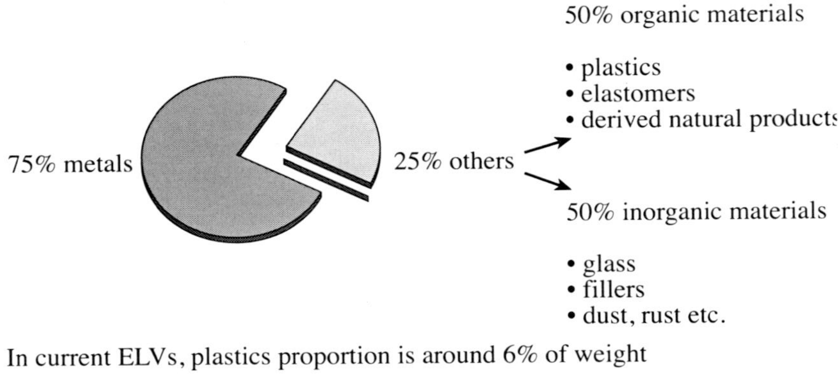

Source: Hook (1998), Summary of the PRAVDA-2 Project.

Figure 3.13 Materials in end-of-life vehicles

as cellulose fibre products or leather. Disproportionate growth in the use of these materials over the last ten years compared with the metallic part of the car has now focused attention on the plastics part. The proportion of plastic components in motor cars has risen from around 5 per cent by weight in 1970 to the present level of around 10 to 12 per cent by weight. In vehicles currently reaching the end of their service lives, the proportion is approximately 6 per cent.

In actual fact vehicles (passenger cars) consist of approximately 15 000 parts. A common trend in the materials composition of a car is towards an increasing use of lightweight materials, especially towards the use of numerous types of plastics and the use of non-ferrous metals like aluminium, copper and magnesium. Table 3.7 shows the material composition of different vehicle types. The generic European vehicle shows a downward trend in metal content, accounting for about 65 per cent of the total weight at the present time. The plastic content of current models has increased fourfold over the last 20 years and it is expected that this will continue to increase to about 15 per cent until the year 2000 (Peters, 1996). The Volkswagen Golf III has already achieved this level of plastic content.

The activities of dismantlers are very important for achieving a quantitative reduction in the amount of ELV waste: they remove re-usable parts and some recyclable materials from the vehicles for resale or recycling before sending what is left – the 'hulks' – to the shredders. For a more detailed dismantling practice, information about materials and parts used by the motor industry is needed. In this matter an International Dismantling Information System (IDIS) has been established.[20] IDIS intends to provide dismantlers with valuable information for an environmentally sound treatment of ELVs.

Table 3.7 Passenger cars' material ratio

Material	Material Ratio (% by weight)			
	Generic US vehicle	Generic Japanese vehicle	Generic EU compact vehicle	Golf III
Steel and iron	67	72.2	65	64
Plastic	8	10.1	12	16
Glass	2.8	2.8	2.5	3.1
Rubber	4.2	3.1	6	4
Fluids and lubricants	6	3.4	2.5	5
Non-ferrous metal	8	6.2	8	1.6
Electric cable				1.3
Insulation				1.1
Paint				0.9
Other materials	4	2.2	4	3
Total weight (kg)	1438	1270	1210	1025

Source: Kuhndt and Bilitewski (2000).

The increasing use of plastics, composite materials and other non-metallic materials (such as ceramics) increases the amount of shredder residue, which has to be disposed of. In Germany, 550 000 tons of shredder residue are generated every year that largely end up in municipal landfills or incinerators. Approximately 400 000 tons result from the salvaging of cars, the remaining 150 000 accumulate from general scrap collections. The shredders rip the hulk into small pieces and recover much of the metal for recycling (Spicer *et al.*, 1996). What is left, known as the automotive shredder residue (ASR), is a low-density material consisting of textiles, rubber, glass and plastics. Tests conducted on shredder fluff indicate that the material is predominantly contaminated with PCBs and hydrocarbons, with PCB levels averaging around 50ppm (parts per million).

The results of the PRAVDA 2 Project (Hook, 1998) show that in certain cases (depending on local conditions and technical, economic and ecological aspects) the mechanical recycling of some plastic parts may be feasible. But the target of reducing effectively the amount of shredder fluff cannot be reached only by mechanical and feedstock recycling and energy recovery. A design for recyclability is needed to meet these challenges. In the interests of more efficient recycling, it is also necessary to mark the plastic parts systematically and to reduce the different components generally. To deal with this, since 1995, information about dismantling has been passed on to the recycling industry. A first step in this direction is the IDIS, which was developed at the end of 1999. The consortium's 20 manufacturers distributed free of charge an IDIS CD-ROM in eight languages to more than 2500 ELV recyclers all over Europe.[21] This CD-ROM contains dismantling information about 364 different vehicle models and approximately 20 000 different components. Already, the motor industries are using recycled plastics in the production of new vehicles.

In future this mixed waste has to be recycled or recovered, as German environmental policy no longer allows its disposal at landfill sites. The new targets for recycling, re-use and recovery are a great challenge for the motor industry.

Reduced input in the national recycling system

The total annual quantity of end-of-life vehicles requiring disposal in Germany during the period 1997 to 1999 has been estimated at between 1.1 and 1.7 million units (ARGE, Monitoring Report 2000). Taking into account the 3.4 million vehicles cancelled from registration every year, it is obvious that a large number of old vehicles are sold to foreign countries. The reason for this is that, at the present time, the consumer may decide either to give the car directly to a dismantling facility or to try and find a dealer who will pay a price for the car even if it has a small market value.

In actual fact it can be seen that most consumers prefer to sell their old car rather than take it directly to a dismantling and recycling facility. Furthermore, an increasing number of car dealers resell the old cars to export dealers who transport them to Eastern Europe, Northern Africa and the Middle East. As a result of this, the recycling operators (dismantlers and auto-scrap shredders) are faced with a reduced scale of input and a reduction in the use of their enterprise's capacity. Only approximately 60 per cent of the cars that are cancelled from registration in Germany are currently being returned to dismantling and shredding facilities.

Targets of the Environmental Regulation

The ELV Act in Germany (Altautoverordnung)

After years of discussion in Germany about regulation and responsibility for end-of-life vehicles, on 1 April 1998 the ELV concept finally became law. In particular, the minimum technical requirements were laid down for the disposal of end-of-life vehicles. The aim was to establish basic standards to be observed by the companies on the utilization of ELVs:

1. measures for deconstruction and drainage,
2. the removal of specific parts (as advice),

3. the inclusion of liquids taken and parts removed in re-use or recycling,
4. the inclusion of 15 per cent of total weight of an ELV in re-utilization.

A concrete producer's product responsibility has been renounced. In particular, a binding procedure to share the costs has not been established.

The ELV voluntary agreement in Germany (Freiwillige Selbst verpflichtung)

In the 13th legislative period, following a review of the available environmental policy options, voluntary agreements were accepted as being a practical way of realizing the producer's responsibility. A total of 16 associations from different sectors including vehicle/passenger car manufacturers, importers, producers and recyclers of parts and raw materials, got together to thrash out the 'voluntary agreement regarding the environmentally compatible management of end-of-life vehicles (passenger cars) within the concept of the Ecocycle Act' (see Figure 3.14). This agreement between the government and industrial associations advised the car manufacturers to reduce the quantity of harmful materials as a part of waste. Thus the German model for an environmentally friendly restructuring of end-of-life vehicle management comprises voluntary, cooperative measures for the industrial sectors involved, combined with lean regulations in those cases where certain restrictions on freedom of trade are unavoidable. The following targets were laid down:

1. improving recycling capability in construction;
2. development, creation and optimization of material cycles and re-utilization possibilities;
3. improvement in the re-utilization advice given to car manufacturers;
4. decrease in the waste from vehicle disposal to 15 per cent by 2002 and to 5 per cent by 2015 on average per car manufacture;
5. qualified assurance of taking back free of charge ELVs not older than 12 years, and under certain qualifying conditions;
6. building up of a monitoring report system to control the devices.

Car manufacturers have agreed to take back end-of-life vehicles made by them on the usual market terms and to further improve the capability of their products for recycling. They have also agreed that, subject to certain defined conditions, any vehicle up to 12 years old which was newly registered after the end-of-life vehicle ordinance came into force will be taken back free of charge from the last owner.

The core of this German model, as summarized in the voluntary agreement, aims at ensuring that end-of-life vehicles are sent to environmentally friendly recycling plants, at reducing the amount of ELV waste sent to landfills and at

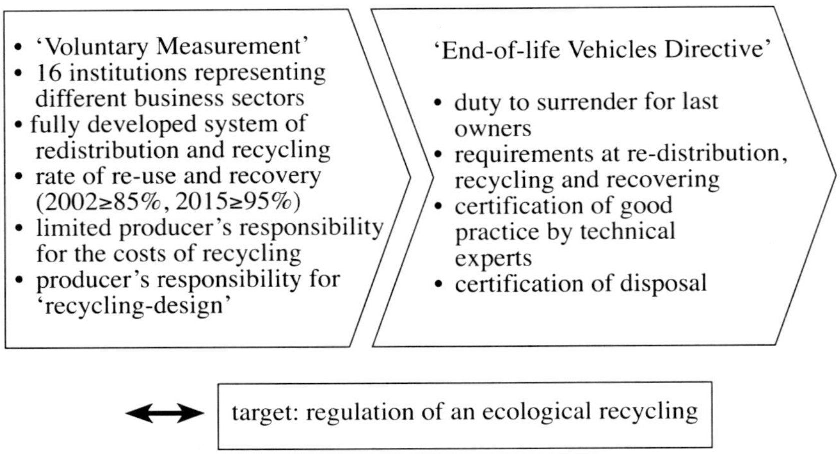

Source: Fried and Scheucher (2000) translation.

Figure 3.14 Treatment, recycling and re-use of vehicles in Germany

ensuring more environmentally friendly draining of fluids. The voluntary agreement allows the sectors involved to decide for themselves how they wish to implement their commitment efficiently and economically. To supervise the voluntary agreement, the Arbeitsgemeinschaft Altauto – ARGE (End-of-Life Vehicle Committee) – was formed.

The EU end-of-life vehicles directive

In the long run, national efforts will be replaced by the EU directive, which takes precedence. It establishes higher-level targets and more concrete advice on the producer's responsibility. Generally, the directive gives advice on recycling, re-use and recovery. It establishes the necessary requirements for collection and treatment facilities to ensure that economic operators set up systems for the collection, treatment and recovery of end-of-life vehicles. Member states should ensure the following:

1. The last holder and/or owner has to deliver the end-of-life vehicle to an authorized treatment facility (without any cost even if the vehicle has no or a negative market value: as from 1 July 2002 for vehicles put on the market after this date; as from 1 January 2007 for any vehicles on the market.
2. The producers have to meet all or a significant part of the costs for the implementation of these measures; the normal functioning of market forces should not be hindered.

3. Hazardous substances in vehicles should be reduced and controlled to prevent their release into the environment, in particular the use of lead, mercury, cadmium and hexavalent chromium (by 1 July 2003).
4. The recycling of all plastics from end-of-life vehicles should be continuously improved; the Commission is currently examining the environmental impacts of PVC.

The major problem of the common position is in our view that the current definition of recycling quotations is entirely weight based. This is essentially

BOX 3.1 CONCERNING RE-USE AND RECOVERY (DIRECTIVE IN ARTICLE 7)

Member States shall take the necessary measures to encourage the re-use of components which are suitable for re-use, the recovery of components which cannot be re-used and the giving of preference to recycling when environmentally viable, without prejudice to requirements regarding the safety of vehicles and environmental requirements such as air emissions and noise control.

Member States shall take the necessary measures to ensure that the following targets are attained by economic operators:

- no later than 1 January 2006, for all end-of-life vehicles, the re-use and recovery shall be increased to a minimum of 85% by an average weight per vehicle and year; for vehicles produced before January 1980, Member States may lay down targets, but not lower than 75% for re-use and recovery and not lower than 70% for re-use and recycling. Member States making use of this paragraph shall inform the Commission and other Member States of the reasons therefore;
- no later than 1 January 2015, for all end-of-life vehicles, the re-use and recovery shall be increased to a minimum of 95% by an average weight per vehicle and year. Within the same time limit, the re-use and recycling shall be increased to a minimum of 85% by an average weight per vehicle and year.

Source: EU (2000).

not correct, as one kilogram of a specific material will not necessarily result in the same environmental burden as one kilogram of another material. Therefore, environmentally weighed recycling quotations could reflect the burden on the environment in a better way. Current research at the Delft University of Technology in the Netherlands is focusing on redefining recyclability by using weighing material percentages by their environmental impact over the life cycle (Plante, 1999; Tempelman, 1999).

In its second reading of the proposal on 3 February 2000, the European Parliament corrected the common position specifically with respect to the question of free taking-back of vehicles already on the road. Although the Parliament agreed that the last owner of a vehicle should be able to surrender an end-of-life vehicle free of charge, and that the vehicle manufacturer should be either solely or largely responsible for covering the costs of disposing of new vehicles, it did not express an opinion about responsibility for the cost of taking back vehicles already on the road. This would have left it up to the member states to decide what measures to adopt, in accordance with the principle of subsidiarity.

The EU directive must be incorporated into national law within 18 months.

Fund models

At the moment the various possible ways of returning a vehicle without any cost to the last owner are being discussed (Wallau, 2000). One is the fund model, which is actually being practised successfully in the Netherlands. Three pillars are significant for this kind of fund: pay-in modalities, fund management and pay-off modalities. The idea is to establish a managed fund that acquires cash from each actor of the motor sector and distributes the money to the recyclers according to their recycling volumes and activities.

The actors paying can, for example, be the first owner, any of the owners in part or the motor industry. With this solution the costs can be shifted to the various actors and distributed most effectively. The distribution can be organized under different aspects. A specific sum for each car is considered as well as a specification according to age, weight, condition and so on.

The management can be organized either by one or more automobile producers or completely externally by the government. In any case, the fund's management makes a controlling of the cash flow easy (Wallau, 2000). Recently, the Volkswagen AG published their currently favoured model (see Figure 3.15), which is similar to the fund solution (Volkswagen AG, 2000). In this model the costs of dismantling will be divided between the producers and car owners. The contribution of the latter will preferably be charged as a lump sum and, periodically, together with the insurance charges. In the case of a negative market value of the ELV (costs of dismantling are higher than profits from selling parts and materials), the payment of the producer will be

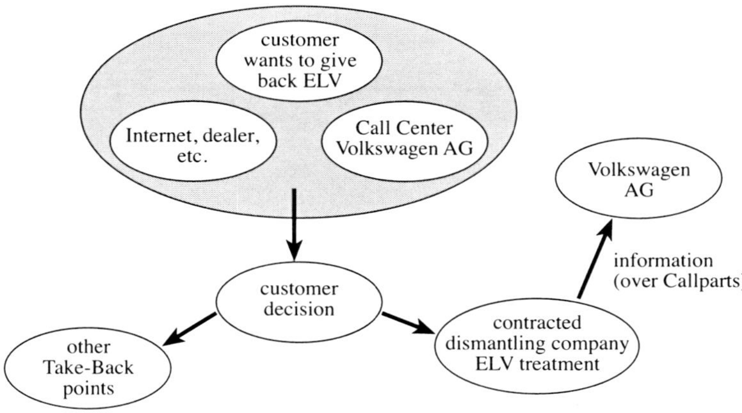

Source: Volkswagen AG, 'Political News', 2000.

Figure 3.15 Outline of a return and dismantling system in Germany

reduced. The contribution of the owners should be calculated so that half of the dismantling costs expected will be covered by them. Whether this system is in accordance with the legal advice of the EU ELV directive is questionable.

ELV Regulation as seen by Various Stakeholders

Progressive environmental policy cannot just be based on laws and regulations. Responsible, flexible participation by all the various stakeholders within society is increasingly important. Sustainability is related to the idea that business, consumers and the state are partner-stakeholders in environmental protection. In view of this we would like to give an overview of the stakeholders involved and their actual positions. The stakeholder approach shows that the strategic question (regulation by law or regulation by market) is embedded in a functional and a normative ruling system (Figure 3.16).

The motor industry (manufacturers, suppliers)

The EU council directive is currently being debated by the motor industry. Whilst the legislators propose a minimum re-use and recycling percentage of 80 per cent by weight per vehicle no later than 1 January 2005, the motor industry advocates that, from a life cycle environmental perspective, the environment will not benefit from following this course of action. The motor manufacturers criticize the directive especially in terms of recycling quotas, return of ELVs free of charge and exclusion of specific materials.

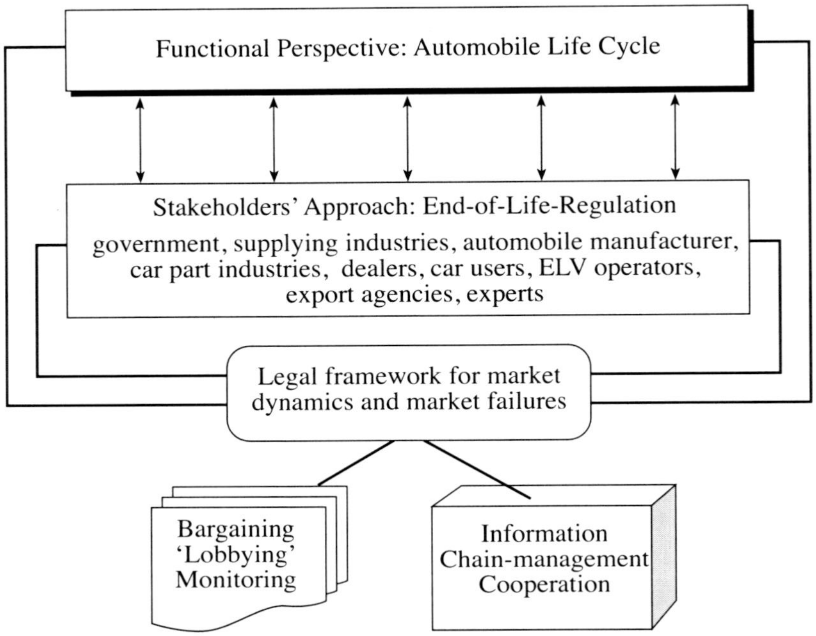

Source: Lucas, 2001.

Figure 3.16 The system of ELV regulation

Recycling quotas, the free return of ELVs and the exclusion of specific materials are rejected by the following arguments.

Recycling quotas The high material recycling ratios stipulated in the EU directive on end-of-life-vehicles intensify the conflict between the objectives of safety, comfort and environmental protection in car manufacturing. A high recycling ratio can collide with the motor industry's objective of reducing fuel consumption. Lightweight construction, one way of fulfilling this objective, is significantly hampered by enforced recycling ratios, since the cost of plastic parts and composites would be particularly affected by a high material-recycling ratio.

The use of naturally grown materials will be excluded, as they cannot be recycled. It may not be environmentally sensible to recycle all materials for re-use. Energy recovery can be a substitute for the use of fossil fuels and can be performed in clean state-of-the-art facilities.

Free-of-charge return Delegating the costs for recycling to the motor industry will take away incentives to dismantle ELVs efficiently and may encourage the exaggeration of costs and neglect efficiency and economy in view of the fact that the industry will bear these costs. To control the costs of dismantling, car manufacturers would have to take back the vehicles themselves or monitor their partners. The losers might be the small and medium-sized dismantlers.

The price of new cars would increase as the costs of establishing additional dismantling and recycling facilities would have to be financed. Finally, introducing the responsibility for cars already in use is legally questionable.

Exclusion of specific materials Lead is a necessary component of steel and aluminium alloys that are mostly light metals and which therefore contribute to a reduction in fuel consumption and lower emissions. Hexavalent chromium serves to improve rust-proofing and helps to produce long-lasting products (ACEA, 1998).

Recycling industry (dismantlers, shredder operators)

In Germany the dismantlers have not built up a strong lobby. Moreover, several dismantlers have clung to the 'ARGE-Altauto' committee, which is dominated by the motor industry. A different position of the recycling industry from the above mentioned arguments could therefore hardly be found.

Meanwhile the EFR (European Ferrous Recovery & Recycling Federation) has expressed its concern about the EU ELV directive and has recently established some basic principles. The first is that certified and fully licensed EFR member companies have developed a highly efficient system for collecting and processing end-of-life vehicles, and that they have both the technology and the know-how to recover and recycle car materials. Another very important precondition for recycling ELVs is that there is a market for recovered materials. The federation rejects a funding system subsidized by the car manufacturer or car purchaser since this would likely lead to market distortion.

The medium-sized companies mainly fear that, in being forced to pay for the recycling costs, car manufacturers will be encouraged to control the recycling process totally. This form of producer responsibility would inevitably result in moves to change the existing car dismantling industry with its many small and medium-sized companies.

German car manufacturers are already considering the possibility that only around 300 of the 1000 certified car dismantling companies in Germany will remain as contract partners of the car manufacturing industry. Moreover Volkswagen, for example, recently hinted that the industry might even move more into the dismantling and shredder industry.

German government, Ministry of Environment

The German Ministry of Environment states that, since the German ELV Act and Voluntary Agreement have become law, successes and difficulties can be identified. As successes, technical and organizational standards stand out. With these standards in place, many dismantlers have made changes necessary to fulfil the requirements. Meanwhile, some experiences have led to criticism of the implementation of the concept, which needs to be changed in the short term. This concerns, in particular, assurance of a standardized qualification of the technical experts examining standards and awarding certification; control of the existing declaration showing the ELV's country of destination in relation to the administrative costs; providing information for the controlling administrators; and, finally, establishing measures for collection and evaluation of information to verify quantification targets of resource flows from vehicle recycling.

Council of experts on environmental questions (SRU – Sachverständigenrat für Umweltfragen)

The 'Sachverständigenrat' mainly criticizes the deficits concerning the ecological deconstruction and drainage of ELVs, the avoidance of 'wild' disposal (dumping or illegal disposal) and effective reporting on the achievement of aims. Deficits in this area can temporarily be solved by a change of product responsibility, which would be difficult to manage with different legal instruments. Recent statistics of the Umweltbundesamt show that the number of ELVs processed at dismantling facilities has decreased since the beginning of the 1990s. Although of course not all the cars cancelled from registration are ELVs and there are no reliable statistics on the destination of these deregistered cars, it can be concluded that the legal system is pervious and suffers from an incomplete monitoring. To make an effective implementation of the 'voluntary agreement' possible, the transparent monitoring of the destination of ELVs should be implemented immediately. Efficient monitoring is the most important element in ensuring the ecological recovery of ELVs.

Conclusions

In Germany, a modernized infrastructure of receiving stations and recycling plants for end-of-life vehicles has been established since 1998. Today, this network comprises approximately 1400 accredited recycling plants and some 15 000 accredited receiving stations to ensure environment-friendly disposal of end-of-life vehicles. A nationwide infrastructure has also been set up for taking back and recycling end-of-life parts following vehicle repairs. In order to fulfil the requirements of the end-of-life vehicle ordinance and to provide an extensive network for taking back and recycling ELVs, more than DM0.5

billion has been invested in receiving stations, recycling plants and shredder plants since 1997. A monitoring concept has been developed to quantify the amount of landfill waste arising from end-of-life vehicle disposal and to chart the progress in reducing it.

In Germany, basic criteria for an environment-friendly disposal of ELVs were laid down in 1998 and modified in 2001 by integrating the new issues of the European regulation. This environmental regulation had a strong influence on the medium-sized dismantlers sector. A lot of small enterprises were not able to realize the high investments necessary and were forced to quit. Nearly 70 per cent of the former 5000 dismantlers still exist, but structural change is still going on. It can be expected that after establishing the new regulation system, within five years only 300 to 500 dismantlers will remain. Thus, in the long run, it can be expected that the motor industry will organize the whole system of recycling itself with central dismantling facilities, and will try to minimize costs in the short term and economize profitably in the long term. The result will probably be that even more dismantlers will disappear from the market and the whole dismantler branch will be put under pressure. At the same time, the centralized organization of dismantling is in conflict with the endeavours of a sustainable decentralized economic structure without long-distance logistics.

On the other hand, the opening of the frontiers to Eastern Europe and the different levels of welfare between eastern and southern countries and the so-called 'western hemisphere' lead to increasing export rates of used cars. It is obvious that a national regulation system cannot solve this problem. A main topic of discussion is that the export of products goes with the export of environmental burden. A solution would be a national law that creates technical standards for the export of ELVs. Furthermore, international appointments should be made to support these countries in building up a modified ELV infrastructure.

The recent initiatives to change the regulation of ELVs in Europe (and in particular Germany) are marked by different and mainly opposing demands of the various stakeholders concerning the effects of an environmentally friendly policy. With regard to a material flow approach it is important to know that there are frequent conflicts between the reduction of fuel emissions and recycling quotas. No general environmental solution can be derived by following a one-way strategy, as by changing one element of the product or its manufacture may cause serious detrimental impact in another. Therefore the improvement strategy of the EU Council has to be evaluated carefully, while there are no clear indications that the approaches being taken actually lead to a more environmentally beneficial product. Lightweight materials, such as polymer composites and aluminium, while reducing the kerb weight of the motor car, also can reduce the recyclability of the vehicle. And how is vehicle safety maintained, when the vehicle's mass is reduced by 50 per cent? Is the reduction of landfill consumption through increased recycling worth the net increase in energy used to run recyclable vehicles? In the absence of a regulatory framework for decision making, progress towards any of these goals will be problematic. These questions cannot be solved by recycling quotas. Rather, it will be necessary for the motor industry to evaluate the technological alternatives in such a fashion that all three of these criteria (manufacturing, use and disposal) are addressed, over the entire 'life' of the product.

Another question is how to finance the ELV measures. The car producers do not accept complete producers' responsibility for ELVs. As with the German 'ELV Voluntary Agreement', they want to take back free of charge only a small number of cars, excluding all cars older than 12 years. These cars should only be taken back under common market conditions. The last owner should assume the risks of the low market value and the costs of recycling. All the other, newer, cars will follow the market rules anyway.

Contrary to the position of the automotive industries, the common position of the EU definitely strengthens the producers' responsibility for the handling of all ELVs. The directive will force the car manufacturers to accept recycling quotas and to exclude toxic materials. This will lead to further costs that will have to be borne by the millions of car owners when they buy a new car. On the other hand, this will force eco-innovations in the motor industry for renewable and recyclable car parts and materials.

Summing up, we have to face the fact that the regulation of end-of-life vehicles in Germany and Europe is in fact confronted by several problems:

- In 1998 German law and voluntary agreements established new standards for the dismantling and recycling of end-of life vehicles. This leads to a structural change in the dismantling and recycling sector and new practice at a higher environmental level.
- An increasing number of old cars are being sold to internationally operating car dealers. Therefore only a reduced number of old cars are reaching the modernized recycling infrastructure of Germany.
- There is no consensus between the various stakeholders on which environmental targets and measurements will lead to better environmental results.
- It remains unclear who will bear the costs of a forthcoming European system based on the producers' responsibility.

What Japanese regulators might learn is that the changes in ELV management that have been initiated by law also have consequences for the management culture. To solve the problems shown, a corporate network culture is needed. Corporate culture requires a management based on common goals and rules. Every company/sector in the ELV chain should be given the chance to strive for self-realization. The newly developed fund system will lead to a new kind of transaction between the motor industry and the recycling branch. Therefore a common understanding of material fairness and performance has to be established. The system of monitoring should be developed into a system of information about economic, social and ecological performance. More ecological information especially is needed to create transparency of material flows. It is necessary to deal with this matter in a spirit of partnership whenever problems arise.

Corporate culture in ELV management generates tremendous performance potential if it is no longer understood as a system that is only ruled by the motor industry. The concept of common responsibility is a challenge for more partnership and decentralized structures. This not only generates a potential for greater performance, but is also of unaccountable value to the stability of the whole ELV management system.

We end this section with a brief overview of research demand.

1. In our opinion it is necessary to analyse the current situation of ELV management in Japan (we started with this research during this case study, but we need further information about the economic relevance and consumers' acceptance of the recycling activities in Japan).
2. On the basis of these facts we could give some advice on how to organize a monitoring system and establish some new information instruments.
3. Also it might be useful to develop new information and marketing systems in order to have more transparency in the market for used parts. In Germany, the bigger dismantling operators are using e-commerce and e-marketing to sell used parts (tested und certified) nationwide.

3.7 FORMULATING TARGET-ORIENTED POLICIES: FACTOR FOUR AND MORE

Policy making is always a process full of uncertainties. Targets provide some orientation for economic agents and allow for stabilized expectations about possible future directions. At least according to the theoretical tradition of welfare economics, a proper target setting stands at the beginning of any 'policy cycle'. Clearly defined targets facilitate the implementation of any policy. In practice, target setting and policy making (that is, problem analysis, anticipation of potential effects and implementation of appropriate measures) are often interwoven. As WI would claim, a general strengthening of sustainable development policies requires target-oriented policies. These targets can partly be conducted from the normative requirement of preserving natural capital and should always rely on latest scientific findings: resilience of ecosystems, sustainable yield of renewable resources, minimal use of non-renewable resources. The various Dutch Environmental Policy Plans starting from 1989 are very close to such target-oriented policies. However, given the complexity of ecosystems, a range of information deficits and uncertainties remain.

As a solution to the ensuing dilemma, target-oriented policies will have to act on different levels of commitments. Below the level of some strict targets for certain harmful substances, two further levels arise throughout European policies. One level is for *quantitative targets* which are related to certain environmental problems and can be based upon scientific evidence. One can identify quantitative targets which are concrete and operational (such as reduction of CO_2 emissions by 25 per cent between 1990 and 2005 as a result of German climate policy). These quantitative targets are related rather to policy makers, although policy makers sometimes hesitate to set these targets since this makes politics 'accountable'. Quantitative targets are clearly defined through a definite indicator, a numerically defined direction and a defined period. They, however, might also have the disadvantage of being too static and less flexible. They are overwhelmingly legally binding and can partly be linked to individual liability of firms.

Another level arises from the demand for strategic *open targets*, which are plausible, but cannot be stated with full scientific certainty. They rather serve as orientation, having a 'leitmotiv' character. This is the level for material flows and, perhaps, land use-related targets. Though there is wide agreement about the environmental relevance of material flows, there is almost no scientific evidence that a certain amount of material flows is less harmful than another. Also the Hotelling rule of individual resources' scarcity or the depletion of limited disposal space are helpful devices, but do not lead towards precise reduction goals for material flows. Any goal, be it a 5, 20 or 35 per cent reduction of current levels, will require a political decision. This level of goal-oriented policies thus leads to the formulation of open targets.

Open targets serve as orientation for current businesses, industrial research and development. In doing so, they facilitate individual decision making under uncertainties by indicating a desired direction for technical progress. While they impose some constraints upon totally undirected search, open targets leave the primary wellsprings of discoveries and knowledge creation as well as individual adaptation processes of firms untouched. They steer the market–economic and societal search process, and offer decision support in cases of uncertainty and a pluralistic variety of options. They indicate, rather broadly, the way or the overall direction in which society might move (for example, a 'sustainability corridor'). Open targets for material flows and energy use are closely related to several concepts around the paradigm of sustainable development introduced in WI's first interim report, such as

Environmental Space and Dematerialization. In this context, they serve as general decision rules for non-governmental actors such as producers and consumers. Competition and technical progress need these rules for their processes of discovery (according to New Institutional Economics: see Furubotn and Richter, 1997; Metcalfe, 2001; Ostrom, 2000). A Factor Four (or Ten) may serve as such an open target. It must not be legally binding, but rather part of a sustainability action programme, of technology policy or of some industrial policy programme.

Since open targets only partly rely on scientific methodologies, they have to be formulated discursively by society within the policy-making context. The target-setting process involves several societal stakeholders such as governmental organizations, non-governmental organizations, industry stakeholders, political parties, media and science. Thereby, scientific insight plays a consultative role. In the end, it is up to society, with the help of its democratic institutions, to decide normatively about the degree of environmental risks they are willing to accept: 'The question of where the "limits" of sustainability lie is thus directly coupled with the question of what environmental risks society is ready to tolerate' (Sachs *et al.*, 1998: 28). To this end, establishing the 'right' institutional frameworks plays an important role. Democratic and pluralistic institutions help to facilitate a societal search process. The foundation of multi-stakeholder institutions, like the German sustainability council, which is in charge of developing a national sustainability strategy (or its Japanese counterpart), is one example of such an institutional setting with regard to sustainability.

Quantitative Targets

In distinction from open targets, which serve rather as an orientation, a set of quantitative targets can be more precise in helping to support policy making in practice. Deriving quantitative targets calls for more detailed scientific efforts and validity. Their implementation and achievement have to be realistic and feasible, which is of particular relevance to those policy makers in administrations who are in charge of the implementation.

Quantitative targets are dependent on indicators, statistical variables indicating a certain problem, which should be addressed by policy measures. The selection of appropriate indicators is often dependent on scientific support. On the one hand, indicators have to capture the problem accurately, for example being based on a scientific cause and effect relationship. For instance, the combustion of fossil energy carriers induces CO_2 emissions, which again increases the CO_2 concentration of the atmosphere. This in turn causes a man-made greenhouse effect, which finally leads to a global climate change seriously threatening human beings and global eco-systems. On the other hand, indicators need to remain understandable for politicians and society. In a considerable number of cases, these cause–effect chains for certain environmental problems are not known exactly, which hampers identification of appropriate indicators.

The Wuppertal Institute presented a first set of quantitative environmental targets for a sustainable Germany in the mid-1990s (see WI, 2001). The proposal was embedded in a broader report entitled 'Sustainable Germany' (Sachs *et al.*, 1998). Meanwhile, several proposals of smaller sets of environmental and sustainability indicators, associated with quantitative targets, have been established all over Europe. These sets of indicators are often referred to as 'headline indicators'. In 1998, the German Minister for the Environment launched a draft programme on priority areas for environmental policies. Within this context, a set of environmental headline indicators has also been established – the so-called 'German Environment Barometer'. The Environment Barometer's total of six indicators stands for the fields of climate, air, soil, water and the cross-sectional field of resources (energy/raw materials). For each of the six environmental headline indicators, quantitative targets have been set (see WI, 2001). In addition, the six indicators have been aggregated to one single figure, the German Environment Index, or DUX (Deutscher Umwelt Index). Related to dematerialization and eco-efficiency, for instance, the targets have been set to increase energy efficiency by a factor of 2 and raw material productivity by a factor of 2.5 by the year 2020. So far, the entire government has not adopted the proposal put forward by the then Minister for the Environment. However, it is expected that, in the context of a German Sustainability Strategy, a more binding set of headline indicators and associated quantitative targets will be launched in the near future. In this context, a draft from November 2001 refers to a Factor Four energy productivity increase in the energy sector.

Similar sets of environmental headline indicators have also been presented in the Netherlands[22] and Sweden[23] and a European set, covering all 15 member states of the European Union, is in preparation. Finland[24] and the United Kingdom[25] have even gone further in developing sets of headline indicators for sustainability covering also economic and social aspects. The UK example is of particular interest since it has been adopted by the entire government and is closely linked to the UK sustainability strategy presented in May 1999.[26] Recently, Environment Minister Michael Meacher presented a progress report on the development of the 15 UK headline indicators of sustainability.[27] A baseline assessment on the development of the 15 headline indicators is given in WI's first interim report (WI, 2001).

Factor Four (or more) as an Open Target

Factor Four refers to a four-fold improvement in eco-efficiency in the medium term (10–30 years). The rationale is to halve worldwide resource use while doubling the welfare. At the business level, Factor Four serves as a heuristic stimulus for the individual search for solutions. Each company devoted to Factor Four acts as a pioneer, aiming at a steady improvement of eco-efficiency, including some spectacular breakthroughs. At the individual business level, the feasibility of Factor Four has been demonstrated by numerous pioneering examples. Factor Ten, introduced by Friedrich Schmidt-Bleek (1994, 2000) refers to a ten-fold absolute reduction of material input (resource use) in industrialized countries in the long term (50 years). It can be interpreted as a target for absolute de-linking in developed countries that involves a ten-fold absolute reduction of extraction of natural resources, leading to a 50 per cent reduction on the global scale. Simply stated, the 'resource productivity' has to be increased.

Both Factor Four and Factor Ten are normatively based on the environmental space concept (see WI, 2001). The basic assumption in these concepts is that the globally available environmental space is already overused by large, that is, environmental pressure needs to be halved. Factor Ten, in addition, takes into consideration that around 80 per cent of current global environmental space is 'occupied' by industrialized countries, representing only 20 per cent of world population. Combining the imperative of halving global environmental space with an equal per capita allocation then leads to an open target of a factor of ten for industrialized countries.

At the policy maker's level, Factor Four and Factor Ten have been adopted as open targets in a variety of programmatic policy documents. Factor Four to Factor Ten was adopted by the special session of the United Nations (1997) and the World Business Council for Sustainable Development (WBCSD, 1998). Also the environmental ministers of the OECD in 1996 expected progress towards this end. Several European countries (for example Austria, the Netherlands, Finland, and Sweden) included the strategic objective in their political programmes. The European Commission, in its recent draft of the 6th Environmental Action Programme, commits itself to the objective to ensure that the consumption of renewable and non-renewable resources and the associated impacts do not exceed the carrying capacity of the environment and to achieve a decoupling of resource use from economic growth through significantly improved resource efficiency, dematerialization of the economy, and waste prevention (European Commission, 2001e: 50). The German National Sustainability Strategy calls for a doubling of resource productivity by the year 2020 (baseline year 1994).

We may conclude from these debates that open targets such as a Factor Four serve a certain function in policy making; that is, to give orientation to economic actors. This intention is well in line with recent debates on economic policy (Dixit, 2000; Matzner, 1994) and technology policy (Weaver *et al.*,

2000) and it certainly acknowledges the remaining scientific uncertainties. If, however, states adopt the precautionary principle in one sense or another, these uncertainties cannot be used for postponing action. Those businesses that are willing to act as pioneers, second-movers, or imitators need exactly that kind of orientation, which can be derived from open targets. Hence, open targets, are essential parts of sustainability policies.

NOTES

1. Raimund Bleischwitz is grateful for an input made by Otto Linher.
2. The government is currently consulting on best design and use of this Sustainability Fund.
3. Though a EU-wide agreement on a CO_2/energy tax has not yet been reached (2002), it seems that some member states are willing to take the lead regarding material flows. In doing so, these member states look for a tax on certain materials in light of their national priorities, and not for overall taxation. They also combine their eco-taxes with tax reductions in other fields.
4. Calculation according to 'engineering equivalence method'; by taking the 'substitution equivalence method' as a basis there is a share of 2.6 per cent today.
5. The exact classification of what organic substances are according to the spirit of the law is settled in the organic substances ordinance, which came into force in May 2001. Above all, the use of highly contaminated timber as an organic substance is excluded.
6. According to the version of the law new plants are also existing plants provided that they have been considerably reactivated or renewed. This condition is fulfilled when the costs incurred amount to more than 50 per cent of costs for new plants.
7. There is a maximum productivity quantity of $1MW_{el}$ for solar stations which cannot directly be connected with structural measures on buildings.
8. While power generation in Germany can be described as a competitive market after the amendment of the EEG (although the market tends to be more and more oligopolistic because of constant mergers of former group companies; of the previous 11 group companies, four remain which generate more than 90 per cent of power in Germany), in the area of transport and distribution of power there is in practice still a kind of monopoly.
9. In StrEG, remuneration rates were attached to the average development of power profits which vary year by year.
10. A description in tabular form of individual support programmes is in the appendix to this chapter.
11. Regarding renewable energies, there are around 38 000 jobs, which is more than in the whole nuclear energy branch (Fischedick *et al.*, 2001).
12. We do not use a definition of 'energy services' in a broader economic sense. Instead, we will call these energy-related services which are aimed at final customers, such as energy efficiency services, advice on efficient equipment, financing, system services (for example keeping frequency and tension constant), measuring and billing. Neither will we use the WTO terminology which classifies transmission, distribution and supply as services (as opposed to the generation function of electricity, which the WTO classifies as production), so these functions of the supply side of energy could themselves be understood as 'energy services'. For this study, this is still the provision of energy, not of energy services.
13. Demands on the health quality tolerance of building products are listed in the building regulations of the federal states of Germany through the Building Products Act.
14. http://www.kompetenzzentrum-iemb.de.
15. http://www.bmvbw.de/Leitfaden-nachhaltiges-Bauen-.565.htm.
16. LEGO is a good example because it is made of only one material, is easy to maintain and could be adapted to the current demand of the user because of its various colours, forms and so on.

17. http://www.sozialestadt.de.
18. Environmental reports from the following enterprises have been researched: Nissan (1998, 1999), DaimlerChrysler (2000), JAMA (1998), Opel (1998), Toyota (1998).
19. After the legal regulation had been passed, the ARGE-altauto was ended and the information service linked to it was interrupted.
20. In 1999, the IDIS 2 Consortium numbered 20 members, representing the interests of BMW AG, Daewoo Motor Corporation, Daihatsu Motor Corporation, DaimlerChrysler AG, Fiat Auto S.p.a, Ford Motor Company, Fuji Heavy Industries Ltd. (Subaru), General Motors, Honda Motor Corporation, Hyundai Motor Corporation, Mazda Motor Corporation, Mitsubishi Motors, Nissan Motor Corporation, PSA Peugeot Citroën, Renault, Rover Group Ltd., Suzuki Motor Corporation, Toyota Motor Corporation, Volkswagen AG and Volvo Car Corporation.
21. www.idis2.com.
22. Ministry of Housing, Spatial Planning and the Environment, Ministry of Economic Affairs, Ministry of Agriculture, Nature Management and Fisheries, Ministry of Transport, Public Works and Water Management, Ministry of Finance, Ministry of Foreign Affairs (1998), 'National Environmental Policy Plan 3 – The Summary', The Hague.
23. Ministry of the Environment (1998), 'Key indicators for ecologically sustainable development. A proposal from the Swedish Environmental Advisory Council', Stockholm.
24. Ministry of the Environment (2000), 'Signs of Sustainability – Finland's indicators for sustainable development 2000' (http://www.vyh.fi/eng/environ/sustdev/indicat/inds2000.htm).
25. http://www.sustainable-development.gov.uk/indicators/headline/index.htm.
26. Department of the Environment, Transport and the Regions (1999), 'A better quality of life: a strategy for sustainable development for the UK, (http://www.sustainabledevelopment.gov.uk/).
27. http://www.press.detr.gov.uk/0101/0028.htm.

APPENDIX: OVERVIEW ON CERTAIN ENERGY MEASURES IN GERMANY

	Grant (DM m)	Basis of calculation
Renewable Energy Sources Act/Feed in Act	980	Feed-in of 13.2bn kWh at a medium feed-in payment of 16.7Pf/kWh and a value of power of 9.28Pf/kWh
Programme to encourage the market of renewable energies (subsidy)	200	Analysis made in this book assuming that 20% of the plans are not realized
Programme to encourage the market of renewable energies (loan)	49	Granted loans for new stations, DM 182mn, cash value of 8.3% with an assumed reduced interest rate over 10 years of around 1.5% p.a. as well as corresponding to the granted loans average support equivalent from the department relief of 19%
100 000 umbrella solar power programme	115	New installed power, 42MW_p, volume of investments DM 460mn, cash value of 25% with an assumed reduced interest rate over 10 years of around 4.5% p.a.
ERP environment programme	76	Volume of loans for new stations, DM 1.38bn, cash value of 5.5% with an assumed reduced interest rate over 10 years of around 1% p.a.
DtA-environment programme	81	Volume of loans for new stations, DM 0.98bn, cash value of 8.3% with an assumed reduced interest rate over 10 years of around 1.5% p.a.
Additional pay for owner-occupied dwellings	3	Only new stations
State programmes	186	

continued

	Grant (DM m)	Basis of calculation
Tax exemption on hydrocarbon fuels, bio-diesel	450	On the basis of a sales volume of 410mn litres and a tax on hydrocarbon fuel of DM 1.10 per litre
Exemption on eco-tax for heat-generating renewable energy systems	182	Provision of final energy, 45TWh, and assuming that corresponding to the heat structure in the ratio of 1.27 to 1 natural gas and heating oil, respectively, is saved (rate of taxation 0.32Pf/kWh natural gas and 4Pf per litre heating oil, plus VAT)
Total grant (approx.)	2 300	Without local and private grant

4. Sustainable business and consumption strategies

Justus von Geibler, Michael Kuhndt, Eberhard K. Seifert, Rainer Lucas, Sylvia Lorek and Raimund Bleischwitz

4.1 INTRODUCTION

The arena of policy makers is at the heart of the conclusions drawn in the previous chapter on emerging regulatory policies. Nevertheless, addressing policy makers does not necessarily presuppose that this arena holds sufficient steering capacities for any sustainable development of an economy and a society as a whole. Governance across multiple arenas implies rather that business bears responsibility for the economy and its various impacts on humans and nature. Analysing management tools for sustainable enterprises is a logical device following such a governance approach. Here, SMEs may be of special relevance as they often tend to be neglected while offering considerable potential for productivity increase. For the sustainability debate and the proposed eco-efficient services, these features lead to the acknowledgment of consumption and life styles too. Both arenas are addressed in the following chapter.

4.2 STRATEGIES FOR SUSTAINABLE BUSINESS DEVELOPMENT

Introduction

From industry's perspective, framework conditions that governments set in the area of sustainable development have been changing over recent years. So far, conventional environmental approaches have almost predetermined the corporate response. With the emergence of emissions trading, other market-based instruments, voluntary approaches and the rest, in recent and coming years business is facing a wider range of response options. In order to benefit from the emerging flexibility, however, companies have to engage in formulating strategies and implementing these through appropriate management approaches.

In this context, proactive strategies for sustainable business development are of increasing relevance for companies and markets, and for future business opportunities, as with, for example, the adoption of environmental management (sustainability) objectives even though there is no apparent attempt by governments to regulate the issue under consideration. A company may act proactively because, for example, it wishes to position itself as environmentally friendly (or more broadly sustainable) on the market, or because it has realized that achieving environmental objectives is linked to economic gains (win–win solutions). These driving forces are a relatively recent phenomenon: companies are starting to realize the power of stakeholders (and the underlying power of consumers and shareholders). And financial markets are starting to direct investments towards environmentally friendly (more sustainable) companies, as they acknowledge that better environmental performance (more sustainable performance) is typically associated with higher returns on investment.

Growing pressure from customers, investors, governments and global supply chains is shaping new corporate models that increasingly incorporate social, economic and environmental responsibility. While a large body of corporate environmental strategies exists, the recent years have also seen a growing number of activities in the area of sustainable business development, covering a range of social, economic and environmental issues. Hereby sustainable business development depends on innovations within the company. The innovation potential of enterprises for sustainable development is influenced by internal factors, such as knowledge and learning abilitities, and the framework conditions in which the companies are operating, such as existence of management tools, competition and regulation as well as their interaction. Therefore it is reasonable to consider these internal and external conditions for the promotion of sustainable business development.

This section has three parts. The first focuses on a model for sustainable business development, which derives green, (eco-)efficient and responsible entrepreneurship as different phases of business development depending on the characteristics of the enterprise. Secondly, for each type of business selected, European framework conditions and external drivers for business development and lessons learned will be presented. The section concludes with ways to promote sustainable business development.

Approaches to Sustainable Business Development

In order to move towards sustainable development, business, like all other actors of society, needs to rethink its behaviour. Companies start from various

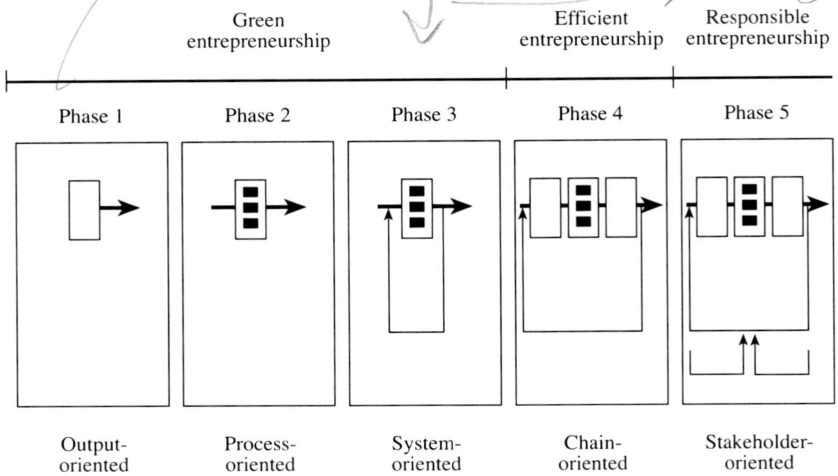

Source: Adapted from Klinkers et al. (1999).

Figure 4.1 Different phases for sustainable business development

stages of development and corporate culture as regards environmental and social issues, as the five phases of Figure 4.1 distinguish.

The different phases can be summarized as follows.[1] Green entrepreneurship's focus is on internal environmental improvements. In the output-oriented phase 1, management emphasis is placed on the outputs, not on the process. Here errors can become apparent after they have been made. Companies in this phase can be labelled reactive with respect to the environment. Process-orientation is a characteristic element of phase 2, in which the focus is on the production process and its management. Here major mistakes can be corrected by using measurements and knowledge of the process. During phase 3, system orientation, the entire organization, including support processes and their management, is the focus of performance improvement measures. In this phase a system is set up which controls the production processes and aims at preventative measures including corrective action if mistakes occur. In contrast to the previous phases with internal focus, the efficient entrepreneur pays attention to the economic relevance of environmental issues, including the external effects within markets. Here companies relate their organization to other parties in the product system. In a cooperative way, win–win situations are created for the entire chain. For responsible entrepreneurship, in the stakeholder-oriented stage (phase 5), companies base their vision and policy on stakeholder expectations, as a sense of responsibility towards society.

The order of the different phases (from green, to (eco-)efficient and then responsible entrepreneurship) seems to be the path for most of the companies on their way towards sustainable development. Often companies first begin to address internal environmental issues (realizing cost saving potentials by internal environmental management). Then companies start looking beyond the companies' boundaries to address environmental issues in the product chain. Thus the product improves. These companies also involve stakeholders, such as the community and NGOs, in the internal decision-making process. However, as Klinkers *et al.*, (1999) state explicitly, it is not necessary to focus first on internal environmental management before taking the step in the chain. Companies can bypass the first phases and start directly with, for example, phase 3 or 4.

As the management has addressed sustainable business development, so the related management tools have evolved. According to UNEP (1995), environmental management tools can be broken down into tools for analysis and evaluation, tools for action and tools for communication (Table 4.1). This typology is used to present tools that are relevant in today's discussion.

The toolbox presented reflects an evolution from purely environmentally related tools (for green entrepreneurship), to tools that mix both environmental and economic aspects (for efficient entrepreneurship) and tools that go further by integrating social and ethical dimensions (for responsible entrepreneurship). These management tools seem to be an important element of a sustainability strategy. However, the mere existence of tools for sustainable business development does not necessarily lead to improvements of environmental, social or economic business performance (Bartelmus *et al.*, 2001, European Commission, 2001c; Hroch and Schaltegger, 2001). Thus the following text will focus more on the interaction of sustainable business developments and sustainability policies, with a focus on the European experiences.

European Experiences from Sustainable Business Development

Here we summarize lessons learned for green, (eco-)efficient and responsible entrepreneurship in Europe and elaborate on the hypotheses related to sustainability policies. The approaches to green entrepreneurship have been subjected to intensive research over the last 20 years and the issues of standardization have been highly debated. Thus, for green entrepreneurship, the institutional perspective will be focused upon.

Green entrepreneurship: formal environmental management systems

The 'semi-public' EU regulation EMAS (Eco-Management and Audit Scheme) and the 'private' ISO 14000 series, with its flagship the ISO 14001 standard, have been practised in parallel as formal environmental management

Table 4.1 Overview of corporate management tools

	Green entrepreneurship	Efficient entrepreneurship	Responsible entrepreneurship
Type of tool / areas of focus	Environment	Economic and environment	Social, environmental and economic
Analytical tools	Ecological footprint Environmental performance evaluation Life cycle assessment Material flow analysis Material Input Per Service Unit (MIPS) Environmental auditing	Full cost accounting Life cycle costing Resource efficiency accounting Cost–benefit analysis	Social accounting Stakeholder value approach
Tools for action	Environmental management systems Eco-design tools	Green procurement Efficient entrepreneur calendar	Companies' and sectors' pass to sustainability (COMPASS) Suppliers accreditation
Tools for communication	Eco-labels Environmental product declaration Environmental reporting Eco-benchmarking/rating	Eco-making Environmental aspects in financial reporting Eco-efficiency–benchmarking/rating	Social reporting Sustainability Assessment for Enterprises (SAFE) Triple bottom-line benchmarking/rating

Source: Adapted from Wuppertal Institute (2001).

systems (EMS) by companies and organizations in Europe since 1995/1996. On the one hand, there is growing concern about the coexistence of two such systems and their future prospects, especially with regard to acceptance by SMEs. On the other hand, the increasing challenges to organizations concerning improvements towards sustainability are on the agenda, in particular in view of the double events of the tenth anniversaries of ISO TC 207 and Rio+10 conferences in Johannesburg in 2002.

EMAS: lessons from the first round of application and novelties As a new kind of 'semi-public' yet voluntarily applied policy instrument, EMAS admittedly is experienced mainly in the German-speaking area (Germany and Austria) with about 80 per cent of all registrations in Europe.[2] A survey by the German Environmental Protection Agency (EPA) in 1999 evaluated the first phase (1995–8) with some implications for the revision process (Umweltbundesamt (2000), finalized in 2001).

- Requests for improvements: top priority was given to better information for the public with regard to the significance and relevance of the EMAS system. A second priority for about 87 per cent was 'a more constructive attitude and improved recognition by the authorities, including the exercise of discretion'. The larger the site (in numbers of employees), the greater the desire for improvement: 'Less administrative work load by reducing legal measuring and reporting requirements' was placed third (83 per cent).
- Continuation with EMAS: this key question for a second registration round (every three years according to EMAS I) was answered by 59 per cent with 'yes, preparation already in progress' and by 29 per cent with 'very probably', with a much larger proportion of bigger sites already tackling preparatory work for 'revalidation' than smaller ones.
- The trump card of EMAS 'continuous improvement of environmental performance': nearly 90 per cent of companies referred to this criterion, followed by particular emphasis on high performance targets, increased legal certainty, strong emphasis on employee participation, preparation of an environmental statement and independent verification.
- There was particular concern about the mandatory environmental statement: interest fell short of companies' expectations with respect to local residents and authorities, media and public as well as to industrial customers, banks and insurances – in contrast to scientific institutions and academia, business consultants and NGOs. The quality of EMAS statements varied greatly during this first round of experiences with such a new system and the mandatory disclosure in a comprehensive and validated 'statement' (according to EMAS I only every three years, with only updates in between).

In 1998, Germany allowed additional organizations to enter the EMAS system, including the service sector. By summer 2001, about 2670 sites in total had been registered in Germany under the EU system (three-quarters of all sites in Europe), indicating a declining rate of additional participants since 1998/9. The stagnation can be observed regarding the first EMAS registrations (monthly figures since September 1999 below 40) as well as for validated EMAS sites (up to July 2000, 140 enterprises had dropped out of the scheme). This reluctance is thought to be due to both rising uncertainties concerning a long-lasting and undecided EMAS revision process and rising interest in ISO 14001 certification, which is 'easier' to realize.

Finally, in late April 2001, the new EMAS II regulation was released. In Germany, it was massively promoted by a coalition of politics, industry, trade unions and NGOs. The main intentions of EMAS II focus on improving the EU system as a (still voluntary) instrument of self-responsibility of organizations as well as enhancing its attractiveness and practicability. Main innovations are the following:

- extension to all kinds of organizations (like ISO 14001),
- inclusion of ISO 14001 in the EMAS management system to provide organizations with a much easier way into EMAS,
- yearly validation as an enforcement of the 'controlling' role of the auditor on real environmental performance activities,
- stronger participation of employees,
- simpler administration for companies/organizations and authorities (in Germany, 'Priviligierungsverordnung' in September 2001) as an incentive for participation, and
- introduction of a new EMAS logo for advertising purposes (which was not allowed in EMAS I).

With this new offensive and the incentives in favour of the EU regulation, broader acceptance by organizations and the public all over Europe of this real 'performance' oriented system is aimed at. But it is still too early for any assessment of the fate of EMAS II, especially concerning SME application and competition from the number of applications of ISO 14000 standards as well as broader sustainability concerns and disclosure demands.

ISO 14001 revision: Japanese and German experiences Up to March 2001, more than 27 000 organizations world-wide have been certified to ISO 14000 standards in about 100 countries, Japan taking the lead with 6072 certified organizations, followed by Germany with about 2400[3] and the UK with about 2000 certified organizations.[4] If the growth rates of ISO 14001 certifications could be extrapolated to future certifications equivalent to developments of the 'forerunner', the quality standard ISO 9001 (with about 408 600 certificates worldwide since 1987 in 158 countries at the end of 2000), huge potentials are to be envisioned for the ISO 14000 series.

Concerning real first experiences, one of the first national evaluations was presented by the Japanese National Committee for ISO/TC 207/SC1 (1998) at an early stage (April 1998, based on 'only' 924 certificates) – too early to draw firm conclusions on some evidence but useful as input into the international revision process. Users and interested parties cited interpretation difficulties due to unclear requirements, such as on 'environmental aspects' or 'communication', or even missing advice, for example on 'performance' (not required in ISO 14001). Whereas opinions on including 'performance' requirements in the standard have been divided, most advocated disclosure of information for building confidence in EMS, related to the commitment issue to be taken up in discussions on the role of ISO standards in general.

In the preparation of the first revision process of ISO 14001 (following introduction in 1996, periodically every five years), German industry also launched a survey of German users of ISO 14000 standards at the end of 1999/beginning of 2000 (in principle according to the issues that arose in the review process of ISO TC 207 SC1 at that time, starting in June 2000; about 400 companies participated in that survey). The main findings (of the preliminary results in June 2001 by EPA) add to early Japanese experiences some interesting pros and cons concerning the overall acceptance of world-wide EMS standards.[5] For further improvements, some issues were of special interest.

- External communication (reporting) as a 'new' element in ISO 14001: this issue, allowed in ISO 14001 but not detailed and facing increased interest at ISO level in incorporating this topic as well, was rejected by a small majority (167), whereas a considerable number (142) thinks positively about such an amendment.
- Integration of the (released) ISO 14031 guidelines: 65 per cent were against integration, still doubting that a standardization in ISO 14001 would be helpful.
- Stronger orientation towards 'product-related' environmental protection: a slight majority in favour (158:147), not surprisingly regarding the European discussion on integrated product policy (IPP) – already discussed and integrated into the EMAS revision (IPP is highlighted by the 6th EU Environmental Programme).

In view of the importance of the 14001 revision, in January 2001 a study was initiated by the German Environmental Ministry and the EPA to supply valid recommendations based on a survey of all 2300 companies certified to ISO 14001 at that time, as well as all 34 accreditation organizations.[6] In general, the survey is quite positive and promises the quick spreading of ISO 14001 world-wide (DIN German Institute for Standardization *et al.*, 2001).

Given such business support for moderate improvements in ISO 14001, strong concerns on SME application (expressed by continual SME workshops over obstacles and improvements at annual ISO TC 207 conferences attracting lots of experts) as well as a world-wide tendency of snowball effects along the whole supply chain (urging suppliers to certify), a continuous if not stronger increase in world-wide ISO 14001 certifications is expected in the short and middle term.

Concerning the relationship between EMAS and ISO 14001, many companies were taking a dual approach. About 30 per cent already had been certified to ISO 14001, nearly 15 per cent planned to do so, and one in five were still in internal discussions with regard to the criterion of 'world-wide validity' and there was widespread agreement on the positive effects of combining ISO 14001 and EMAS.

BOX 4.1 LOW ACCEPTANCE OF CERTIFIED EMS: SOME EXPERIENCES

Generally, the number of companies with certified EMS is still low. In Germany, currently fewer than 0.2 per cent of the companies have certified EMS. According to Keddie (2000), the reasons for the low acceptance of EMS include the complexity of the certification processes, a perception that systems are irrelevant or ill-suited to most companies' needs, competition with other demands on managers' time and resources and a lack of credibility in government campaigns to encourage adoption. There are even some studies identifying disbenefits from implementing a certified EMS.[1] Some of those disbenefits are shown in the following figure.

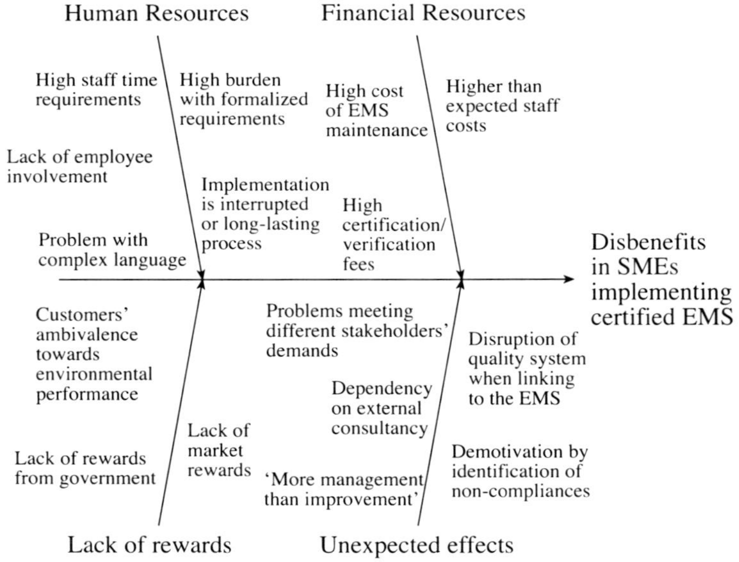

Source: adapted from Hillary (2000).

The disbenefits of implementing certified EMS can be grouped into four categories: human and financial resources, lack of rewards and unexpected effects. Internally, the human and financial resources needed, based, for example, on aspects like the high burden with formalized requirements or the high cost for EMS maintenance, are major disbenefits. Also the lack of market or governmental rewards or unexpected effects, such as dependency on external consultancy or problems with meeting different stakeholder demands, can be disbenefits to a company.

NOTE

1. The probable cause of the low number of studies focusing on disbenefits is that many reports present best practice case studies and seek to 'sell' EMS to the SME sector.

ISO 14031: Guidelines on 'environmental performance evaluation' (EPE)
Besides the best known 'flagship' ISO 14001, a whole series of about 20 standards has already been developed within the ISO 14000 family since Rio 1992 according to the original mandate (see Interim Report from February: Bartelmus *et al*., 2001). The last standard released is the ISO 14031 guidelines on 'environmental performance evaluation' (EPE).

This standard intentionally defines 'environmental performance' differently from ISO 14001,[7] reflecting concerns also mentioned in some national reviews on shortcomings in the 14001 standard in contrast to the explicit 'performance' orientation of EMAS as outlined earlier. After difficult international consensus processes on the new ISO 14031 guidance standard, its release was finally agreed by accepting some 'unsolved' or insufficiently elaborated issues such as assessment, reporting or micro–macro links between corporate environmental performance and environmental condition indicators. Meanwhile, continuous presentations of successful ISO 14031 implementations by organizations of all sizes and sectors during the annual ISO TC 207 conferences period of 1999–2001[8] demonstrate rising awareness of this beneficial but still relatively unknown ISO tool for performance evaluation (Seifert, 2001).[9] With this recent EPE standard, ISO TC 207 is closing a widely criticized gap in the 14000 series concerning 'performance', although ISO 14031 is not a certifiable standard. But this 'disadvantage' in first implementation experiences is turning out to be a benefit for organizations which profit from real performance results in a well structured EPE process without being obliged to make (cost-intensive) certification commitments immediately. Further improvements are promoted by ISO 14031, for example with regard to the 'reporting' issue.

As a pioneering example of a real 'performance'-oriented evaluation process according to ISO 14031 and elaborating its reporting guidance[10] towards a 'lean reporting' approach, the case of the Kunert company was highlighted at the ISO–EPE workshop 2001. This hosiery manufacturer, given an award by UNEP for environmental reporting, has already presented a third ISO 14031 Environmental Performance Report on the occasion of its 10th anniversary of environmental reporting in 2001, experiencing also the application of the 'micro–macro link' recommendations of the standard (linking performance indicators with condition indicators: Seifert, 2001). The experience gained from cooperation with SMEs highlights the importance of environmental (cost) information within the organization, as in the Furniture Workshop Kambium, a medium-sized furniture enterprise, which was awarded the 'Eco-Manager of the Year' prize by the business magazine *Capital* and the WWF Germany (Liedtke *et al*., 1998). The new and easy to handle ISO 14031 standard on EPE, together with stakeholder-oriented communication and reporting activities, would strongly support such requirements, especially with regard to SMEs.

Institutional activities of ISO: challenges and 'future visions' regarding sustainability Within the ISO, so-called 'new work items' entered the work agenda, among them in particular 'Design for the Environment' (DFE), the recently started work on 'Environmental Communications' (internal and external reporting) and a Task Force for Climate Change (TFCC), stimulating the 2001 ISO host, Malaysia, to announce preparations (together with Canada) of a 'new work item' on this issue for an ISO voting process (still in progress).

On the product side, new concepts like the IPP (integrated product policy) urged by the EU is stimulating aspirations among consumer-oriented parties and is partly integrated already into the forthcoming ISO 14062 on DFE; real performance criteria for overall production processes towards goals such as 'dematerialization' or 'zero emission' still have to be developed and implemented at large.[11]

A further topic which would be a really new one within the ISO 14000 series is EMA, environmental management accounting. This issue, mentioned by the TFFV (see below), already has remarkable support outside ISO TC 207 and it would be a timely approach to react to such market developments and to complement the ISO family with such a tool to realize 'win–win' solutions based on eco-efficient accounting procedures as for example promoted by the UN–EMA group (2001)[12] or other organizations like the EMAN network.[13] Referring to the many theoretical and practical experiences, especially in Japan and Germany, this issue would be a suitable common ISO initiative for experts of both countries as well as for additional experts from business, academia and stakeholders. Germany at least, via its ISO mirror body to ISO SC 4 on EPE, has developed such an initiative for the Johannesburg conference to launch this issue and to receive reactions on a possible new work item.[14]

Facing challenges for the next phase of an institutional process of enlarged multi-stakeholder dialogues, the ISO/TC 207 chairman advisory group (CAG) established a small 'Task Force on Future Vision/Planning, Rio+10 and Sector Policy' (TFFV) to prepare a draft strategic plan for ISO/TC 207. This acronym, according to *Tomorrow* magazine (2001), is the most important one in TC 207's history as the first serious attempt at policy making since its start in 1993. Subjects discussed so far are:

- assessment of the current situation: where do we stand?
- what are the current trends and what does the future look like?
- how do trends and future developments influence TC 207's current and possible future activities/products?
- to what extent can ISO/TC 207 absorb and influence these external developments?

With regard to one of the more hotly debated agenda points during the 2001 ISO/TC 207 conference on the pros and cons of the general approach of TC 207 in favour of 'generic' standardization rather than considering 'sector-specific' challenges (as for example by the forestry industry), the 'vision' paper recommends dialogue processes.[15] However, final conclusions will not be drawn before the Task Force has submitted corresponding recommendations.

The open agenda of this TFFV goes beyond environmental issues in view of the wider challenges of sustainability. The range of such issues which are beyond the original scope of the ISO 14000 standards and even their environmental mandate is increasingly being discussed inside and outside ISO TC 207. This issue of reporting, deliberated on only by subcommittee (SC)4[16] and included to some extent already in the 14031 guidelines,[17] resulted finally in a new working group on 'environmental communication' for an additional ISO 14063 guideline (starting at the ISO conference 2001 and for three years' work maximum). Best practice examples on corporate environmental performance and disclosure to interested parties have been referred to at the Rio+10 United Nations World Summit in Johannesburg in 2002.

Evaluating the Agenda 21 as well as new challenges, the summit presents a timely opportunity also for the evaluation of the 'role of business' (according to Agenda 21) and the corresponding mandate given to ISO for the development of a 14000 series. Besides a future new work item (NWI) on climate change, a crucial issue in multi-stakeholder dialogues is 'communication' within organizations and between business and its various stakeholders to enhance credibility, especially with respect to 'standardization' activities outside ISO TC 207 as recently started by ISO COPOLCO (Consumer Policy Committee)[18] or by the Global Reporting Initiative (GRI). These guidelines, still in progress and experienced by some pioneering companies mainly in the USA and Europe, very soon included the comprehensive triple bottom-line approach towards sustainability, that is environmental as well as social and economic concerns. This reflects the fact that a growing number of (multinational) organizations are moving beyond pure environmental reporting and towards sustainability reporting.

The evolution from marketing brochures in the early 1990s to serious disclosure approaches (documented periodically by SustainAbility-London on behalf of UNEP) is seen as a response to certain market needs as well as stakeholder concerns (NGO pressures), including those of financial analysts. A recent survey of reporting practices of the firms on *Fortune* magazine's current list of the top 100 companies in the world (the Global 100, or G100) confirms such trends. But, in contrast to such positive trends, actual performance data, especially in areas that are not regulated by law, remain rather thin: fewer than 25 per cent of companies report global figures for waste generation, water use or air emissions – a strong confirmation of the potentials and necessity of ISO 14031 application and implementation. Obviously, there is a need to bring into this landscape of diverse reporting and communicating practices of even the top 100 multinationals (not to mention SMEs) some rational structure and comparability and basics for benchmarking. This, indeed, also reflects the different phases of sustainable business development as outlined here.

Beyond green entrepreneurship or pure environmental concerns, real challenges to Rio+10 achievements lie in integrated approaches towards sustainability as experienced by business with new integrated management systems and disclosure, encouraged by NGO initiatives like GRI. To this end, in addition to formal environmental management systems (EMS), 'simple' but tailor-made approaches are needed, especially for SMEs to keep them on track towards sustainable development. These approaches are dealt with in the next sections in more detail.

Efficient entrepreneurship

This section elaborates on (eco-)efficient entrepreneurship, the enterprise phase in which companies relate their whole organization to other parties in the product system and thereby include the economic relevance of environmental issues in decision making. As SMEs are seen to be critically important in the product chain and for macroeconomic aspects like employment and overall innovation, specific attention is given to SMEs under the hypothesis that certified EMS as green purchasing criteria do not fit all SMEs to improve their environmental performance.

It has been shown in a number of case studies that a management system that integrates environmental and economic performance measures can help to improve business-to-business customer relationships along the chain, to reduce risks that result from external effects and inefficiencies, to reduce the total cost at company level by 2 to 5 per cent (Gege, 1997; Liedtke and Weizsäcker, 2000) and increase the shareholder value considerably (see Schaltegger and Figge, 1997). An example of potential cost savings is given in the Box 4.2 and illustrates the importance of transparency for internal efficiency improvements.

BOX 4.2 TRANSPARENCY OF COST STRUCTURE

The relevance of cost caused by waste streams within a company is shown by Strobel et al. (1999) for a company in the pharmaceutical industry. The hidden cost of non-product outputs (third row) is here more than ten times higher than the obvious output cost.

	Input cost	Support function cost	Processing cost	Disposal cost	Output cost	Σ Cost
Production materials	350 000 000	6 000 000	15 000 000	3 000 000	2 200 000	376 200 000
Product packaging	20 000 000	4 000 000	13 000 000	3 000 000	4 000 000	44 000 000
Non-product output	**20 800 000**	**670 000**	**1 220 000**	**450 000**	**2 300 000**	**25 440 000**
Waste	15 000 000	480 000	1 100 000	250 000	2 000 000	18 830 000
Product materials	6 000 000	80 000	300 000	80 000	300 000	6 760 000
Product packaging	1 000 000	200 000	600 000	50 000	400 000	2 250 000
Rejects	3 000 000	50 000	200 000	40 000	50 000	3 340 000
Reclaims	5 000 000	150 000		80 000	250 000	5 480 000
Other waste					1 000 000	1 000 000
Waste water	2 300 000	80 000	100 000	200 000	300 000	2 980 000
Product materials	2 000 000	30 000	100 000	200 000	300 000	2 330 000
Water	300 000	50 000				650 000
Emissions to air	500 000	10 000	20 000			530 000
Heat losses	3 000 000	100 000				3 100 000
Σ Cost	390 800 000	10 670 000	29 220 000	6 450 000	850 000	445 640 000

Knowledge about the economic gains of environmental activities for many enterprises is essential to improving efficiency. SMEs especially depend on external information to gain a balance of ideas, information, technological options and financial power to improve efficiency. Here networks are crucial for SMEs, as owners and managers of small firms are less likely than their larger counterparts to have undergone formal management training and may be less familiar with analytical techniques associated with the strategy formulation and decision making that underpin efficiency improvements. Therefore the importance of disseminating appropriate information as a primary strategy for encouraging the efficiency of SMEs is virtually unchallenged. In a meeting of experts specializing in communicating environmental information to enterprises (particularly SMEs), the model illustrated in Figure 4.2 was compiled explaining how companies currently receive information.[19] One conclusion has been that information efforts not taking this flow into account are likely to be less effective or influential.

Following this model, information campaigns are most effective in reaching SMEs when they use the existing information routes through local-level information sources such as municipal authorities, business organizations,

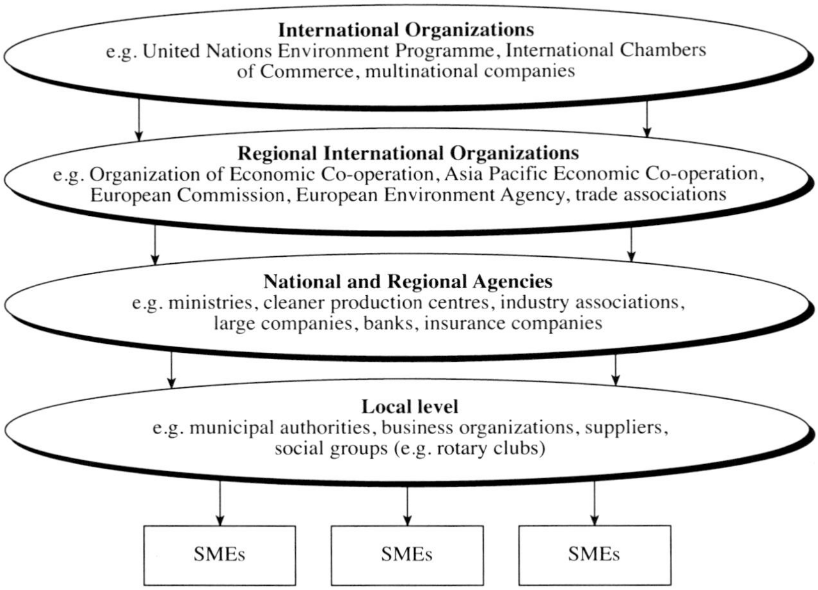

Source: Adapted from UNEP Division of Technology, Industry and Economics (1997).

Figure 4.2 Levels to reach SMEs

business partners of SMEs, rotary clubs and local chambers of commerce. Campaigns directed at industries, especially SMEs, via other information routes, from the international level, for example, do not have the same chance of success. In order to inform SMEs world-wide, to invest in local and regional networks where no information routes exist and to inform existing networks in which SMEs participate, a diverse set of information 'gatekeepers' at the international, national, regional and, especially, local level is necessary. Partners that need to get involved are trade associations, employer associations, business associations, direct business partners of SMEs, chambers of commerce, local authorities, training institutions, academia, insurance companies and banks.

Taking the product chain approach As SMEs, and industry in general, prefer to receive information from business to business,[20] the most effective way of disseminating information is seen to be through existing information channels, such as local business organizations and supplier chains. The reputation of large companies, the success of international voluntary and business initiatives and the commitment to continuous improvement in environmental management systems are closely related to SMEs. A poor environmental performance of SMEs within the supply chain will negate the environmental success of large partners.

Green purchasing is one form of cooperation to improve the environmental performance of the product chain actors. Green purchasing goes beyond internal efficiency and can promote the supplier's efficiency, as well as demonstrating the responsibility of the purchaser.[21]

There seems to be a common global trend for companies to act, not alone, but in networks of companies, cooperatives or partnerships along the value chain. Monczka and Morgan (1997) claim that there seems to be increasing recognition that, in the future, it will be the whole supply chain that will compete, not just individual firms. A supply chain is a network of producers and distributors which buy materials, make them into intermediate and finished products and distribute them to customers. The key elements within the supply chain are the actors and the flows (material, informational and monetary), as illustrated in Figure 4.3.

(Eco-)efficient entrepreneurship incorporates the coordination of these actors and material, informational and monetary flows with the aim of achieving economic and environmental objectives. Well-established objectives of supply chain actors are the value creation from increased customer satisfaction and shorter delivery time. An increasing number of companies are also beginning to consider the reduction of environmental impacts along the supply chain as an objective for their supply chain management and to communicate and cooperate with all actors in the supply chain. This integrated approach seems

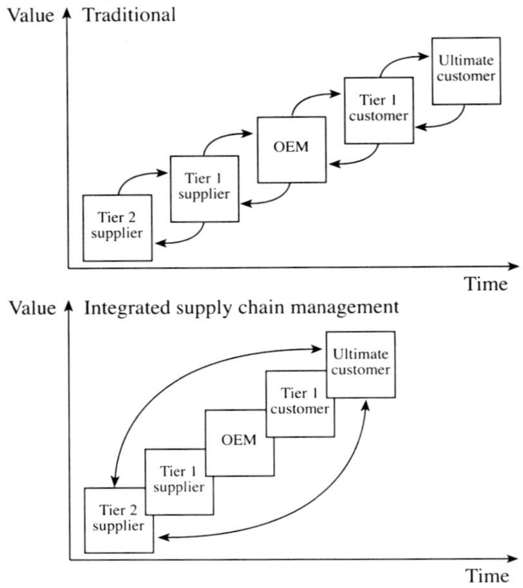

Source: Adapted from Powell (2000).

Figure 4.3 Comparison of the traditional and integrated model of supply chain management

to be a promising approach to improve the environmental performance of entire product chains. Most companies begin to establish purchasing policies as a first step towards integrated product chain management, as illustrated in Figure 4.4. This process refers to vertical coordination of firms.

Another option for eco-efficient entrepreneurship can be seen in horizontal coordination among firms, following the problem-solving framework for certain locations. Eco-industrial parks are one example of such coordination (Bleischwitz, 2001a).

Green purchasing strategies European product chain actors and governmental organizations are begining to exert greater influence on the general environmental performance of companies, specifically medium-sized companies. Green purchasing is an often-discussed factor as a means to promote improved environmental performance.

Green purchasing – the integration of environmental considerations into purchasing policies, programmes and action – has recently been identified as a possible driver for environmental improvements in the product chain (for

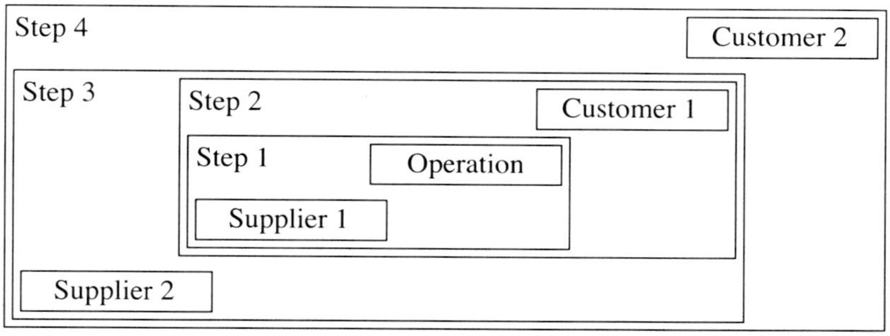

Figure 4.4 Stepwise approach to integrated product chain management

example Russel, 1998). Green purchasing, including aspects such as vendor selection, material selection, negotiations, buying or delivery scheduling, is a relevant strategy for private and public organizations to promote sustainable development.

There is a range of green purchasing approaches available. They can be grouped into three major categories: product standards, behaviour standards and collaboration (Table 4.2). A public or private organization should select the most efficient purchasing approach according to suitability to the target group. The use of certified environmental management standards is one purchasing criterion commonly used, for example in the automotive industry. However, this approach does not necessarily lead to significantly improved environmental performance among suppliers (Hamner and del Rosario, 1997). Firstly, the commitment to performance improvements depends on the standard being applied; for example, ISO 14001 does not require improvements in environmental performance, whereas the EMAS standard does. Secondly, different studies conclude that certified EMS are not essentially the best means to improve the environmental performance of companies. A European research project, 'Measuring Environmental Performance of Industry' (MEPI) investigated the correlation between EMS and environmental performance and concluded that companies with certified EMS do not perform significantly better (European Commission, 2001c). The same conclusion has been arrived at by Hroch and Schaltegger (2001) when investigating CO_2 and energy indicators published in German environmental reports. Regarding the effectiveness of EMS in SMEs, a study from the Wuppertal Institute (Klemisch and Rohn, 2002) found that almost all SMEs with fewer than 50 employees have used financial support to implement EMAS and identified negative evaluation of EMS by SMEs.

Thus those buyers who simply require suppliers to meet an external environmental management standard as a kind of 'low-cost' strategy to introduce

Table 4.2 Green purchasing approaches

Product standards	Purchase products that have environmentally friendly attributes (recycled materials or non-toxic ingredients)
	Purchase products that disclose their environmental attributes (eco-labelling)
Behaviour standards	Require suppliers to disclose information about their environmental practices, pollution discharges and so on
	Audit suppliers to evaluate their environmental performance
	Require suppliers to implement and maintain an environmental management system
	Require suppliers to have an EMS that meets recognized standards (such as EMAS, ISO 14001 or Responsible Care)
	Require suppliers to obtain formal certification of their EMS
Collaboration	Work with suppliers to help them reduce environmental impacts through changes in product design and materials use
	Product stewardship: active management of all aspects of the product from raw materials to final disposal

Source: adapted from Hamner and del Rosario (1997).

environmental criteria in the purchasing policy need to consider that this should only be taken as a first approach. Later they should request performance measures and targets.

Responsible entrepreneurship

An increasing number of European companies are promoting strategies for responsible entrepreneurship as a response to a variety of social, environmental and economic pressures. They aim to send a voluntary signal to the various stakeholders with whom they interact: employees, shareholders, investors, consumers, public authorities and non-governmental organizations (NGOs). In doing so, companies expect that their voluntary commitment to stakeholder consultations will help them to perceive and avoid future risks and to increase their future profitability.

This section elaborates on the nature of responsible entrepreneurship, the phase of the approaches described above in which companies manage their social performance in addition to economic and environmental issues. It also elaborates on internal and external drivers to promote responsible entrepreneurship.

Taking the stakeholder approach Responsible entrepreneurship is a concept whereby companies integrate social and environmental concerns in their economy-driven business operations and in their interaction with their stakeholders on a voluntary basis. Being responsible means not only fulfilling legal demands, but also going beyond legal compliance and investing in human capital, the environment and the relations with stakeholders. The existing experience with investment in environmentally responsible technologies and business practice suggests that going beyond legal compliance can contribute to a company's competitiveness (Kerber, 1997; Langlois and Robertson, 1995). Going beyond basic legal requirements in the social area, for example training, working conditions and management–employee relations, can also have a direct impact on productivity. It opens the way for improved corporate social performance while improving competitiveness. (European Commission, 2001b).

Compared to the business strategies described above for sustainable development, responsible entrepreneurship incorporates improvements of corporate social performance, which has been defined and interpreted in different ways. According to Figge *et al.*, (2001), three different approaches to social performance can be distinguished. There is an ethical approach (Hoffmann *et al.*, 2000; Takala and Pallab, 2000), the social management approach with the focus on employee involvement and workers' safety (for example, Pischon and Liesgang, 1998) and a stakeholder approach (for example, Freeman, 1984). In the following the stakeholder approach as a means to manage corporate social performance will be focused upon. The stakeholder approach can cover workers' health and safety, as well as ethical questions, when employees or ethical NGOs are addressed in the stakeholder process. Recently, there have been a number of public initiatives promoting sustainable development, which have drawn on the stakeholder approach as a means of getting a broad consensus among different societal groups on the issues where each initiative is concerned (UK Roundtable on Sustainable Development, 1998; Global Reporting Initiative (GRI), 2000; German Council for Sustainable Development, 2001; UN Global Compact).

Stakeholder approaches can range from informing processes to monitoring processes and mechanisms, implementation processes and processes which include not only dialogues but also consensus building, decision making and implementation (Hemmati, 2001). At the beginning of an effective stakeholder dialogue is the definition of stakeholders (Starik *et al.*, 1996). Freeman (1984) suggests that stakeholders include any group or individual who can affect or is affected by the achievement of an organizational purpose. This definition is rather broad as it includes interested parties as well as affected parties. Therefore some argue for restricting the term 'stakeholder' to those who have a 'stake' or vested interest in the firm (Carroll, 1993). In management practice, however, for instance in sustainability reporting and social auditing, stakeholders are defined as primary or secondary, depending on an assessment of whether they are immediately affected by, or can immediately affect, a firm's operations (Bendell, 2000).

European experiences regarding responsible entrepreneurship European businesses and governments over recent years have promoted a number of stakeholder consultations. Thus CSR Europe, a European business-driven membership network, was established as a result of the European Declaration of Business against Social Exclusion. The network was initiated by the former President of the European Commission, Jacques Delors, and 20 business leaders (www.csreurope.org). The European Commission is promoting the stakeholder approach in its recently released green paper on corporate social responsibility. It aims at launching a multi-stakeholder debate in order to promote a new European framework for corporate social responsibility (European Commission, 2001b). Also the activities in the area of integrated product policy (IPP), as mentioned in Chapter 3, take and promote the stakeholder approach to reduce the environmental impact of products (European Commission, 2001b).

Several member states of the European Union have taken active steps to promote responsible entrepreneurship. In Denmark, the Minister for Social Affairs launched the campaign 'Our Common Concern – the social responsibility of the corporate sector' in 1994 and set up the Copenhagen Centre in 1998. In the UK, a Minister for Corporate Social Responsibility was appointed in March 2000. The Eco-efficiency and Sustainable Enterprise Group of the Wuppertal Institute is applying a stakeholder approach on an industry sector level. The project 'Towards a Sustainable Aluminium Industry' is conducted on behalf of the European Aluminium Industry. Here, using the COMPASS methodology (Kuhndt and Liedtke, 1999), stakeholders' expectations related to sustainable industrial development for the European aluminium industry are gathered and visualized. Core indicators for the aluminium industry are identified and brought into the stakeholder discussion. The results are used in defining important sustainability issues and possible measures (sector report) within the aluminium sector in the context of the European/international debate. Another sectoral multi-stakeholder project is managed by the International Institute for Environment and Development in London, under contract to the World Business Council for Sustainable Development. It is seeking to understand how the mining and minerals sector can best contribute to the global transition to sustainable development. A key element within this project is stakeholder involvement, a process of non-discriminatory participation and involvement with stakeholders affected by all aspects of the mining and mineral cycle.

From a business perspective, there are some critical factors explaining why enterprises are still reluctant to move towards a sustainable industry as outlined in Box 4.3. On the other hand, there are a variety of different drivers for responsible entrepreneurship, which can be distinguished in internal and external issues. The internal objectives of stakeholder involvement are to promote better business decisions by means of wider input; to integrate diverse viewpoints; to bring together the relevant stakeholders; to create trust through honouring each stakeholder group as contributing a necessary component to the bigger picture; to create mutual benefits (win–win rather than win–lose situations); to develop shared power with a partnership approach; and to create commitment through stakeholders identifying with the outcome and thus increasing the likelihood of successful implementation (Hemmati, 2001).

External factors driving this move towards responsible entrepreneurship (European Commission, 2001b) are new concerns and expectations from citizens, consumers, public authorities and investors in the context of globalization and large scale industrial change; social criteria increasingly influencing the investment decisions of individuals and institutions both as consumers and as investors; increased concern about the damage caused by economic activity to the environment; and transparency of business activities brought about by the media and modern information and communication technologies.

The experience with stakeholder consultations shows that these are putting people into the centre of decision finding, decision making and implementation. Thus the consultation reflects the different basic values or hierarchies of values of the stakeholders involved. Whereas for many NGOs, for example, transparency and equity are high priorities, some businesses and governments may place more importance on speeding up processes and producing outcome within a short time period.

There is general criticism of voluntary initiatives such as stakeholder consultations, particularly from NGOs. Stakeholder consultations may be criticized as 'talk-shops' and as being misused as legitimization while not having to do anything. Setting specific objectives and monitoring the outcome and the follow-up is important, otherwise the process may not lead to much. It turns out that the early involvement of a diverse stakeholder group can better take into account the different viewpoints throughout the process. Where stakeholders have not been involved from the beginning, they sometimes question whether much effort has been made to be inclusive.

BOX 4.3 FACTORS HINDERING THE PROGRESS TOWARDS SUSTAINABILITY

The main reasons for most businesses still hesitating to move faster towards a sustainable industrial development are as follows:

1. Business lacks the gateway to sustainability

Business fears sustainable development (SD) in general ('It will limit our competitiveness and thus endanger jobs'). Business only has limited information about the concept of SD and does not have access to front-line expertise. And if companies have access to relevant information, it is often not available in business-oriented language, so that decision makers in SME, in particular, cannot use it.

2. Business lacks a clear understanding of what stakeholders expect them to do

Business has difficulty in understanding the broad range of expectations of their stakeholders towards SD. They are lacking clearly defined macro and meso sustainability goals that would provide a coherent set of indicators to subscribe to. Some pieces of the puzzle can be deciphered from existing initiatives (for example, the UN's Agenda 21, international conventions, national environmental plans, Factor 10) but these pieces have not yet proved to be enough to provide a clearly defined set of integral sustainable development goals and indicators backed up by the broad-based societal support needed to help enterprises on a more sustainable path.

3. Business lacks a broad recognition of its achievements

Business needs information channels to communicate its efforts and achievements in SD to its stakeholders ('The majority of our stakeholders do not reward our efforts and achievements'). That does not mean that every single measure has to pay, but that the public and stakeholders should take notice of these efforts. Up to now hardly any efficient system could be found that systematically provides this kind of information to the relevant stakeholder groups.

4. Business lacks support on the path to sustainability (policy/NGO/consumer)

Business feels that governments need to create a framework which makes investments in support of sustainable development economically worthwhile. Business needs incentives (such as deregulation) to move forward. Sustainability has to be promoted to consumers in order to arouse their awareness and increase their demand for more sustainable goods. Last but not least, NGOs (especially research) must become aware of business problems, capacities and needs, and provide business-oriented concepts and strategies on SD.

Conclusions on Strategies for Sustainable Business Development

This section has outlined the variety of different approaches to sustainable business development. Conclusions can be drawn for both the institutional level of ISO and business/government.

Conclusions on the institutional perspective of ISO

After a full decade of experiences with Agenda 21 and related programmes, Johannesburg 2002 served as an appropriate occasion to take these issues into account *within* ISO and to continue *outside* dialogue at a high political level.

ISO TC 207 is well advised (as for example by *Tomorrow* magazine on three crucial issues[22]) to face these discourses by evaluating the achievements that have so far been realized in 'strengthening the role of business' according to Agenda 21 on the road towards sustainable development.

Looking to the Rio+10 summit in Johannesburg in 2002, evaluations of achievements and challenges to sustainable development to be considered in the TFFV have resulted in more ambitious agendas for multi-stakeholder processes of civil society, to be fostered by formal standardization institutions. Many urgent issues are on the agenda of the TFFV, but TC 207 has to decide in June on a future roadmap.

The GRI guidelines as well as the new ISO work on environmental communication could contribute to harmonization in international experiences and stakeholder communication actually experienced in environmental (or enhanced) reports by about (only) 2100 companies around the world which voluntarily disclose their economic, environmental or social policies, practices and performance. Stronger cooperation between ISO and outside 'proto-standardizing' initiatives like GRI would benefit comparability in general, thus also sustainability requirements.[23]

Conclusions on business strategies

Given the increasing influence of business in a globalized world, corporate responsibility for sustainable business development needs to be promoted. The framework conditions for innovations in business gain increasing importance. Thus the mere existence of microeconomic tools for sustainable business development such as environmental management systems, life cycle assessment, material flow accounting or social audits does not necessarily lead to improvements in environmental, social or economic business performance. A reasonable choice of strategy to promote sustainable business effectively should consider the characteristics of the enterprise in focus. Through their role as innovator and employer, SMEs play a crucial role in achieving sustainable development (Kuhndt and van der Lugt, 2000; European Commission, 1995).

One generic framework condition governments can set to promote efficiency in business activity is linked to the economic instrument of environmental taxes. For cost-driven companies, the taxes can increase the awareness of environmental cost due to the economic incentive. Once the internal cost of environmental aspects of corporate activities are known and related to the corporate decision-making processes, those companies are likely to act more efficiently. Here, raw material taxes as implemented in some European countries can play a crucial role in promoting the long-term integration of environmental cost. For a company, input-oriented approaches might be more cost-efficient. Focusing on material input savings in production processes even has a twofold economic benefit: reduced input costs and reduced end-of-pipe/waste-treatment/disposal costs.

Governments as well as large (and proactive) enterprises influence the framework conditions for SMEs through their strong buying power. Thus governmental and business purchasing policies focused on environmental performance can have a more direct effect on SMEs than any other type of environmental pressure. Governments may be constrained in the selection of supplying SMEs by rules regarding low bid selection; nonetheless, supplying SMEs may be questioned regarding their environmental performance. Thus certified EMS are not necessarily the most efficient green purchasing criteria to promote environmental improvements in SMEs, as there may be some deficits of certified EMS in SMEs, such as high demands on human and financial resources and limited effectiveness. Using their power, larger companies and governments might promote environmental improvements in SMEs by taking measures such as developing purchasing policies that reward corporate performance improvements and collaboration (not only certified EMS). Also, if an EMS is required in SMEs through supply-chain pressure (for example in the automotive industry most enterprises are forced by the market to have certified EMS), SMEs should be supported when implementing an EMS, for example by incremental approaches for implementation with rewards on the way or joint EMS and group certifications. Additionally, existing purchasing policies may be expanded to further areas, such as canteens or cleaning products, which are not commonly integrated into procurement guidelines.

A number of companies with good social performance indicate that stakeholder processes can result in better performance and can generate more profits and growth. Performed well, a stakeholder process can underpin a powerful change process with trust, facilitation of collaboration, market creation meeting future customers' needs, reduction of future risks or enhancement of the corporate value. Badly handled, it can be an expensive, time-consuming and counterproductive activity. Effective stakeholder consultations can be a critical element in a socially responsible business strategy. Whilst, so far, stakeholder consultations are mainly promoted by a number of large or multinational companies, they are relevant in all types of companies, from SMEs to multinational enterprises, and in all industry sectors. Although many SMEs already take a stakeholder approach, particularly through community involvement, further promotion by government is needed. Focusing on relevant drivers, possible measures might be to disseminate good practice of responsible entrepreneurship to raise awareness among companies and stakeholders. Here the European policy approach on IPP (stakeholder involvement in product panels) points in the right direction. Additionally, supporting minorities in society can give them a stronger voice in the discussion and create a balanced stakeholder arena.

The involvement of industry associations to begin sectoral dialogues on their sustainable development is another promising way to disseminate information to SMEs and promote sustainable development at the macro level. Further actions could be the incorporation of social and ethical criteria in public procurement and socially responsible investment to promote the uptake of responsible entrepreneurship in companies.

The behaviour of enterprises has important implications for all economic and social actors as well as for public authorities, who should consider them when determining their own actions. Efficient and responsible entrepreneurship is a key to achieving socioeconomic and environmental goals at the macro level and sustainable development in the long run.

4.3 SUSTAINABLE CONSUMPTION: POLICY STRATEGIES, CONSUMERS' BEHAVIOUR AND MARKET DEVELOPMENT

Introduction

Agenda 21, the major policy document issued by the United Nations Conference on Environment and Development in 1992, states, in chapter four, that 'the major cause of the continued degradation of the global environment is the unsustainable pattern of consumption and production, particularly in industrialized countries'. It then goes on to demand that 'consideration should also be given to the present concepts of economic growth and the need for new concepts of wealth and prosperity which allow for higher standards of living through changed life styles and are less dependent on the Earth's finite resources and more in harmony with the Earth's carrying capacity'. It is evident that Agenda 21 expects any theory of sustainability to include an analysis of the scale and pattern of consumption in society for the purpose of exploring changes in demand that could help to bring about a resource-light economy.

But it must generally be said that in reality the consumption patterns of industrialized countries do not meet the challenge of Agenda 21 targets: most of the important ecological indicators show that recent consumption patterns are far from being sustainable, and the environmental progress made as a result of eco-efficient strategies has been cancelled out by a rising consumption level.

In order to approach the difficulties, the following sections explore some solutions in the field of changing consumption patterns and new markets. The introduction of the analytical framework is followed by two market-based case studies referring to energy and food consumption of private household members.

Research Approach

Consumers' behaviour and change of consumption patterns

It is common knowledge in social science that, over the last 20 years, environmental problems have led to a change in consumers' attitudes and behaviour in Germany and elsewhere. 'However, the diffusion process of ecology was accompanied by a more or less marked discrepancy between attitudes and behaviour and with clear differences in behaviour in the different areas of life relevant to ecology. We are living in a plurality of an ecologically ambivalent patchwork of life styles' (Empacher *et al.*, 2000). A positive attitude towards ecological targets only is just a weak indicator for the behavioural tendency to adopt new life styles, and there are incidences of environmentally responsible behaviour without a corresponding positive attitude (Kuckartz, 2000).

For the following examination of relevant market segments, these findings are important in two ways. First of all, it must be taken into account that the verifiable consumption behaviour of people is embedded in a more comprehensive context of values, attitudes and cultural impact: 'We shall assume that the essential function of consumption is its capacity to make sense' (Douglas and Isherwood, 1978: 62). Secondly, it is apparent that consumption behaviour plays an important part in everyday actions, which is expressed in the demand for goods and services. Everyday actions, however, cover much more than only economically relevant behaviour.

People's behaviour is continually changing because of social changes. In this process of change the functional structures of society and individual preferences influence each other. Marketing-oriented consumer research regards the following points as the fundamental factors influencing this change in Germany and elsewhere (Hansen and Bode, 1999).

- Demographic factors: stagnating or sinking birth rates, partial compensation of naturally weak population growth rates through immigration from other countries, changes in ethnic population structure, increase in life expectancy, increasing proportion of senior citizens to total population.
- Socioeconomic factors: changes in family structures, increase in single-person households, structurally continuous unemployment, structural change from industry to services and internationalization of employment, increasing polarization between low-income and high-income households (new poor, segregation).
- Sociocultural factors: loss in significance of traditional values, change in values, pluralistic life styles, individualization, ties/loyalty to established organizations such as the church, trade unions and parties diminish, employment is no longer regarded as the grounding centre of life, reduction in working hours leads to increased recreation, recreation time increasingly becomes consumer time, consumption takes on social and symbolic importance.
- Technical factors: technology push through the emergence of new technologies and high innovation dynamics, change in everyday life and employment through information and communication technologies.

Having turned the debate around these points it is clear that the primary challenge is to understand the shifts and innovations of demand structures. How are 'new' and 'ecological' market fields constructed, how do expectations of comfort and convenience evolve? And how do they relate to 'green enterprises' (see section 4.2)?

Definitions and methodological context

Sustainable consumption In short, from a demand-oriented perspective on consumption the following social targets are important: fulfilling basic needs for all, building human capabilities, the consumption of some must not compromise the well-being of others, and no mortgaging of the choices of future generations.

Including these points in the concept of sustainable consumption is more than just the greening of products and services: 'It must be perceived as a multi-staged process of need fulfilment where each stage is seen as relevant: The consumption process starts with the perception of a need, which is transformed into a specific want, then a concrete demand, and finally into an act of purchase or into other forms of procurement, e.g. leasing, sharing, pooling, trading in, or self-production. Thus, product use schemes, e.g. for household appliances, can tremendously influence resource use. In accordance with the "cradle-to-grave" approach of sustainable consumption, also the final stage of disposal is relevant' (Scherhorn and Reisch, 1999: 11f).

Life style and environment Life styles are fundamental and distinctive modes of living and working that are accomplished by individuals and groups through socially sanctioned and culturally intelligible patterns of action. Life style possibilities for individuals are constrained by available (and appropriate) choices. While durable, life styles are changing – historically, regionally, globally and generationally – and differ between societies with a different cultural background (Burgess, 1992).

Different life styles have differing consumption requirements and environmental impacts. Life style researchers (Mitchell, 1983; Sobel, 1981; Underhill, 1999) have ventured that life styles associated with higher positions in social stratification systems are likely to consume more and this consumption is related to higher requirements of resources (Lorek and Spangenberg, 2001c). Also consumption choices are more constrained for those in lower-status life styles, and life style experimentation and flexibility is more likely to occur in marginal life style groups. The environmental effects of life styles cannot be tied only to individual behaviour. Individual behaviour itself is at least partially a 'product' of 'life style engineering' by business supply strategies, supported by government action (for example through subsidies for consumption of new housing, highways and infrastructure for communication). And life styles, and their environmental impacts, are also shaped to a significant degree by mass media portrayals of 'how we live' and 'how we want to live'.

Consumers as social actors Looking systematically at consumers as social actors, it first becomes obvious that consumers' decisions are important for the kind and volume of material flows in society. Behind this decision making there are a lot of steering factors such as income, needs, knowledge and symbolic attitudes. Secondly, it is obvious that private household members are more than just consumers. As citizens they vote in elections and thereby indirectly influence the legal framework of product and consumer policy. The strength of this kind of influence in practice became clear in the debate on BSE that led to new standards for meat production in Germany and elsewhere in

Europe. Both selecting products and acting as citizens in an open society indicate the offers made by companies (whether their offers are accepted or not) (Hansen and Schrader, 1997: 447).

Private households The household is understood as an economic unit of people (one or more) who live together and spend a common budget. To divide it into units that can be handled analytically, consumption researchers have focused on different household functions and household types. These functions serve to satisfy the needs of household members and could also fulfil – with many different options – sustainability targets. The role of private households in the policy field of consumption could be better understood in a conceptual framework which recognizes the intermediate influence of different spheres such as the interaction between supply and demand, and the ruling influence on these interactions of frameworks like legislation and cultural impact.

Stakeholders Stakeholders in the field of consumer policy can be defined as 'all those people or organizations who are either affected by or who can affect the performance of various functions at the household level', leading to the following differentiation (Pacchi, 1998: 1):

- supply-side stakeholders (companies and trade associations from various industrial sectors),
- demand-side stakeholders (household members, consumer organizations),
- regulators/policy makers (at different levels),
- researchers, experts and media,
- independent organizations (such as environmental NGOs).

The integrated user perspective and stakeholder analysis are two important 'tools' for structuring the acting fields of sustainable household consumption. The following analysis is based on an integrated approach reflecting the reciprocal influences between legal framework, supply–demand, and values–attitudes–cultural impacts.

Analytical framework

The German discussion of sustainable consumption often aims at formulating new targets and values and their social integration (see Neitzel *et al.*, 1994; a brief overview can be found in Scherhorn *et al.*, 1997). From a practical perspective it becomes clear that governmental frameworks are to be seen as useful measures to stimulate ecologically oriented consumption. Value-based dimensions of behaviour patterns on the one hand, as well as governmental frameworking on the other, affect the economic relationship between supply and demand which Scholl and Zundel refer to as a 'utilization regime' (see Scholl and Zundel, 1999). In order to explain the market dynamics and the market success of individual products and product groups, the utilization regime must be taken into account. It is therefore important to formulate a far-reaching theoretical concept that extends the economic market-related context of utilization regimes and incorporates the institutional settings of governmental frameworking on the one hand and promoters of value change on the other. The following research aims to investigate the prospects for sustainable market(s). This is done within the analysis of intermediate connections and influences of values/attitudes/cultural impact, legal framework, the demand side and the supply side of the market. The innovative aspect of this analytic view is that both supply and demand are influenced by the same frames. But often these frames are only seen as the background to sectoral policies, likewise:

- Legal framework is seen mostly only connected with the supply side (production)
- Values, attitudes and cultural impact are mostly seen as relevant to consumers' policies (consumption)

The intention of the following analytic frame (Figure 4.5) is to overcome these viewpoints and to draw attention to the synergetic potentials in the interlinked areas of the model.

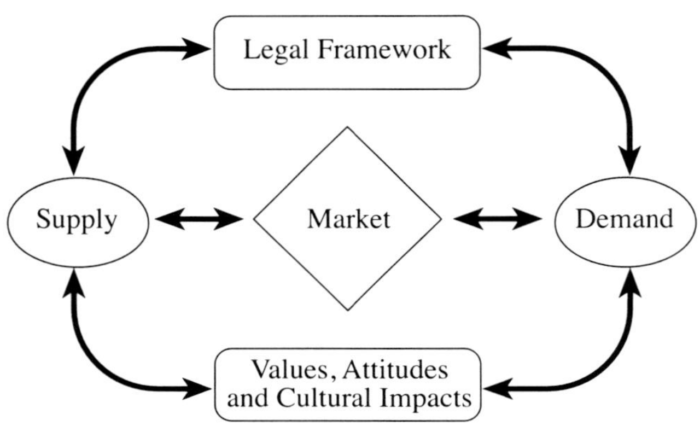

Source: Lucas and Lorek (2003).

Figure 4.5 An integrated approach for market analysis

Against this background it is of great importance for a national strategy of sustainable development to determine what measures can succeed in reducing material and energy demands without having to accept a loss in the quality of life. In this area of different values and targets, important markets for ecological products and services have been established in Germany and elsewhere in Europe. In the following sections this development is looked into, taking selected market fields as examples. Finally, tentative conclusions are drawn regarding conditions for success and any applicability to Japanese conditions.

Taking these arguments and definitions seriously, the necessity for an integrated approach is obvious. Therefore the following research analysis investigates especially the intermediate connections and influences between values/attitudes/cultural impact, demand and green market development, bearing in mind that the game is also ruled by policy making and business offers on the supply side.

Market Fields of Sustainable Consumption

The rest of this chapter summarizes the activities in selected market fields, focusing on market structures, market volumes for green products and services and decision making on the demand side. The first case study relates to the consumption of energy.

Driving forces of residential energy consumption

Over the last 20 years, there have been significant gains in energy efficiency; however, total energy demand in most European countries has increased over the same period (and in most cases has increased per capita as well). Currently, households are the most important final energy consumption sector in Germany (BMWi, 1999: 24). Within households the biggest share of the final energy consumed is for heating (77.5 per cent). In private households heating is responsible for around half of all emissions (Figure 4.6). On average, 209.6kWh of heating energy are consumed per square metre in Germany annually. Being 170kWh/m^2 above the average of a low energy house of current standard, this reveals a considerable potential for improvement.

Fossil energy carriers for heating like fuel oil and coal are still very widespread. Coal, for instance, was still the number one final energy carrier for heating in the east of Germany in 1997, with a share of almost 40 per cent (Federal Statistics Office, 1999). With improved insulation and making buildings airtight as in low and passive houses, however, ventilation technology and thus energy consumption for airing and ventilation are predicted to become more important in the future.

The development of heating energy is driven by three main factors: dwelling size, comfort and convenience (Wilhite *et al.*, 2000).

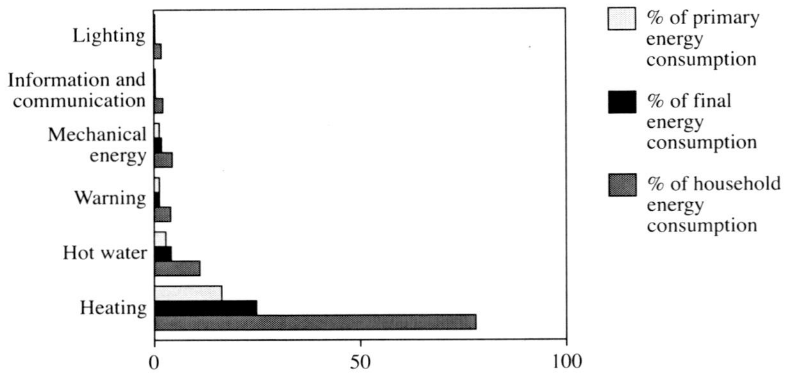

Source: Lorek (2001).

Figure 4.6 Shares of household energy purposes

Dwelling size Dwellings and the residential space occupied or used per person are getting larger. The number of specialized rooms is growing (offices, second bathrooms, separate bedrooms for each child, entertainment rooms and so on), as is the number of appliances and the physical space needed to accommodate them, particularly for entertainment, information and kitchen services. Bigger volume means larger space heating and cooling needs, two of the strongest drivers of energy demand. Statistically, in 1998, an average household in Germany consisted of 2.2 persons occupying 86.7m^2 of living space (German Federal Statistical Office, 2000c). On average, a person in Germany occupies 39.3m^2 or 1.98 rooms, while 1.22 million singles live in five or more rooms; among these the over 65 age group is of particular relevance (BMVBW, 1997). There is a strong trend towards smaller households (German Federal Statistical Office, 2000c). In the early 1990s this development ruled out any positive energy saving effects from energy-efficient improvements (DIW, 1998).

Comfort One example for the link between comfort and energy consumption is space cooling in Japan. In Japan, air conditioners are technically very efficient, but the space cooling demand has still been increasing dramatically owing to increases in dwelling size, changing tastes and modern building designs which do not support natural cooling (Wilhite *et al.*, 1996). Other examples are the increasing use of hot water as a provider of pleasure (hot tubs, jacuzzis, Roman-sized bath tubs) and space heating and lighting to provide atmosphere.

Convenience Energy-efficient technology is often incorrectly used or not optimal, such as with an appropriate airing behaviour or a non-economizing

	resident	owner	communes	housing construction companies/corporate owners	politics	planning	services
heating energy kWh/m^2 and year	+	+	o	+	+	+	+
living area size m^2/person	++	o	+	+	o	o	o

Source: Lorek *et al.* (1999).

Figure 4.7 Actor influences on different housing indicators

thermostat setting (Eicke-Hennig, 1998). Residents' behaviour in identical dwellings can result in a difference in energy consumption for heating of a factor between three and nine (Fraunhofer Institut für Systemtechnik und Innovationsforschung *et al.*, 1997; Eicke-Hennig, 1998).

Figure 4.7 illustrates the diversity of actors involved in the determinants of heating energy consumption as well as their different but overlapping spheres of influence, according to the reasoning above. These results are based on common sense; for a validation of these estimates, or even for their quantification, detailed social science studies would be required.

Policy context and market development

Many governments are putting specific policies, initiatives and regulations in place to increase the percentage of eco-efficiency market volume. Government policies still represent a dominant driver for renewable energy markets, but the trend is increasingly to unleash market forces to achieve policy objectives (Figure 4.8).

Besides these special initiatives in general,[24] the energy market in Germany is dominated by two developments which are both related to the legal framework: first, the liberalization of the national and European energy market starting with the Energy Industry Act from 1998 and, second, the introduction of an energy tax in 1999. The liberalization was followed by fundamental changes for supply-side actors and gradual changes also for the demand side, primarily for business customers but, starting in summer/autumn 1999, also for private households. While the liberalization resulted in price reductions, the energy tax on electricity, gas and heating oil almost cancelled out this effect for private consumers.

United States

- Production tax credits ($1.5 c/kWh) for renewables but only valid until the end of 2001
- Million Solar Roofs Initiative
- Renewable portfolio standards (RPS) in eight states and renewable energy funds in 14 states
- Introduction of green pricing and alternative fuels incentives in several states
- 80+ utilities offer green pricing programmes
- 30 states with net metering programmes

India

- Commitment to source 10% renewables by 2010

China

- Renewables are included in the 10th Five Year Plan for the first time
- Low-interest loans are available
- Planning to instal six GW of renewable capacity by 2010

Europe

- Commitment to source 12% renewables by 2010
- 100 000 rooftop programme for photovoltaics (PV) in Germany
- Guaranteed buy-back prices and preferential feed-in laws (as high as $0.50/kWh for PV in Germany)
- Effective 1/1/01, six countries will have trading of 'Green Electricity Certificates'
- Green pricing programmes
- EU reduction goal of 8% for greenhouse gas emissions by 2008–12
- EC 'Renewables Campaign for Take-Off' to focus on public–private partnerships (2000–2003)

Japan

- Subsidies for PV purchases until 2003
- 70 000 rooftop PV programme
- Subsidize up to 1/3 the cost of wind turbines
- Commitment for 2% of power generation to the renewables by 2010

Note: Examples given are not exhaustive within countries or regions and many other countries are not listed.

Source: Little (2000, sheet 7).

Figure 4.8 Governmental initiatives and regulation unleashing market forces

Environmentally friendly energy policy seeks to change the structure of household energy consumption in order to strengthen the share of renewable energy carriers in comparison to the existing composition (Table 4.3). In the following the potential will be described for wind energy and solar energy as the most important examples for renewable energy carriers that can be promoted by private households.

Structure of household energy consumption As well as for the whole economy, mineral oil and natural gas are the most important energy carriers of household energy consumption in Germany. Both have a share of about one third. Since the mid-1990s, natural gas has taken the lead. Electricity accounts for about one-sixth of the total energy consumption (Table 4.3). Coal and mainly brown lignite coal are losing importance in Germany's household energy mix. In 1999, only 0.7 per cent of household energy consumption was still from coal, and 1.0 per cent from brown coal.

There are reasonable efforts to change this carrier structure and to establish new green markets for renewables (see Chapter 3 on the Renewable Energy Act). Consumer demand for green power has led many companies to develop a 'green line' of electricity supply with the possibility to influence the household's composition of energy carriers. In Germany, this small niche market occurred with the deregulation of markets in 1999 and is therefore quite a new experience. In the USA there is a longer tradition of selected Green-e Certified Electricity Products.

The Danish consultancy firm BTM Consult, forecasting 35 000MW of green power by the end of 2004 and 70 000MW by the end of 2009 in a survey in 2000, (even more optimistic). In Germany, the record growth of the past two years will continue in the medium term. According to BTM Consult, the annual growth rate will be 2000 MW by 2004, an increase of around 18 per cent on the record-breaking results of the year 2000, of almost 1700 MW.

While the growth rate can be expected to level off gradually in Germany in the second half of the decade, countries such as Spain, Portugal, Italy and Ireland will outperform Germany in terms of percentage growth rate. This growth is politically substantiated by the intention of the EU and its individual member states to promote the expansion of renewables.

Overcoming the barriers: the importance of eco-oriented behaviour and new energy services Experts evaluated the following aspects of the current situation as core problems and barriers to a sustainable development in this field (Pfeiffer, 2000: 27).

1. There is a user–investor dilemma: the person who would have to invest in energy-efficient modernization often does not have any (financial)

Table. 4.3 Energy carrier of household energy consumption (%)

	1990	1991	1992	1993	1994	1995	1996	1997	1998	1999
Coal	1.6	1.8	1.6	1.5	1.4	1.5	1.2	1.0	0.8	0.7
Brown coal	13.7	8.3	5.7	4.5	4.0	2.5	2.4	1.7	1.1	1.0
Other solid fuel	2.7	1.6	1.7	1.6	2.2	3.6	3.4	5.5	5.6	6.0
Mineral oil	31.0	34.6	35.1	36.2	35.7	33.9	33.0	35.2	33.6	30.9
Natural gas	26.6	29.5	31.0	32.6	32.7	34.8	37.5	34.3	35.9	37.6
Electricity	17.6	17.5	18.2	17.3	17.5	17.2	16.7	16.4	16.8	17.6
Remote heating	6.8	6.6	6.7	6.2	6.4	6.4	5.7	5.8	6.1	6.2
Total	100	100	100	100	100	100	100	100	100	100
PetaJoule	*2377*	*2507*	*2433*	*2609*	*2556*	*2815*	*2869*	*2882*	*2801*	*2648*

Source: Lorek, S. (2001).

Table 4.4 Comparative analysis of wind energy usage in Germany, the USA and Japan

	Germany	USA	Japan
Wind energy till Sept. 2000	5,432	2,495	81
Wind energy till 1999	4,443	2,473	68
Wind energy till 1998	2,875	1,820	40
Wind energy till 1997	2,081	1,673	18
Rate of increase till Sept. 2000 in %	22.3	0.9	19.1
Population 1997 in millions	82.1	267.6	126.1
Area in km^2	375,021	9,809,155	377,819
Installed power in W per inhabitant	66.19	9.32	0.64
Installed power per unit of square measure in kW per km^2	15.25	0.26	0.21
GNP 1997 in billion $	2,321	7,783	4.812
Installed power per GNP in MW per billion $	2.34	0.32	0.02

Source: Bundesverband Windenergie (2001).

advantages from the investment (for example in rented dwellings). Compared to other industrialized nations the number of owner–occupiers is (a historically determined fact) fairly low in Germany. Spain has the highest proportion of people living in their own dwellings (85 per cent), whereas in Germany there are only 40 per cent of owner–occupiers, which is the second lowest rate in Western Europe and North America (Institut der deutschen Wirtschaft, 1998). This situation makes the aspect especially important for Germany.

2. The users do not have the knowledge about the correct application of the technology as it is too complex or badly described; there seems to be a crucial false estimation of engineers about the effort and time which consumers are willing to spend on understanding and maintaining the appliances. Besides, the energy consumption rate is invisible to the consumer.
3. Furthermore, the habits ('I always did it that way'), the consumption orientation of the users (trend to more comfort) and too little motivation (for example, less feeling of personal responsibility) are a problem.
4. The actors have too little knowledge about energy-efficient, and at the same time financially interesting, technology. Thus, for example, manual workers often recommend conventional appliances; further dissemination of energy-efficient devices is hindered.

5. An overall coordinating management during the construction and refurbishment process is often missing, so that saving potentials are overlooked and not realized.
6. There is still a gap between technology design and user needs and preferences (too little innovation; sale- rather than need-oriented). Systems with more automation easily become very complex and error-prone.
7. Energy prices are too low so that, in comparison with conventional technology, investment in energy efficiency hardly pays off. Prices do not show the ecological truth (ecological damage is mostly non-measurable).

These barriers are a great challenge for market transformation programmes and other demand-side activities (see also Chapter 3 on demand-side management). Full economic and environmental efficiency can only be achieved by including the efficient use of electricity and gas in the competition, and developing a European internal market for genuine energy services. What customers need is not energy, but genuine energy services, that is the physical amenity provided by energy-using equipment, for example cooking or illumination. The provision of such genuine energy services requires a combination of energy-using equipment, energy and energy-related services, which means that the electricity and gas supply industries need to develop further, combining efficiency on the energy supply side and efficiency in the final use of energy, to achieve the economic and environmental optimum and to address the transition to sustainable energy systems at least cost and least environmental damage.

Reflecting these targets in the USA, Jamie Woods (2000) sees a chance to overcome these barriers by introducing equity partnerships with a non-resident investor (which could be a service company). In Germany, this model is discussed under the heading of 'contracting'. This financial arrangement provides both reliable information through the property specification in the partnership agreement, and an expert consumer, the non-resident investor, whose incentives are perfectly aligned with the resident home buyer. These perfectly aligned incentives come from the force of the partnership, prearranged shares of both the purchase and the sales price, with additional contract terms about improvements and expenses. With this, real estate becomes more like a restaurant meal, frequently purchased, frequently criticized and very responsive to sophisticated customer demands. Strategies for developing markets for eco-efficient services and residential renewable energy will increasingly need to focus, not only on utility requirements, technical options and capabilities, but also on financing arrangements, investment incentives and other contemporary customer needs.

The further diffusion of eco-efficient technologies and renewables, and their considerable implications for lower demand levels, shows evidence of social and cultural norms for energy policy. From this point of view the understanding of consumer expectations has to be changed: people do not consume energy, they consume services that make a 'good life' possible. Additional research concerning institutional barriers also needs to be conducted in an effort to promote a more symbiotic, customer-driven approach to future market expansion.

The OECD study on private energy consumption found that the main focus to reduce household energy consumption has to be on the heating energy demand. This calls for effective promotion of efficient energy consumption for heating, behavioural changes towards lower room temperatures and efficient airing, the use of primary energy (natural gas) for hot water production and cooking, demand for and production of renewable energy, and use of energy-saving appliances in an efficient way, which could be the subject of additional initiatives (Lorek and Spangenberg, 2000).

Organic food

Policy context At present, drastic changes are transforming the EU agricultural–political order, which was established after the Second World War, and the agricultural interventionist policies of Western industrialized countries. At the same time, a new biotechnological era has begun which could revolutionize the entire agriculture and food supply sector. In this context, emphasis is placed on the following fields of action by German politics:

- new economic issues arising from the gradual adaptation of structures to conform to these new demand fields, with special emphasis on ecological, social and security aspects;
- modified, liberalized agricultural market regulations that demand greater innovation and flexibility at all stages;
- change in agricultural policy and its implementation – transition from producer's structures to consumer demand and from centrally planned targets/rules to a regional approach;
- new functions for rural areas; in highly developed economies like Germany, the importance of the traditional task of food production is declining. On the other hand, there is a steadily increasing demand for agriculture to supply public services (care of arable land, creation and maintenance of leisure and recreation areas and so on);
- new economic fields such as food assurance, biotechnological developments, the utilization of natural resources and the production of renewable raw materials and sources of energy.

With the new organization of national agricultural financing, public funds are allocated in such a way that agricultural operations can orient themselves to the principles of organic farming and thereby receive support in the form of subsidies. Government funding is thus used as a market control instrument to steer away from problematic or socially undesirable developments. Germany, for example, intends to concentrate on awarding subsidies to those farms practising free-range farming and which keep animals in their natural environment. At the same time, the expansion and professionalization of the market structures of organic farming are planned. This should encourage an area-wide supply of organic food for consumers.

Market analysis of organic food The European market for organic food has grown rapidly in terms of both supply and demand during the 1990s. However, national markets vary considerably. In some countries, the market share is quite high, while in others the market for organic products hardly exists. In Germany, the status quo of the development of organic farming is as follows.

On 1 January 2001, 12 740 farms managed 546 023 hectares ecologically in accordance with EU Ordinance No. 2092/91, corresponding to 2.93 per cent of farms and 3.2 per cent of agriculturally used land in Germany (Table 4.5). Compared to the previous year, the number of farms thus increased by 22.2 per cent (2315) and land by 20.7 per cent (93 696 ha.). In the following data, the reporting date is 1 January of the respective year.

Behind this growth there are some interesting qualitative developments on both sides of the market. On the demand side, a study by ZMP (1999) looks at the following questions:

- Who is buying organic food?
- What kind of food has been put in the shopping basket?
- What expectations and motives are behind the consumer's decision?
- What can be said about the consumer's behaviour in the future?

The results of this study are as follows. First, 22 per cent of those interviewed reported buying organic food (Figure 4.9). It is interesting to note that only a small share of total food requirements is thus covered, which suggests that this buying behaviour does not underlie a self-contained view of life (such as a healthy diet). Second, what is very conspicuous is the ecological buying behaviour of households with children under 18 years of age and, looked at spatially, in the new German states. Clearly below average are persons over 50 years of age, singles and those living in towns with up to 20 000 inhabitants. Third, in general, it can be said that the consumer profile of the typical organic food consumer consists of four main features: (1) consumers are on average young families with small children, (2) they have above average incomes, (3) they have a higher education standard, and (4) they live in cities. Given the rising supply of organic food and the falling prices, the irregular buyer of

Table 4.5 Market development and volume of organic food production in Germany

Year	Number of companies	Area (hectares)
1985	1 610	24 940
1986	1 720	27 160
1987	2 006	33 047
1988	2 330	42 393
1989	2 685	54 295
1990	3 438	90 021
1991	4 274	158 477
1992	4 750	202 379
1993	5 091	246 458
1994	5 866	272 139
1995	6 641	309 487
1996	7 353	354 171
1997	8 184	389 693
1998	9 209	416 518
1999	10 405	452 279
2000	12 740	546 023
2001	14 702	634 998
2002	15 626	696 978

Source: ZMP (2003).

organic food is purchasing more often. That is, the number of regular buyers is increasing. Furthermore, recent surveys have identified that West and East Germans tend to behave differently when it comes to purchasing organic foods. However, there aren't any exact figures available for this yet.

Organic food customers shop on average once a week and cover with this 13.2 per cent of their total food requirements. They visit on average 2.5 shopping facilities. Preferred shopping facilities are supermarkets or hypermarkets, followed by weekly markets and health food shops. An important role is played by buying direct from manufacturers. The customer profile of the various shopping facilities differs considerably (Figure 4.10). For example, the supermarket/hypermarket is especially popular with people up to 30 years of age and singles. The clientele of health food shops, on the other hand, tends to be old.

The share of individual products in organic food shopping is very different. According to the ZMP study, 70 per cent of organic food shoppers report buying organic eggs. Organic eggs are thus bought the most, followed by

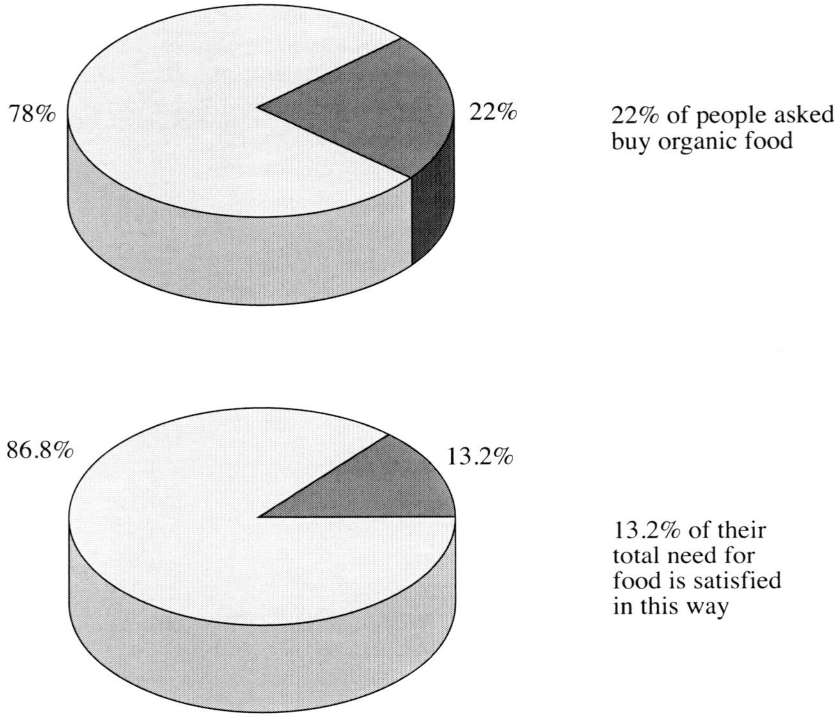

Source: ZMP (1999).

Figure 4.9 Potential of future market volumes in Germany

vegetables (45 per cent), fruit (41 per cent), potatoes (37 per cent) and bread (36 per cent). Approximately every fourth organic food shopper selects butter, milk, cheese and yoghurt. Organic meat, on the other hand, plays a minor role. Generally speaking, organic food shoppers are seen to consume an underproportional amount of meat. Intensive and casual customers have clearly different product affinities.

Depending on the product, the prices for organic foods differ considerably compared with those for conventional foods. A question of the ZMP study and other studies (Hamm, 2000) is therefore what induced consumers to pay more money for these products. The answer to this is very clear. It can be seen that there is one overall motive for 'buying organic': healthy eating, which dominates all other motives, including concern for the environment or animal welfare. Additionally, many consumers, largely because of highly publicized

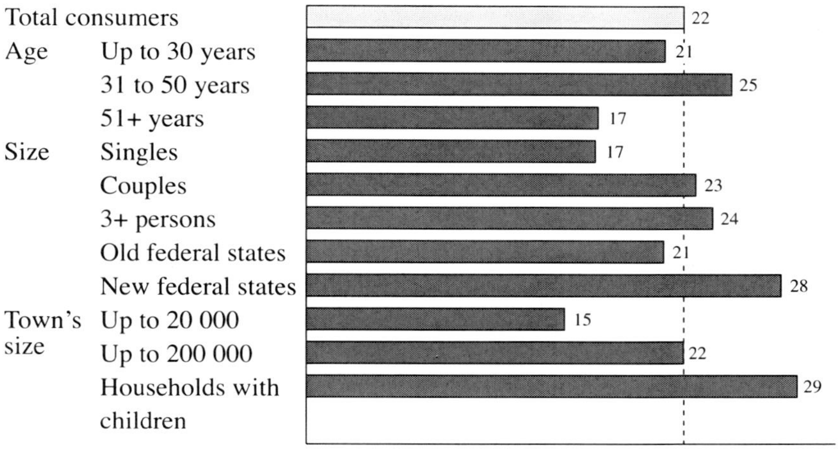

Source: ZMP (1999).

Figure 4.10 Consumers' profiles concerning organic food in Germany

food safety scares, do not trust conventionally produced products. The growing awareness of the prevalence of genetically modified foods (GMOs) and the scope for environmental problems further heightens the consumer's preference for organic food, but there is also a positive motivation: many consumers are being attracted to organic food for the better taste and quality of organic products. This is helping to overcome the initial experience of non-regular buyers of organic produce from traditional natural food stores that tended to be of very variable quality.

The spreading of the 'organic food' market segment can be explained especially by the improved and more extensive supply that is increasingly being marketed and presented by professional means. For a long time in Germany and most European countries the dominant market channel for organic food has been the traditional natural food store. For many consumers these stores were associated with poor product presentation, small range, unreliable continuity of supply and quality and rather high price levels. For these reasons the consumers of organic foods tended to be those committed to the philosophy of the organic movement.

Today, market channels for organic food in Germany and Europe are quite different. The traditional natural food store has been joined by organic food supermarkets and conventional retail chains as the most popular channels for selling organic goods. Even more recently, box schemes, direct sales and Internet sales have grown in popularity as market channels. Channels have largely diversified, the consumer base is broadening and the supply of goods is becoming better managed. The retail chains especially, whether conventional or organic, are becoming a very significant channel for the marketing of organic foods.

Looking at future marketing strategies, there will be a positive emphasis on life styles. This will have consequences for symbols and messages in advertising the goods and services but also for the structure and layout of the stores. At present many retail stores have a coffee and juice bar, offer 'well-being' services (such as a massage centre) and consumer information. Linked to the theme of healthy life style is a concern about social responsibility. A lot of companies emphasize social responsibility in their advertising (see section 4.2). They publicize contributions to local charities and their adoption of 'democratic' models of internal organization and decision making. The linking of healthy food, environmental care and social responsibility is prominent in the advertising of a number of companies. It is also worth noting that the companies tend to favour in-store promotion and information distribution to promote their product range as opposed to public advertising through the general media. This reflects the stated strategy of word-of-mouth advertising that is locally based and suits local market conditions.

To sum up, it can be stated that, in order to meet consumer demand, major efforts in organizing a transparent national and international market and in developing appropriate marketing strategies are still required.

Conclusions

Reflecting the two case studies, the following conclusions can be made. First, the demand for ecological goods and services has increased in Germany and elsewhere. From a company's point of view, it is first of all relevant what market potential can be mobilized for each product or service; that is, how far consumers will actually reward the socioecological design of products and services or sanction inappropriate behaviour. Here it is assumed that the general factors (see p.134) mentioned also influence those markets or market segments in which there is a demand for environmentally oriented products and services.

Second, the market field of eco-efficient housing and heating facilities and the field of organic food differ considerably. The demand for new, eco-efficient energy facilities and services in private households was mostly prompted by a variety of activities. For demand-side policy, new laws fixing new technical standards and changes in the philosophies on the supply side were important. New ecological market initiatives for individual consumer goods, such as organic food and 'eco-clothes', mostly came from critical consumers who, from the mid-1980s, increasingly organized themselves within the general public. The influence of the legislation framework played a less important role in these fields. In spite of these differences, it can be stated that the demand for eco-services and products increased in all market fields researched.

Third, the use orientation of the buyer connected with this however, is, based, not exclusively on ecological motives, but on a variety of use expectations such as better levels of supply, increase in product quality, reduction in costs of use or symbolic attributes such as image effects (see Minsch, 1996). Therefore those goods are successful which embed environmental aspects in a use-oriented strategy. This ought to be embedded in measurements of an integrated product policy, but the use orientation of consumers is not to be based only on environmental aspects such as increased efficiency and improved environmental quality; instead, in the market surveys, it could be testified that increasing the *complete benefit potential* of a product/service is the major factor prompting consumers' decisions. This, indeed, is a key insight of the Factor Four (or Ten) concept.

From the examples investigated, one could already learn about processes of transformation from niche markets to mass markets. It is crucial to the analysis that a given demand setting of different needs can be achieved by different offers (for example, a comfortable dwelling can be created either by heating or by insulation) and that these different solutions imply different social–economic management by different suppliers. In the case of organic food it could be seen that the traditional institutional setting of farmers and trade organizations blocked the choice of environmental products and services in the past. Therefore new institutions and organizations seized the chance to organize the new market of organic food. After ten to 15 years' practice the market for organic food is on the way from niche market to a mass market.

The Institute for Ecological Economics in St. Gallen (Switzerland) has developed a tool that enables a conceptual map of ecological mass markets to be drawn. In this way, an ecological mass market has to be understood as a bidimensional construction whose dimensions embrace on the one hand the market shape and on the other hand the relative ecological quality of products. The target is to reduce the total environmental pressure caused by the products in each market. Starting points can be found in both dimensions, so besides an increase in the market shape of eco-products, there is also a raising of eco-quality standards in mass markets and finally also a decrease in the total market volume (sufficiency, sustainable shrinking) (Wüstenhagen *et al.*, 2000). Similar conclusions can be drawn from the previous sub-section.

The development potentials (eco-growth and upgrading the middle) shown in Figure 4.11 can be promoted all by innovation and communication strategies

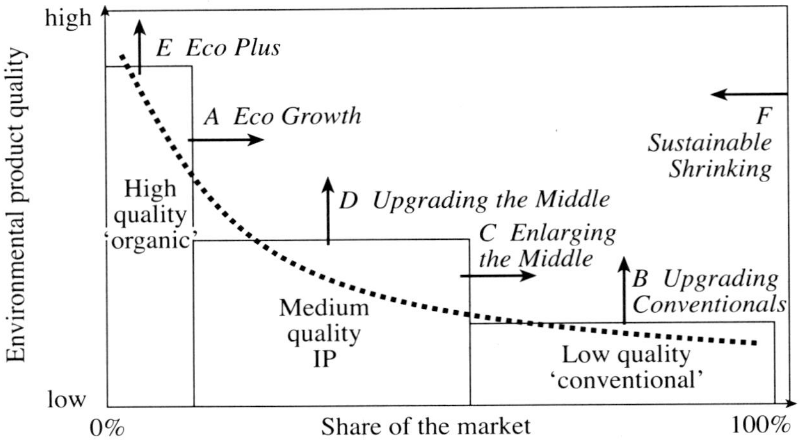

Source: Wüstenhagen *et al*. (2003).

Figure 4.11 Development of eco-markets

reflecting the criteria mentioned. To spread a sustainable pattern of consumption, an extensive use orientation as well as an exact analysis of the actor's spectrum which influences a 'utilization regime' are especially important. Important ecological market volumes can be traced back to the ecological problems at the biophysical level and the ecological stakes of a socioeconomic background.

Finally, the question arises, 'How to get a deeper understanding of the conditions leading to green markets?' The case studies show that there are several ways of conceiving changes in utilization regimes. The first is to consider the multiple, cumulative, often incremental changes that occur within the different regimes. These step-by-step innovations may be seen as a smooth reorientation of producers following the market signals of new consumption patterns. Another way of seeing regime change is to envisage a process of establishing new quality standards by law or other regulatory instruments. Last, and perhaps most contentiously, there may be a normative desire to precipitate or accelerate the process to sustainable consumption. In these cases the emergence of green markets depends on a broad enough range of market actors. The growth of renewable energy markets is an example where both conscious choice and the overcoming of economic and political barriers enable a new market segment for green power. By looking at the case of the green power market we could learn how important it is to create an economic and institutional context for adoption. Innovation of utilization regimes requires the channelling of new life styles and cultural impacts by governments and commercial institutions. If no commitments to the first movers in new utilization regimes were made, the development would be too fragile to emerge.

In summary, the two case studies' emphasize the persistence of change along different pathways for new ecological market volumes. Innovation and eco-quality are seen as being bounded by regulatory assumptions and institutional settings, which are linked in an interactive frame with producers and consumers. But, having argued this, consumers' choices are not only a product of individual needs. So future research has to draw attention to the interlinkages between regulatory incentives, market activities and behaviour.

NOTES

1. For more details on the different phases, see Klinkers *et al.* (1999) and Kuhndt *et al.* (2002).
2. Germany tops the list: up to June 1999, some 2751 industrial sites were registered in the EU, 2085 in Germany accounting for 76 per cent of all participants, followed by Austria with 6.9 per cent, Sweden with 5.6 per cent and Denmark with 3.7 per cent.
3. Mainly in the chemical sector, electrical and optical equipment, basic metals and fabricated metal products, rubber and plastic products, machinery equipment and the food industry.
4. The world-wide number of certifications is available online: (www.14001news.de/14001_ff/Peglau-Liste/body_peglau-liste.htm).
5. Some main findings of this study are that companies endorse the work at ISO level and favour a closer alignment of the ISO management standards on environment and quality in order to enhance the compatibility of the EMS with the ISO 9000ff. series, although not demanding an integration into (only) one Generic Management System Standard. Open to the issue of legal compliance, companies follow the requirement of proving that they comply with legal provisions, expressing their approval of specifying ISO 14001 according to the EMAS regulations. Because EMAS already provides for an initial review as a first step for the establishment of an EMS, there was basic agreement by 50 per cent on also including this system element in ISO 14001.
6. The main reasons for ISO 14001 are promoting the image of the company as well as clients' demands. Internal improvements generally are realized but expected external benefits (improved image, possible market effect) are not (always) reached. ISO 14001 certification is less costly than ISO 9001ff or EMAS. No problem of lack of clarity of the standard or its compatibility with quality management standards was expressed, but there were concerns over time and costs and complaints about the chapters 'Environmental aspects' and 'documentation', followed by 'objectives' and 'targets', main issues of the standard. General concern was about compatibility between 9000 and 14000 series. Certifiers identified serious deviations during the audits concerning correct and complete identification and implementation of legal and other requirements on the one hand and environmental aspects on the other. Users wish ISO requirements to be more concrete and enhanced as well as deepened; further, benefits by public acknowledgment of participation and less efforts necessary for implementation. Concerns of other interested parties (trade unions, NGOs, business in general) are in comparisons with the more challenging EMAS.
7. 'Results of an organization's management of its environmental aspects' (ISO 14031) v. 'measurable results of the environmental management system, related to an organization's control of its environmental aspects, based on its environmental policy, objectives and targets' (ISO 14001).
8. A technical report ISO/TR 14032 prepared by ISO SC4 contains 17 examples of EPE experiences of organizations, three of them already real ISO 14031 applications; further examples

have been and will be presented in the future in EPE workshops at annual ISO TC 207 conferences as well as posted on the ISO webpage.
9. As opposed to pure improvements of the Environmental Management System itself, which some critiques are accusing ISO 14001 applications.
10. At this time, these guidelines on 'reporting' are the only ones within the whole ISO 14000 series and they are not certifiable – in contrast to EMAS I and II where environmental statements are mandatory. Furthermore, guidance on identifying the views of interested parties or stakeholders has been provided quite extensively in this EPE document at the 'plan' stage of the 'plan–do–check–act' cycle which has been welcomed by pioneering companies when applying this new standard and selecting appropriate indicators to measure performance. But to what extent the forthcoming WG 4 document ISO 14063 on 'communications' will benefit from previous SC 4 work (only some SC 4 participants are continuing work in WG 4) is an open issue.
11. ISO: officially 'Ecological Aspects in Product Development'; the forthcoming Technical Report ISO/TR 14062 is expected to be finished in early 2002.
12. UN-EMA working group: http://un.org/esa/sustdev/estema1.htm.
13. For the forthcoming 5th annual conference: http://online.chelt.ac.uk/eman.
14. The German mirror body is chaired by Dr Eberhard K. Seifert from the Wuppertal Institute and interested colleagues might like to get in touch with him directly (e.seifert@wupperinst.org).
15. 'With any sector that approaches TC 207 for development of sector specific guidance an open dialogue should be sought to assess what the problem really is. Distinction needs to be made between proposals brought forward to develop additional sector specific guidance to the application of the specification, sector specific additional requirements or sector specific 'enhancement' of the requirements (e.g. with respect to communication and stakeholder consultation).' (International Organization for Standardization, Technical Committee 27, Chairman's Advisory Group, July 2001).
16. But the dynamics of the SC 4 work forced postponement of further discussion until the final release of the main document ISO 14031 and the accompanying Technical Report ISO TR 14032 with 17 examples illustrating EPE.
17. ISO 14031 has already integrated some general guidance on 'reporting and communication' for providing useful information on an organization's environmental performance. The main text indicates benefits that derive from internal and external communication and reporting.
18. ISO COPOLCO created the Corporate Social Responsibility and Standards Forum in August 2001 to facilitate worldwide discussion of the possible role of standards to articulate and promote the concept of corporate social responsibility (contact Dr Kernaghan Webb at webb.kernaghan@ic.gc.ca).
19. UNEP Division of Technology, Industry and Economics, 'Developing better systems for communicating environmental best practice in business – final report', 1997, Paris.
20. Ibid.
21. For internal efficiency improvements cost transparency has been recognized as an important factor, which was illustrated in Box 4.2. For product chain management downstream from the supply chain, see literature on product stewardship or p.128 this volume with focus on strategies for sustainable consumption.
22. First of all, on taking sector concerns seriously into account, exemplified by the importance of the Basle convention on the chemical industry and internationally accepted definitions of environmentally sound management; secondly, on the speed of changing market needs for standards that ISO could not react to, exemplified by the only recently imitated 'communication' standard in comparison to GRI activities; thirdly, on the contrast of rigid mandates set by TC 207 versus flexibility requirements, exemplified by a simple and flexible platform approach that can be easily adapted to meet unique market needs.
23. An 'optimal' approach in this case might be (as long as the scope of ISO 14000 is restricted to the environment) to see ISO 14000 guidelines for communicating and reporting as the environmental module for a broader approach to 'sustainability reporting' as promoted by GRI at a level of rigorousness, comparability and completeness evident in financial reporting.
24. For a detailed overview of the consequences of the German Renewable Energy Sources Act see Chapter 3.3.

5. Bridging the data gap

Stephan Moll, Stefan Bringezu, Dirk Assmann, Thomas Hanke, Holger Wallbaum and Raimund Bleischwitz

5.1 INTRODUCTION

Research on sustainable development, strategies and actions of policy makers, business and interest groups critically rely on information. In particular long term-oriented scenarios as useful decision support tools (as analysed in the Wuppertal Institute, 2001, first interim report) require data on certain items. In this chapter we attempt to address the data gap in sustainable development policies. The chapter responds to the needs of researchers and statistical offices who insistently demand data for various tasks and focuses on the topics of material flows, energy and buildings in their relation to the concepts of eco-efficiency.

5.2 MATERIAL FLOWS

Policies towards a 'Recycle-Oriented Society' (Clean Japan Center, 2000) or towards the 'Sustainable use of natural resources and management of waste' (CEC, 2001c) have to build on information on the physical performance at the macro-economic level ('You can better manage what you can measure'). In order to design policy measures for increased eco-efficiency and dematerialization it is necessary to know how many and which resources are used by whom for which end-users and how efficient are those resources used.

Material flow accounting (MFA) refers to a number of methodologies to describe national economies in a physical way (WI, 2001). MFA has been developed by research and is increasingly used by official authorities. MFA is part of official statistics in Austria, Denmark, Finland, Germany, Japan, Sweden, the United Kingdom and the European Union, as shown in Table 5.1 (for an overview, see also Bringezu and Moriguchi, 2002).

From an administrative perspective, providing information on the 'industrial metabolism' is a shared task of environmental and statistical authorities.

Table 5.1 Overview on MFA activities in selected countries

Country	Organizations	MFA activities	Selected references
Austria	Ministry for the Environment, Youth and Families Central Statistical Office (ÖSTAT) Department of Social Ecology of the Institute for Interdisciplinary Studies of Austrian Universities (IFF)	Joint publication of annual material balances	Gerhold and Petrovic (2000)
Denmark	Statistics Denmark Danish EPA	Physical input–output tables Economy-wide material flow balance and derived indicators	Gravgaard Pedersen (1999)
Finland	Statistics Finland Ministry of the Environment University of Oulu	Economy-wide material flow accounts Physical input–output tables	Hoffrén (1999), Juutinen and Mäenpää (1999), Muukkonen (2000), Mäenpää (2000), Ministry of the Environment (1999)
Germany	Federal Statistical Office (StBA) German EPA (UBA) Ministry for the Environment, Nature and Nuclear Safety (BMU) Wuppertal Institute	Material and energy flow accounts Physical input–output tables Raw material productivity indicator	German Federal Statistical Office (2000a, 2000b, 2001a) Stahmer *et al.* (1998) Federal Ministry for the Environment, Nature Conservation and Nuclear Safety, Germany (1998)

Japan	National Institute for Environmental Studies (NIES)	National material balance (published in the annual State of the Environment Report)	Japanese Environmental Agency (1992, 1998)
		Physical input–output tables	Moriguchi *et al*. 2000
Sweden	Statistics Sweden	Economy-wide material flow accounts and derived indicators	Bergstedt and Linder (1999), Isacsson *et al*. (2000)
		Material flow accounts of selected materials	
United Kingdom	Department for the Environment, Transport and the Regions (DETR)	Economy-wide material flow accounts and derived indicators	Department for Environment, Food and Rural Affairs (2002)
	Office for National Statistics (ONS) Wuppertal Institute		Bringezu and Schütz (2001b)
European Union	Statistical Office of the European Communities (Eurostat) European Environment Agency (EEA) Wuppertal Institute	Economy-wide material flow accounts and derived indicators	European Environment Agency (2000b, 2000c, 2000d), Eurostat 2001; Bringezu and Schütz (2001a)

In the EU member states, the dossier of material flows may be found at three organizations: the environmental protection authorities (for example EPA), the ministry for the environment, and/or the economic ministry, and the statistical offices. This requires a high degree of coordination between these organizations. Often, as a fourth element, scientific experts are also involved (for example, the Wuppertal Institute has been involved at the national as well as the EU level).

Two outstanding examples of the way in which MFA has been established administratively in Europe are given below. The first case is the German Environmental Economic Accounting unit at the German Federal Statistical Office; the other is the initiative to standardize MFA methods as brought forward by the Statistical Office of the European Communities (Eurostat).

In Japan, the National Institute for Environmental Studies (NIES) has outstanding expertise on the subject of material flow accounting. Yuichi Moriguchi (Head, Resources Management Section, Social and Environmental Systems Division, National Institute for Environmental Studies, Japan) has also been involved in the development of standard MFA methodologies at the international level in cooperation with the Wuppertal Institute (see, for example, Adriaanse *et al.*, 1997, Matthews *et al.*, 2000, Moriguchi *et al.*, 2000).

Integrated Environmental and Economic Accounting at the German Federal Statistical Office

In the light of the Rio Conference in the early 1990s, the German Minister for the Environment established a unit at the Federal Statistical Office dealing with the integration of environmental and economic information for sustainable development, called German Environmental Economic Accounting (GEEA). The objective of GEEA is to add meaningful modules to the traditional System of National Accounts, which are designed to quantify the external (environmental) effects of economic activities.

The purpose of environmental–economic accounting is to represent interdependencies between economic activities and the environment. GEEA shows which natural resources are utilized, used up, devalued or destroyed by production and consumption and how efficiently the economy and society deal with materials, energy and land. The GEEA system makes it possible to determine the pressure put on nature by using it as a source for resources and as a sink for residuals and pollutants. It allows compiling information on the state of the environment and the costs of environmental protection. Following this pattern of issues, GEEA results are structured by the following subject fields: material and energy flows, land use, state of the environment, environmental protection measures and abatement costs (see Figure 5.1).

One important module of GEEA is 'Material and Energy Flow Accounts'.

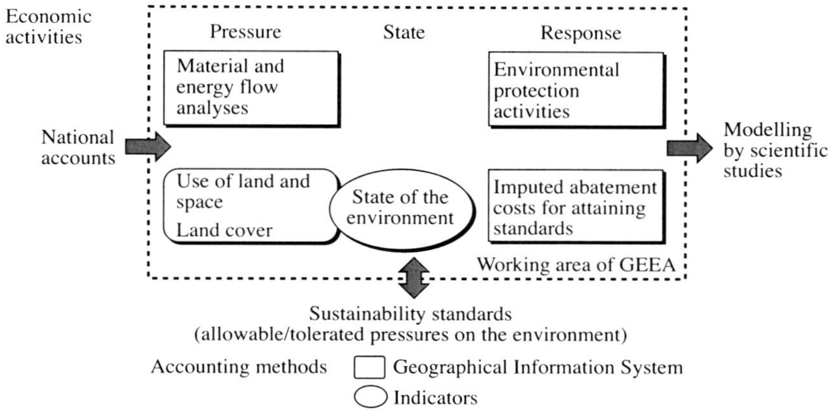

Source: German Federal Statistical Office (2001b).

Figure 5.1 German environmental economic accounting

The conceptual basis was worked out in close cooperation with the Wuppertal Institute and is also embedded in international activities (Eurostat, London Group[1]). Since 1995, the Federal Statistical Office has been publishing comprehensive material and energy flow reports on a biannual basis. These contain material balances of the German economy including imports and exports as well as raw material extractions, energy consumption, emissions to air and water, and waste by industry sectors (German Federal Statistical Office, 2000a, 2000b). An overview of the content of these biannual reports is shown in Table 5.2. In addition, a selection of tables from this module can be found on the Internet (German Federal Statistical Office, 2001c).

Raw material productivity, one indicator derived from GEEA's work on material flows, is part of the German Environment Index (Deutscher Umweltindex DUX;[2] see German Environmental Protection Agency 2001). This indicator, expressed in Euros per tonne, relates the gross domestic product in constant prices to the non-renewable raw materials extracted domestically and the imports of non-renewable goods. It is an indicator used to monitor the resource productivity of the German economy in an aggregated way.[3]

As a target to improve resource productivity, the German Environmental Protection Agency proposes to increase raw material productivity by a factor of 2.5 until 2020. The German Sustainability Strategy includes the target of doubling the resource productivity by 2020 in relation to the base year of 1994.

Table 5.2 Content of the biannual material and energy flow reports of the German Federal Statistical Office

1	National material balance
2	Raw materials
2.1	Raw materials by raw material categories
2.2	Raw materials by economic branches
3	Energy
3.1	Overview (including cumulated energy requirements associated with imports)
3.2	Primary energy consumption (by economic branches, energy carriers)
3.3	Energy use relevant for emissions (by economic branches, energy carriers)
4	Imports of goods
5	Exports of goods
6	Waste
7	Air emissions (CO_2, CO, NO_x, SO_2, PM, NMVOC, CH_4, N_2O, aggregated GHG and acidifying gases)
7.1	Overview
7.2	Direct air emissions by economic branches and energy carriers
7.3	Direct and indirect (cumulated) air emissions, by economic branches and energy carriers
8	Water

Source: German Federal Statistical Office (2000a).

The GEEA also includes hidden flows associated with domestic extractions of raw materials ('unused domestic extraction'). However so far, the GEEA has not been reporting the indirect 'hidden' material flows associated with imports because of data constraints.

> Representing indirect withdrawal of material appears necessary because the principle of sustainability in using nature applies not only at the national but also at the global level. Especially where domestic raw materials are substituted by foreign raw materials or by less material-intensive finished or semi-finished products . . . the withdrawal of raw material in the rest of the world increases despite the decreasing use of material within the country. Indirect use of material, however, is very difficult to determine with a satisfactory degree of accuracy. . . . The Federal Statistical Office intends to improve the database for such calculations to the extent that it will be possible to perform such estimations with sufficient accuracy. (German Federal Statistical Office 2000b: 20)

As another activity, the GEEA has set up physical input–output tables (PIOT) for 1990 and 1995. PIOT account most comprehensively for material flows in a sectoral disaggregated way. They combine the material accounts of the domestic economy, such as raw materials extraction, flows of commodities in the production and consumption activities and discharge of residuals (air emissions, waste and waste water) into the environment (Stahmer *et al.*, 1998). In these accounts the activities of the domestic economy are divided into around 60 branches of production, an additional branch of environmental protection activities (included recycling), and consumption activities of private households. The tables also show in physical units the inputs and outputs of gross fixed capital formation (equipment and construction), stocks and nature. Nature serves the domestic economy with raw materials and at the same time absorbs residues from the economic activities. The material flows are broken down into nine types of raw materials, 49 groups of commodities and 11 sorts of residues.

To summarize, the information provided by the German Federal Statistical Office in the context of GEEA is highly valuable for policies aimed at a sustainable and efficient use of natural resources. Further efforts will probably focus on the improvement of information on the indirect 'hidden' material flows associated with imported goods. However, the exploitation and application of GEEA information by German policy makers is still below its potential use.

Aggregated Economy-wide Material Flow Balances (MFB) as Developed by Eurostat

The Statistical Office of the European Communities (Eurostat) developed a methodological guide on aggregated economy-wide material flow balances and derived indicators for 2000 (Eurostat, 2001)[4] This guide presents a framework and practical guidance for establishing material flow accounts and material balances for a whole economy. The guide is a first step towards harmonized terminology, concepts and a set of accounts and tables for compilers at the national level, which lays the information foundation for an integrated policy on the sustainable use of natural resources and indicators to monitor resource productivity.[5]

The methodological guide is part of Eurostat's work on integrated economic and environmental accounting. It contributes to various EU-wide and international activities in the context of national and environmental accounting, including the revision of the United Nations System of Integrated Environmental and Economic Accounting (SEEA).

The work on material flow accounting is continuing at Eurostat together with the task force on material flow accounting (comprising mainly experts from national statistical offices of the EU). Work is now focusing on pooling the practical experiences of member states with economy-wide material flow accounts that are becoming progressively available and on collecting material use indicators derived from these accounts more regularly from more member states. It is planned to develop further this methodological guide in the coming years through testing by national statistical offices. In a study for the European Commission, the Wuppertal Institute provided for the first time estimates for this set of MFA indicators for the EU15 by member state, based on international statistical sources. The results are published by Eurostat (Bringezu and Schütz, 2001a).

Aggregated economy-wide material flow balances (MFB) represent a consistent accounting scheme for measuring the metabolism of economies (WI, 2001). They provide, in a way similar to energy balances, the appropriate tool for measuring the entire metabolic performance of a national economy in terms of material flows. MFBs also serve as an accounting framework to derive selected aggregated indicators (see below).

Basically, a MFB counts all material flows crossing the functional system boundary between 'environment' and 'economy'. On the material input side, they comprise domestic resource extractions including associated domestic 'hidden flows' (such as mining overburden), imports and, optionally, upstream foreign 'hidden flows' associated with imports. On the output side, they include domestic material releases to the domestic environment, domestic 'hidden flows' and exports. Economy-wide material flow balances further monitor the net material additions to domestic stock (buildings, infrastructure, durable consumer goods and so on) in order to balance material input and output flows.

A set of indicators can be derived from economy-wide material flow balances in order to provide an overview of the industrial metabolism. They refer, respectively, to materials that are extracted domestically or imported and their hidden 'ecological rucksacks' (as for instance in the Total Material Requirement indicator), to materials and substances that leave the economy (emissions and wastes) and to the net accumulation of materials in the economy (indicating the physical growth of the economy).

On the one hand, economy-wide material flow accounts provide a more comprehensive picture of the industrial metabolism than single indicators. On the other hand, they can be used to derive several parameters which, when taken in time series and for international comparison, provide certain aggregated information on the metabolic performance of national or regional economies. Indicators, derived from MFB, can be grouped into input indicators, output indicators, consumption, balance and efficiency indicators (Table 5.3). The set of main indicators derivable from a complete material balance have been briefly characterized in the WI interim report (WI, 2001).

Data for economy-wide material balances are mainly derived from other statistical sources. Some material flows are not statistically captured and have to be estimated. Main data sources for material inputs are Eurostat (2001):

Table 5.3 General accounting scheme for an economy-wide material flow balance with derived indicators

INPUTS (origin)	OUTPUTS (destination)
Domestic extraction (used) Fossil fuels (coal, oil) Minerals (ores, gravel) Biomass (timber, cereals) *Imports*	*Emissions and wastes* Waste landfilled Emissions to air Emissions to water *Dissipative use of products and dissipative losses* Dissipative use of products Dissipative losses
DMI – direct material inputs	**DPO – domestic processed output to nature**
Unused domestic extraction from mining/quarrying biomass from harvest soil excavation and dredging	*Disposal of unused materials domestically extracted* from mining/quarrying biomass from harvest soil excavation and dredging
TMI – total material input	**TDO – total domestic output to nature**
	Exports
	TMO – total material output
Indirect flows associated with imports	
TMR – total material requirements	*Net additions to stock* Infrastructures and buildings Other (machinery, durable goods, etc.)
	Indirect flows associated with exports

Note: Excludes water and air flows (unless contained in other materials).

Source: Eurostat (2001).

- forestry statistics and accounts (timber harvested and removed, other products of forestry, supply and use tables of wood and so on);
- agricultural statistics (cereals, vegetables, hay and so on);
- industry/production statistics (extraction of fossil fuels, crude ores, industrial and construction minerals, identification of recycled materials);
- energy statistics and energy balances (extraction of fuels and estimation of oxygen demand);
- statistics of foreign trade (imports);
- supply–use tables and input–output tables (accounts for individual product groups);
- estimates: for example, air inputs may be estimated, based on combustion of fossil fuels; coefficients for indirect flows associated with imports.

Domestic extraction of raw materials is taking place in the following industries:

- agriculture, hunting and related activities (NACE 01);[6]
- forestry (NACE 02);
- fishing (NACE 05);
- mining and quarrying of coal and lignite, extraction of peat (NACE 10);
- extraction of crude petroleum and natural gas (NACE 11);
- mining of uranium and thorium ores (NACE 12);
- mining of metal ores (NACE 13);
- other mining and quarrying – stone, slate, sand, clay, gravel, salt and so on (NACE 14);
- manufacture of other non-metallic mineral products – glass, bricks, cement and so on (NACE 26); (mainly useful for identifing ancillary extraction and for establishing supply–use tables of materials);
- electricity, gas, steam and hot water supply (NACE 40); (useful for compiling water accounts);
- collection, purification and distribution of water (NACE 41); (useful for compiling water accounts);
- construction (NACE 45); (mainly useful for identifing ancillary extraction and for establishing supply–use tables of materials).

These data sources may be complemented by more specific sources such as reports and statistics published by industry associations (for example, mining associations reports on unused domestic extractions). No direct statistical sources are yet available for indirect flows associated with imports. The Wuppertal Institute has set up a database with coefficients for these based on case studies, LCAs and so on. For the future, an international organization could be established to fulfil this task of gathering, assessing and maintaining such coefficients (see Box 5.1).

Statistical sources for the accounting of material outputs include the following (Eurostat, 2001):

- environmental accounts (especially NAMEAs[7] with air emissions, waste and so on);
- environment statistics (for several output flows including air emissions, solid waste disposal, waste water and, partly, for recycling);
- agricultural statistics (dissipative use of products such as fertilizer on agricultural land);
- statistics of foreign trade (exports);
- energy statistics (domestic consumption of energy carriers to account for additional emissions not reported in emission inventories).

BOX 5.1 EU-WIDE DATABASE FOR INDIRECT FLOWS

Extract from MFA Guide (Eurostat 2001)
5.58 Indirect flows of imports and exports are probably the most difficult to establish in the context of economy-wide MFA. A set of default coefficients for indirect flows would permit estimation of indirect flows regularly and at low costs. Such a set would provide a shortcut to estimating indirect flows from import and export data. Information that could be used for establishing such a default set is partly available but scattered and more work will be needed to establish an easy-to-use database. The coefficients should allow a clear separation of used (i.e., direct) and unused material flows, a condition not universally met by information currently available.

5.59 To improve the accuracy of such a database the following activities may be envisaged:

- collect information on specific indirect flows (e.g. precious metals and precious stones);
- compilation of a database of standard coefficients for indirect flows that can be applied to the volume of traded commodities;
- establishment of a material resource database with direct material inputs and reference values of indirect flow coefficients for the extraction or harvest of raw materials by countries/regions;
- use and further development of global model systems integrating material flows into national economic accounts and interlinked trade models such as NAMEAs and the COMPASS model system.

5.60 The sharing of indirect flow data and coefficients among countries and research institutes is a promising first step. The research community and network that has evolved in the context of the European Commission-funded ConAccount concerted action should act as a catalyst and relevant information should be sent to the following e-mail address: conaccount@wupperinst.org.

5.61 In the interim, a first set of useful information may be found on the Wuppertal Institute's web page at http://www.wupperinst.org/Projekte/mipsonline/download/download.html by downloading the file MIWerte.pdf.

Source: Eurostat 2001

Some output flows will always have to be estimated (for example, emission of water vapour from the combustion of fuels), and data gaps filled by estimates (for example, waste disposal for years not covered by official waste statistics).

Conclusions on the Information Gaps as regards Material Flows

MFA statistics are clearly addressing the level of aggregated national economies and are not designed for the environmental assessment of single products and services (although synergisms between MFA and LCA may be used). As regards data requirements, MFA statistics are widely based on already available statistical sources such as agriculture statistics, industry statistics, trade statistics and so on. In order to assess the environmental burden associated with imported goods and to monitor 'problem shifting' to foreign, in particular developing, countries, it seems worthwhile to establish an international database for coefficients of so-called 'hidden' material flows associated with imports and exports ('ecological rucksacks').

Although many European statistical authorities have started to report regularly on material flows, there is still no harmonized accounting system established as there is for economic statistics (such as the System of National Accounts). First efforts towards this end have been put forward by the statistical office of the European Communities (Eurostat) in developing jointly with member states' statistical offices a common methodology. Further progress may be expected.

The implementation of material flow accounting in official statistics is also dependent on the priorities as set by politics. The rising political awareness of issues like eco-efficiency, resource productivity, dematerialization and so on will probably enhance the process of establishing respective statistical information systems on the 'industrial metabolism' of national economies. In future, indicators derived from material flow statistics might be increasingly put on the political agenda, as with, for example, the German 'headline' indicator on raw material productivity. These efforts will also have to be linked to modelling total factor productivity.

In Japan, MFA methods are already applied and results have also been considered in official reports. However, proper institutionalization can be improved. Results of the Japanese MFA have not yet been discussed with respect to priorities for sustainable resource and waste management.

5.3 ENERGY

The demands on the database of a bottom-up model are in some cases very different from those on top-down or macroeconomic models. The whole system must be modelled on a technology and service-oriented basis with a very high disaggregation. Therefore most countries with good availability of the necessary data needed more than a few years to build up the relevant data collecting and analysis system. With the Energy and Modelling Center and other institutions, Japan is provided with an excellent data system. However, first analysis showed that it is difficult to build up a service and technology-oriented model and to calculate bottom-up scenarios with the existing data. Therefore, in this section, the necessary database for high-quality bottom-up scenario work can be found. Of course, more specific data are desirable as well as the integration of further socioeconomic information. Nevertheless, the following data represent a minimum for getting useful results. The data requirement is divided into general aspects, the four sectors of the demand side, and the supply side.

General Data

Population: past development over the last 20 years, prognosis for the next 50 years.
Total economic development within the last 20 years and prognosis for the next 20 or 30 years.
Statistical data of the mains system (electricity network, natural gas network).

Residential Sector

Entire energy statistics of the sector:

Final energy use by energy carriers (electricity, coal, oil, natural gas, heat and so on) and differentiated between room heating, cooling, hot water and other appliances for the last 20 years.
Electricity consumption differentiated between the most important electric applicances (all together, more than 90 per cent of total demand), saturation rates of electric appliances.
Heated area (in m^2) and space (in m^3).
Water consumption per capita for the last 20 years.
Cooking energy consumption by energy carriers for the last 20 years.
Specific unit consumption and efficiencies of all converting technologies of the residential sector.
Electricity demand curve differentiated between regions.

Industry

Detailed explanation of the differentiation between the branches (necessary for comparisons with international data).

GNP differentiated between all industry branches for the last 20 years. Prognosis of the economic development (same differentiation) for the next 20 to 30 years.
Energy statistics differentiated between all industry branches: final energy use by energy carriers (electricity, coal, oil, natural gas, heat and so on) for the last 20 years; energy intensities for the last 20 years.
Production quantity (in kg) of the most energy-intensive industry branches (primary industry: steel/iron, cement, primary chemical industry and so on) for the last 20 years.
Electricity demand curve differentiated between regions.

Commercial/Service Sector

Detailed explanation of the differentiation between the branches (necessary for comparisons with international data).
GNP differentiated between all service branches for the last 20 years. Prognosis of the economic development for the next 30 years
Number of employees differentiated between all branches for the last 20 years.
Energy statistics differentiated between all branches: final energy use by energy carriers (electricity, coal, oil, natural gas, heat and so on) for the last 20 years; energy intensities for the last 20 years.
Saturation, use and energy demand of the different appliances in the service sectors (electric appliances such as lighting, air-conditioning, in detail).
Area of office space differentiated between all service branches for the last 20 years.
Electricity demand curve differentiated between regions.

Transport in Relation to Energy

Please be aware that the following data only represent the minimum needed for bottom-up scenarios.

Passenger transport
Passenger kilometres: air, rail, individual (motorized four-wheel, two-wheel and so on), public transport for the last 20 years; with international transport, only half of the journey should be taken into account.
Average energy intensity/specific consumption of air, rail, individual (motorized four-wheel, two-wheel and so on), and public transport for the last 20 years (in kJ/pkm and kJ/km).
Final energy use by energy carriers (electricity, coal, oil, natural gas and so on) and differentiated between transport types (air, rail and so on) for the last 20 years (in PJ).

Freight transport

Tons kilometres: air, rail and road transport (absolute in tkm and specific in tkm/GNP) for the last 20 years; with international transport, only half of the journey should be taken into account.

Average energy intensity/specific consumption of air, rail and road transport for the last 20 years (in kJ/tkm and kJ/km).

Final energy use by energy carriers (electricity, coal, oil, natural gas and so on) and differentiated between transport types (air, rail and so on) for the last 20 years (in PJ).

For both freight and passenger transport: electricity demand curve differentiated between regions.

Best Available Technologies on the Demand Side

Technical and economic data of the best available technologies are essential for obtaining reliable scenario results. Therefore comprehensive data assessments should be done for all demand sectors and presented on the same basis and units as mentioned before (for example, kJ/ton steel, kJ/GNP in the chemical industry, kWh/m^2 room heating, and so on). In a lot of these cases, international data can also be used. However, the assessments should strongly distinguish between technical and economic potentials.

Conventional Supply Technologies

Detailed statistics of the existing supply system:

- technological standards (description of the plants and heating systems, actual efficiencies and so on);
- electricity and heat generation as well as co-generation by energy carriers;
- costs of the different types of generation;
- classification of the specific unit power for all supply systems.

Renewable Energy Potential

Potential and generation costs of at least the following renewable energy forms should be available (in TJ final energy):

- hydro power (large- and small-scale),
- wind energy (on- and off-shore),
- solar heating and hot water systems,
- solar electricity generation (photovoltaic and parabolic trough, roof areas and so on),

- bioenergy (wood and other solids, energy plants, biogas, organic waste, fuels and so on)
- geothermal energy (heat and electricity).

All potential factors must be differentiated between regional and temporal. Typical solar radiation, temperature and wind velocity time series (a period of one year with a short-term disaggregation – the shorter, the better) for the different climate zones are especially necessary. The data should be compatible with the demand curve regions.

Potential of Conventional Technologies

Efficiency potential of heating and electricity systems including advanced technologies compared to the actual rates.
Co-generation as well as tri-generation potential in industry, commercial/service sector and residential sector and their costs.
Technological parameter and costs of these techniques.

5.4 BUILDINGS

In the interim report (WI, 2001) a short description has already been given for the scenario model HEAT – the Household and Appliances modelling Tool. Below the HEAT model is examined closely for its operating method as well as for its advantages with regard to the valuation and the founding of renovation measures.

To develop energy conservation measures, it is important to know the initial state of the old buildings and where the potential for saving energy lies. Besides, it is important to know what measures are most simply attainable and at what price. Furthermore, many other viewpoints must be taken into consideration. If the energy conservation measures developed are oriented to a rough aim of a factor four (factor ten) by 2050, an aim corridor can be shown and the basic government condition sets can be derived from it. The dematerialized trading which can be promoted by corresponding general regulations, such as introduction of a resource tax, offer prices of dematerialization as in Germany the VDI[8] offers as a reward, causes innovative drafts which can help the Japanese business. In addition to a significant positive environmental impact, improved energy efficiency will lead to a more sustainable energy policy and enhanced security of supply. However, computer-aided simulation models offer a substantial contribution to expel business potentials and to rank the business options according to their economic viability.

The HEAT Model

The following shows how the energy flow to provide heated floor space and hot water is implemented in the model. In general there are three steps. First, the heat losses of every energy-relevant part of the outer shell of the house (roof, walls, cellar, windows), each separated into north, south, east and west, and the losses through ventilation are calculated for each of 40 typical houses (cf. Table 5.4), using information on the construction of the parts, typical *u*-values and recently made alterations. The calculations are based on the Swiss standard SIA 380/1 which is more precise than the German standard calculation. The definition of typical houses is derived from certain building periods and sizes of houses. Within each of the 40 groups, the energetic standard and so on is quite homogeneous. The calculation for new and future buildings is made in the same way. In the current models for Germany, six typical 'to-be-built' houses are considered (actual standard, low-energy house, passive house: each type for detached and semi-detached houses and bigger houses). This specification was sufficient for the German case and the questions were analysed. But the model is flexible: further 'to-be-built' house types can be defined if necessary.

As a second step, the supply of the heat demand by 11 different heating systems is calculated. Heating systems are defined by energy carrier, efficiency, typical usage patterns, and demand for auxiliary energy for circulation pumps, fans and controls. In the third step, the emissions, the energy costs and, as an option, the material flows are calculated.

The description of future trends in the energy supply of the building stock is made by destruction rates (which are less than 1 per cent in Germany) and renovation rates by building parts. This is a very important parameter as existing houses are responsible for most of the energy consumption and will be during the coming decades. Construction rates, market shares of heating systems and stock exchange (reinvestment) rates are further parameters for calculating future energy demand. For the business-as-usual (BAU) scenarios, the data are mainly derived from a well-accepted prognosis.

For the construction of policy scenarios, the measure-oriented approach and the policy-oriented approach can be used. The measure-oriented approach uses detailed modelling of the representative buildings. For every part of the building several possible retrofit measures are implemented, ranging from simple BAU retrofits to different energy-saving measures. For every measure, technical data, cost data and material intensity data are implemented in the model. Currently, more than 150 different insulation measures covering the whole building stock are programmed. Additional measures can be easily defined by data-masks.

Based on the measures and the technical modelling of energy savings, the

Table 5.4 *Definition of typical houses and their share of floor space in West Germany, 1995*

Built between (share of dwelling-floor space 1995)	Detached/ semi-detached houses	Buildings with 3–6 dwellings %	Buildings with 7–12 dwellings %	Tall buildings > 13 dwellings %
before 1918	8.3	5.8	0.5	–
1919–1948	6.2	3.1	0.5	–
1949–1957	5.9	5.5	1.0	–
1958–1968	10.2	5.9	1.7	0.5
1969–1978	11.3	5.5	2.2	0.6
1979–1983	5.0	1.5	–	–
1984–1987	2.1	1.9	–	–
1988–1995	9.3	5.4	–	–

Note: 100% = 2555.1 million m^2 (West Germany; East Germany: 466.25 million m^2 comparable method, postwar differing periods); every field in the table represents one typical representative building category implemented in the model.

Source: Prognos (1995).

policy-oriented approach consists of different policy measures such as information campaigns, energy-saving regulations with different voluntary or obligatory standards and/or certain energy-saving cost levels for the technical measures. For every policy measure, the dynamic potential of technical measures addressed is estimated, which means that the potential varies during the scenario timeframe, mainly for the sake of specific reinvestment periods. In a second step, for every measure the share of realistically achievable savings is estimated and the measures are categorized for scenario building (for example as 'soft', 'medium' and 'strong' measures). Potential and intensity of policy measures are estimated by expert groups within and without the institute in a kind of Delphi method. This method shows a high variance in experts' guesses but also provides a higher quality of estimates and results which in this form is unique among all currently existing models in Germany and the EU, and probably world-wide.

The 40 building types of the whole German building stock are illustrated separately in the building stock simulation model, where all energetically relevant building components (outer walls, windows according to direction, cellar ceiling, roof) with their absolute surfaces as well as the respective heat transition coefficients (*u*-values) are registered (Institut Wohnen und Umwelt, 1994). On the basis of this information, a benefit design heat loss is carried out for each of the buildings according to the rules of the Swiss standard 380/1 SIA. Table 5.5 shows as an example the data contained in the model for a multiple dwelling.

On the basis of these data, heat-insulating measures can be determined for every building component, and the effects on the heating demand of the building calculated. Here, in addition, the investment figures of the heating insulating measures and the surfaces of the renovated building components can be determined as basic data for further material flow analyses and the determination of the effects on jobs. In order to calculate the costs, an in-depth market and price analysis was carried out. A comparison of BAU costs and additional costs is available too.

Furthermore, the renovation rates which are to be expected as well as building demolition have also to be considered. The model can be expanded to include new buildings by a comparable procedure. A range of typical building standards (WschVO1995, low-energy houses, passive houses) is integrated into the model library and can be linked to any sub-building scenarios.

The next step is to simulate the supply of necessary heat demand. The result of this modelling step is the actual energy demand of the building stock (including new buildings), divided into the energy sources used in each case, either natural gas, fuel oil, wood, coal, solar energy or electricity. The latter is not used just as heating energy, but also as an auxiliary energy to run the heating pumps, burners and regulators (Fischedick and Lechtenböhmer, 1998).

Table 5.5 Characteristic building values

Description	Multiple building with 3 to 6 units, built between 1958 and 1968			
Share of total housing space (%)	5.9			
Number of buildings	53 427			
Number of dwellings	1 900 000			
Housing space (1000 m^2)	152 000			
			Energy loss kWh/m^2	
Characteristic Values	m^2	u-value (old)	before renovation	after renovation
Housing space	2845	–	–	–
External wall	1732	1.54	71	14
Roof	971	1.9	49	5
Cellar	971	0.92	12	4
Window	507	2.6	35	19
Total loss of transmission heating			167	42
Total loss of ventilation heat			38	38
Solar profits			–16	–19
Useful heat			188	61
Original state			246	
Renovation measures	u-value (new)		Description	
External wall	0.3		8cm outer wall insulation	
Roof	0.198		16cm stone wool	
Cellar	0.348		6cm insulation on the underside	
Window	1.4		synthetic window (u-value 1·4)	
		Costs of renovation		
Costs of renovation		DM/m^2	DM	
External wall		200	346.340	
Roof		85	82.544	
Cellar		40	38.844	
Window		238.47	121.018	
Total costs (DM)		588.747		
DM/m^2 housing space		206.94		

Sources: Prognos (1995); HEAT issues WI (1999).

Finally, in the third modelling step the total emissions for the heating of the building stock for each scenario year can be determined, based on the end-energy use and differentiated by energy carriers with the help of emission factors of the energy carriers. On the basis of set energy prices, the resulting heating costs can be calculated.

Advantages of Computer-aided Design Heat Loss with the HEAT Model

In this section the advantages of computer-aided design heat loss are described on the basis of four modelling principles in general and the HEAT model in particular.

Systems and their parameters as well as the manner in which the system works (as with the system building–heating–user including meteorological parameters) are usually extremely complex as regards the interesting procedures. Such complex systems are usually not available to a simple building model and the attempt to convey such a system in its full complexity stands in the way of gaining any real knowledge. Only the analytical method which consciously dispenses with the description of the complex overall system creates visible and verifiable models. It is clearly shown in the assignment that the model has to show all fundamental, interacting components of the building and the heating system used. Every part of the model has to be looked at with regard to the parameters which are being strongly influenced by other components.

With regard to the classification of the analytical methods, a number of points have to be considered. First, a computer model has to work closely with the physical basic equations of the processes involved. Models that are based on empirical data are frequently subject to a high number of uncertainties with regard to the knowledge gained (passive houses, experimental buildings and so on).

In the HEAT model, the illustrated buildings are modelled bottom-up with regard to their heat consumption and their heating behaviour, starting with the separate components of the wall construction and going down to the individual user behaviour. This procedure enables an exact reproduction of the physical as well as the behavioural aspects.

Second, the computer program must allow a sufficiently high flexibility with regard to the spatial and temporal solution. One must assume that the qualities of component parts will gain a much higher importance (badly insulated windows in a low-energy house). Because the behaviour of these components is likely to change in interaction with other components, the model must allow at least an examination of the influences of differently fine spatial and temporal solutions.

In the HEAT model, the exogenous data as well as the corresponding model parts are structured flexibly with regard to the spatial and temporal

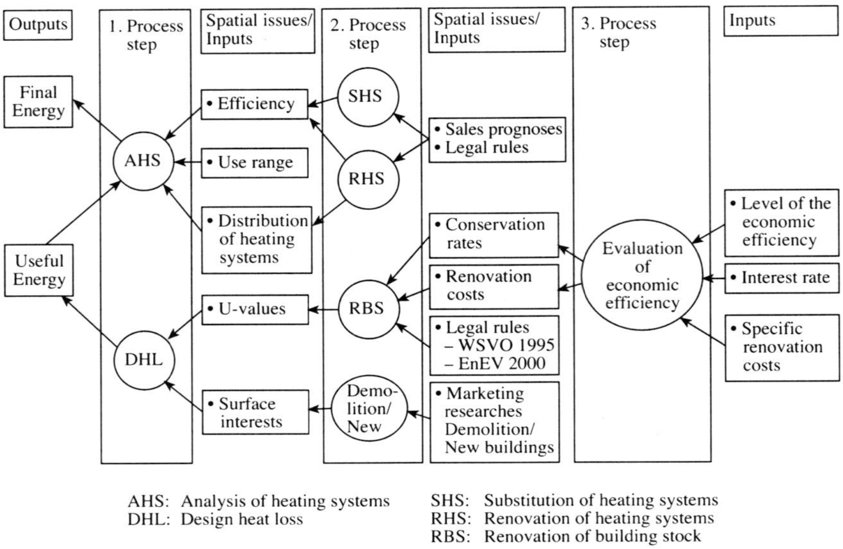

Source: Wuppertal Institute (2001).

Figure 5.2 Organization of data and process steps of the HEAT model

differentiation, which makes a gradual refinement of the modelling depth and modelling width possible at any time (see Figure 5.2).

Third, the program must be able to illustrate whole buildings; that is including the interactions between zones with different rules for heating.

The HEAT model works with the so-called 'usage range' which on the one hand shows heating behaviour of the inhabitants, and on the other a simulation of partial heating of extensions.

Finally, the program has to be comparable with other models in its algorithms and (partial) results. Only when the chosen methods and the results match the real conditions can the knowledge gained from the simulation be transferred to real conditions.

The HEAT model works on a tables-oriented data structure and every intermediate result and its algorithms are documented. Therefore the greatest possible verifiability of results gained is guaranteed.

The Necessary Database

The HEAT model is used for two main purposes, which differ substantially according to their required data demands. First, it is used for determining and balancing energy and emission quantities which are necessary to cover the demand for room heating in a financial year. In this case the differentiated data of the current building stock as well as the market shares of the heating systems and their technical indexes are necessary.

Second, it is used for updating the functions mentioned above, taking into account certain general assumptions (population development, energy prices) and scenario settings (renovation ratio and renovation measures, costs of renovation and so on). In this case, additional indexes are necessary, apart from the data mentioned above, which allow a temporal development of the leading indicators.

The database of the HEAT model is presented below, referring first to influences on heating demand and then to the updating of the model.

Climatological factors

The amount of energy sources used (oil, coal, gas and so on) to cover the heating demand depends on different influences which appear at different levels. At the beginning of the supply chain is the demand for well-heated living space (so-called 'energy service'). In Germany, the inside room temperature is set at 20°C. Another influence is the so-called heating level. It indicates at which outside temperature the average inside temperature, disregarding inside heating gains or solar radiation, has to drop for the heating system to produce the necessary warmth. The heating level for Germany is set at 15°C.

The average temperature course for a whole year is reflected in the so-called 'heating curve'. It indicates over 8760 hours what average outside temperature was measured at a particular hour of the day. By relating this to the heating level, the number of hours recorded which are under the heating level can be added together, as well as the sum of temperature differences which in the course of one year fall between the heating curve and average inside temperature. These parameters are called degree-day numbers or heating degree days. The regional peculiarities (regional climate zones) affect the course of the heating curve to such a degree that it is necessary to determine a separate degree-day number for each area. In Germany alone, there are approximately 40 different areas for which a degree-day number has to be calculated.

In Japan, the climate shows wide variations between regions, ranging from cool and temperate in Hokkaido to subtropical in Kyushu, where the annual average temperature ranges from 6°C to 22°C (Japan Information Network, 2000).

Existing building stock

Heating demand is a building characteristic for which the choice of heating system is not considered to start with. Its calculation is costly and requires

Table 5.6 Building issues

Building	Description
1 house unit (HU)	Single-family house
2 HU	Family house with two units/terraced house
3–6 HU	Small multiple houses
6–12 HU	Large multiple houses
More then 12 HU	Apartment house

Source: Japanese Statistics Bureau and Statistics Center (2000).

specific knowledge of the building. At the same time, certain buildings with similar construction and building design can be combined into so-called 'building types'. The building age and the number of units per building are appropriate for classifying the German building stock. From there, a first classification into single house units and multiple house units follows. In Germany, the building stock can be differentiated between the classes of building size and building age groups shown in Table 5.6. A similar classification can be made for the Japanese building stock (Table 5.7).[9]

Transmission heat requirement

The heating demand is calculated by coefficients of heat transition based on living space or, in short, the u-value for each building type. At the same time, it must still be differentiated between the different parts of a building which can differ substantially according to the building design (window surfaces in outer walls and so on). The HEAT model distinguishes between the following building components: RO (roof), OW (outer wall), CE (cellar/basement), WI (windows).

Table 5.7 Age of buildings in Japanese building stock

Date of building of Japanese building stock	AU	Number
Before 1945	1 000	1 646
1945 – 1980	1 000	19 556
1981 – 1990	1 000	11 964
1991 – 1993	1 000	3 694
1994 – 1998	1 000	5 950
Total buildings	1 000	42 810

Source: Japanese Statistics Bureau and Statistics Center (2000).

The transmission heat loss (*Qt*) for each respective building part is calculated by multiplying the parameters: *Qt* = surface (building component) × *u*-value (building component) × heating degree hours.

The ventilation heat requirement

Ventilation heat losses occur through the supply of colder fresh air and the removal of used warm air. Depending on the quality of the building, the losses can vary in some cases by up to 24 per cent of the total transmission heat losses. Parameters that influence the ventilation demand apart from fixed parameters like the specific thermal conductivity of the air (= $0.33\text{Wh/m}^{3*}\text{K}$) and the heating degree hours, are the air change rate (which indicates how often the air in a room is exchanged per hour) and the air volume. These ventilation losses (*Ql*) can be calculated as follows: *Ql* = air change rate × volume × warmth conductivity × heating degree hours.

Heating gains

To calculate a specific heat balance, heat losses and heat gains have to be compared. These occur by solar radiation, heat emitted by people, thermal radiation of electrical appliances, particularly, and thermal radiation of lighting systems. The dimension of typical passive solar heat gains in Germany according to the cardinal points is as follows: south = 370kWh/m^2, east/west = 225kWh/m^2, north = 140kWh/m^2.

The total heat given off per person at an average inside temperature is approximately 118 watts. The contribution of these heat gains by people is low in the case of buildings with today's average thermal quality. With highly insulated buildings (like the passive house), this corresponds to a heat contribution of almost 80–90 per cent. Typical conditions in Germany differentiated by single house units and multiple houses are $10\text{kWh/m}^2 \times a$ for a multiple family house and $8\text{kWh/m}^2 \times a$ for a single family house.

Development of the leading indicators

To develop a prognosis, the modelling assumptions have to be valued temporally and qualitatively; this means they have to describe a consistent temporal development as well as describe a consistent path to each other. Apart from the above-mentioned parameters, other factors influencing the heating demand have to be considered:

- the population development,
- the development of the active and passive household sizes,
- the standard of comfort (expressed in square metres of housing space per person),

- the development of qualitative renovation standards in old buildings and their conversion rates,
- the development of heating systems (efficiencies and so on) and their market shares.

An essential factor influencing the development and choice of qualitative renovation standards in the old building stock is the cost aspect. This is why the following description shows the data requirement as well as the systematic approach to acquire the cost-optimal renovation measures.

Economic Criteria for Choosing a Heating Insulation Measure

Apart from the ecological necessity to carry out thermal renovation measures in existing buildings, it is wise in economic terms to implement measures for the economic and rational use of energy when they also lead to net savings.

During the analysis of energy-saving measures, one looks at the question whether a positive interest rate on the invested capital, in the context of the component's life expectancy, is the outcome and which of a number of possible investments is the most economical. Depending on the required accuracy of the statements, two types of methods are available. The *static methods* are useful when the database is inaccurate or incomplete and are only suitable for estimates. The *dynamic methods* consider the future changes of expenditure or economic developments. For the analysis of the economic viability of an energy system, the use of dynamic methods is recommended, taking into account the annually changing expenditure (due to price increase, interest and so on), since an investment in energy systems usually implies a long-life expectancy.

The basis for the cost calculation is the annuity method. Here, annual costs or annual cost savings are calculated, based on the level of the investment, taking into consideration the calculation interest rate and the life expectancy of energy-saving investments. With the help of the compound interest calculation, the investment is converted into annual equal instalments. The annuity method enables in particular the comparison of investments which have a varying life expectancy.

An investment is economically viable if the average annual net cost savings result in a positive value (or if during its life span an investment shows lower average annual costs than any alternative method). To determine a ranking of renovation measures (so-called 'supply curves'), this energy expenditure has to be compared to the energy expenditure which would occur annually if these measures were not implemented. Dividing the annual additional costs by the annual additionally attainable energy conservation results in the price per saved kilowatt hour (DM/kWh):

$$P_{Save} = \frac{a \times I + Z}{E_{Save}}, \tag{5.1}$$

where

P_{Save} = price of the saved kilowatt-hour in DM/kWh,
a = capital recovery factor,
I = investment costs in DM,
Z = additional running costs in DM (maintenance/auxiliary electrical system for the control units and pumps,
E_{Save} = saved energy per year in kWh.

This procedure enables a direct comparison between the energy conservation costs and the supply costs. If the energy conservation costs are below the usual market energy costs, the measure is profitable:

$$P > P_{Save} \tag{5.2}$$

where

P = average price of an energy unit during its life expectancy,
P_{Save} = price of the saved kilowatt-hour in DM/kWh.

Some basic conditions and factors influence the result P_{Save} and should be considered separately. An important factor influencing the result is the underlying amortization period. This period differs substantially between different investors.

NOTES

1. The London Group on Environmental Accounting was created in 1993 to provide an informed forum for practitioners to share their experience of developing and implementing environmental satellite accounts linked to the economic accounts of the System of National Accounts. It convened its first meeting in March 1994 in London. Successive meetings have been held in Washington (1995), Stockholm (1996), Ottawa (1997), Fontevraud, France (1998), Canberra (1999) and Voorburg, Netherlands (2001). Participants include representatives from statistical offices and international organizations. The meetings are hosted voluntarily by each participant in turn and each has provided facilities and secretarial functions for the meetings. Japan is represented by Professor Kimio Uno, Keio University.
2. The German Environment Index is a joint initiative of the German EPA and the Ministry for the Environment, Nature and Nuclear Safety (http://www.umweltbundesamt.de/dux-e/index.htm).
3. Energy productivity is the second indicator to monitor resource productivity in the German Environment Index.

4. The guide was drafted by the Wuppertal Institute and the set-up was assisted by a task force of European experts.
5. Resource productivity indicators can be derived by relating GDP to material flow aggregates such as TMR (total material requirement) or DMI (direct material input) (see, for example, EEA, 1999).
6. NACE = Statistical classification of economic activities in the European Community.
7. NAMEA = National Accounts Matrix including Environmental Accounts. A statistical framework developed by Statistics Netherlands. It divides the economy into industry and household categories and shows how each industry or the households contribute to a variety of environmental concerns such as emissions of pollutants to air, waste water and waste. It is also possible to include environmental protection expenditure, eco-taxes, use of natural resources and land use in the framework.
8. VDI (Verein Deutscher Ingenieure), the association of engineers, is a financially independent and politically unaffiliated non-profit organization to represent engineers in the profession and in the public area.
9. The division of the time frames is a result of different historic processes and standards and adapted to the particular specifications of both Germany and Japan.

6. Concluding thoughts

Raimund Bleischwitz

The study has revealed some interesting results for any sustainable development of an economy. Putting an emphasis on the concept of eco-efficiency, it has spelled out various benefits resulting from pursuing such a strategy. Business makers may like the idea of combining innovations with less use of nature. By and large, companies can save costs via the reduction of energy and materials input. Innovations are likely to emerge when companies revise their production chain and develop new products and services that require fewer natural resources and lead to lower levels of emissions and waste. Driven by pioneers and early imitators, a Factor Four (or more) increase in eco-efficiency may occur for whole economies in the long run.

Because of such self-interest, the scope of environmental regulations may become leaner compared to previous times of pollution control policy. A general conclusion, however, that self-interest will almost automatically drive firms and markets towards a Factor Four would be misleading. Typical market failures such as information deficits, negative externalities and low prices for the use of nature call for a review of framework conditions. Eco-efficiency still demands some regulatory policies. The study explores via empirical analysis different kinds of regulatory approach towards increasing eco-efficiency in Europe. Though these approaches differ and can even be seen as heterogeneous, further general remarks can be made. There is, firstly, no general tendency towards one single instrument. Economic incentives, however superior they might be seen to be from the standpoint of economic theory, are usually embedded in a larger set of legal and other institutions. Such cross-cutting instruments and institutions deserve more attention by research. Raw material taxes are an interesting feature leading towards broadening the scope of eco-taxes beyond certain pollutants and energy. Scandinavian states and the UK have initiated attempts towards raw material taxes, leading to higher prices for natural resources and, thus, to incentives for increasing resource productivity.

Other regulatory approaches favour the provision of information combined with financial incentives where a lack of knowledge coincides with conservative investment behaviour (demand-side management, building law); they provide better conditions for doing business in oligopolistic markets (renewable energy law). Waste law increasingly provides incentives for recycling and for a review of whole production chains. Recent environmental targets include not only those well-known targets for combating certain risks, but also strategic targets that combine innovations with less use of nature. The German National Sustainability Strategy calling for a doubling of resource productivity by 2020 is but one example for such a tendency towards open and strategic targets.

All these approaches may have in common that they favour eco-efficiency rather than reducing single pollutants and that they call for a shift of attention towards the inputs of production processes. As regards the aim of a recycling economy, the conclusion is that regulatory approaches increasingly deal with material flows rather than with packages, other wastes or certain substances. Such a regulatory framework may still entail some restrictions for doing business because the quality of substances and their specific impacts can never be neglected. But increasingly the governmental paradigm is changing towards incentives for the 'good': innovation, information, learning processes. The latter is perhaps the most striking conclusion for policy makers – incentives for learning processes at the micro level of society and among actors are at the heart of any governance for sustainable development.

The two chapters on sustainable business and consumption in this book may have shown promising tools and examples of the way these actors might behave in a sustainable manner. Given that these attempts will likely be imitated by others, but still may need some additional incentives, the policy conclusion is as follows. Any regulation by governments should aim at stimulating learning processes of these pioneers and early imitators. While governments usually lack knowledge about the various options for action emerging throughout open development processes, this is a call for some kind of 'responsive' regulation. What such a governance structure that enables private actors and lower levels of policy making might look like and how it may absorb their various responses is not yet part of our study. The plea for learning processes on multiple arenas, however, might serve as an important criterion for any governance for sustainable development. Towards that research aim, additional efforts should also be devoted to an analytical framework for evaluating existing policies. Our analysis has been based upon some insights from policy analysis combined with experience, but it surely can be improved by more thorough research.

While these concluding thoughts deal with incentive structures between the state and private actors, another conclusion refers to information and data. Private actors as well as governments depend upon sound, reliable, and easy-to-access information. The study has revealed some data gaps that need to be addressed by official statistics. Though statistical offices can be considered to run well in most industrialized states, almost every area still falls short in providing sufficient information for action towards sustainable development.

The study has pointed out some specific deficits with regard to material flows, energy, and buildings, which might be considered in revising prevailing statistics. In this context, policy-oriented research ought to carry out research in terms of the way these statistics might fit into a broader monitoring and reporting system on sustainable development and how these statistics might provide better guidance in future transitions processes. After all, there will be a long and winding way towards governance for sustainable development, but it will be a fascinating journey.

References

ACEA (The European Automakers) (1998), 'Position Statement on the Commission's proposal for a Directive on End-of-Live Vehicles', Brussels (http://www.acea,be/ACEA/position_papers.html).

ACEA (2000), 'Monitoring the New Car CO_2 Agreement between the European Commission and ACEA – ACEA's 1999 Progress Report', Document MNCCO2AECACEA (pdf from www.acea.be/acea/position_papers.html).

ACEA (2001), 'Monitoring ACEA's Commitment on CO_2 Emission Reduction from Passenger Cars (2000), Joint Report of the European Automobile Manufacturers Association and the Commission Services', Final Report 28 June 2001, Document CO_2 2000 (pdf from www.acea.be/acea/publications.html), Brussels: Association des Constructeurs Européens d'Automobiles (ACEA).

Adriaanse, A.S., S. Bringezu, A. Hammond *et al.* (1997), *Resource Flows: The Material Basis of Industrial Economies*, Washington, DC: World Resources Institute.

Allenby, B.R. (1999) *Industrial Ecology – Policy Framework and Implementation*, Englewood Cliffs, NJ: Prentice Hall.

Arbeitsgemeinschaft (ARGE) Altauto (2000), '1. Monitoringbericht gemäß Punkt 3.6 der Freiwilligen Selbstverpflichtung zur umweltgerechten Entsorgung von Altfahrzeugen (PKW) im Rahmen des Kreislaufwirtschafts-/Abfallgesetz der Bundesregierung vorgelegt am 31. März 2000', Frankfurt a. Main: ARGE Altauto.

Ayres, R.U. (1989), 'Industrial Metabolism', in J. Ausubel, H. Sladovich (eds), *Technology and Environment*, Washington, DC: National Academy.

Ayres, R.U., and L.W. Aayres (eds) (2002), *A Handbook of Industrial Ecology*, Cheltenham, UK and Brookfield, US: Edward Elgar.

Ayres, R.U. and U.E. Simonis (eds) (1994), *Industrial Metabolism*, Tokyo and New York: United Nations University Press.

Bartelmus, P. (ed.) (2002), *Unveiling Wealth – on Money, Quality of Life and Sustainability*, Dordrecht: Kluwer.

Bartelmus, P., S. Bringezu and S. Moll (2000), 'Dematerialization, Environmental Accounting and Resource Management – main issues and how they can be translated into public policy initiatives', final report to the European Commission (DG ENV), Wuppertal Institute.

Bartelmus, P., R. Bleischwitz, S. Bringezu, M. Fischedick, J.v. Geibler, P. Hennicke, M. Kuhndt, R. Lukas, F. Merten, S. Moll, W. Sachs, K.O. Schallaböck and E. Seifert (2001), 'Application of European-Based Policies on Resource Flows and Energy to Japanese Sustainable Development Policies. Interim Report for the Economic Planning Agency of Japan and Mitsubishi Research Institute', Wuppertal Institute.

Bartelt, H. (2001), 'Rahmenbedingungen zur Windstromerzeugung in Deutschland'.

Barthel, M. and K. Boehmer (2001), 'ISO and Climate Change: Identifying Opportunities', ISO 9000+ISO 14000 NEWS 1/2001, Geneva, pp.27ff.

BCSD (Business Council for Sustainable Development) (1993), 'Getting Eco-Efficient', report of the Business Council for Sustainable Development, first Antwerp Eco-Efficiency Workshop, Geneva: BCSD, November.

Becktepe, C. and T. Strütt-Bringmann (eds) (1992), *Der Stoff, aus dem die Kleider sind. Die Verbraucher Initiative*, Bonn: Bundesverband Die Verbraucher Initiative.

Bendell, J. (2000), 'Talking for Change? Reflections on Effective Stakeholder Dialogue', a paper for New Academy of Business Innovation Network, October.

Bergstedt, E. and I. Linder (1999), 'A Material Flow Account for Sand and Gravel in Sweden', Eurostat working paper 2/1999/B/4.

Bleischwitz, R. (1998), *Ressourcenproduktivität: Innovationen für Umwelt und Beschäftigung*, Berlin: Springer Verlag.

Bleischwitz, R. and E.U.v. Weizsäcker (2000), Vorbeugen durch umweltpolitische Maßnahmen – Institutionen und Konzepte der Umweltpolitik im Wandel', in Wichmann, Schlipköter and Füllgraff (eds), *Handbuch der Umweltmedizin*, vol. 3, ch. IX, Munich: Ecomed-Verlag, pp.1–17.

Bleischwitz, R. (2001a), 'Joint Environmental Management: A Look at the Business Institutions of Eco-Industrial Parks', Contribution to the IHDP Conference, Berlin, December (www.environmental-policy.de).

Bleischwitz, R. (2001b), 'Rethinking Productivity: Why has Economic Analysis Focused on Labour Instead of Natural Resources?', *Environmental and Resource Economics* (EARE), **19** (1), 23–36.

Bleischwitz, R. (2002a), 'Governance of Eco-efficiency in Japan – An Institutional Approach', Wuppertal papers, no.124.

Bleischwitz, R. (2002b), 'Cognitive and Institutional Perspectives of Eco-efficiency – A New Research Landscape towards Factor Four (or more)', Wuppertal papers, no. 123; also in *Ecological Economics*, **46**, 2003, 453–67.

Bleischwitz, R. (2003), 'Governance of Eco-Efficiency in Japan – An Institutional Approach', *International Asian Quarterly*, **34** (1–2), 107–26.

BMU (Bundesministerium für Umwelt, Naturschutz und Reaktorsicherheit/ German Federal Ministry of the Environment) (1997), 'Klimaschutz in

Deutschland. Zweiter Bericht der Regierung der Bundesrepublik Deutschland nach dem Rahmenübereinkommen der Vereinten Nationen über Klimaänderung' (Climate Protection in Germany. Second Report of the Government of the Federal Republic of Germany according to the United Nations' Framework Convention on Climate Change), Bonn.

BMVBW (Bundesministerium für Verkehr, Bau- und Wohnungswesen) (2001), 'Guideline for Sustainable Building', Bonn: BMVBW.

BMVBW (German Federal Ministry for Building) (ed.) (1997), *Haus und Wohnung im Spiegel der Statistik 1997/98* (House and Flat as reflected by Statistics 1997/98), 9th rev. edn Bonn: BMVBW.

BMWi (Bundesministerium für Wirtschaft und Technologie/German Federal Ministry for Economic Affairs and Technology) (1999), 'Energie Daten 1999. Nationale und internationale Entwicklung' (Energy Data 1999. National and International Trends), Bonn.

Boltho, A. and J. Corbett (2000), 'The Assessment: Japan's Stagnation – Can Policy Revive the Economy?', *Oxford Review of Economic Policy*, **16** (2), 1–17.

Bringezu, S. (1993), 'Towards increasing resource productivity: How to measure the total material consumption of regional or national economies?', *Fresenius Environmental Bulletin* (2), 437–42.

Bringezu, S. (1997a), *Umweltpolitik – Grundlagen, Strategien und Ansätze ökologisch zukunftsfähigen Wirtschaftens*, Munich and Vienna: Oldenbourg Verlag.

Bringezu, S. (1997b), 'From Quantity to Quality: Material Flow Analysis', in S. Bringezu *et al.*, *From Paradigm to Practice of Sustainability*, Wuppertal Special 4, Wuppertal: Wuppertal Institute for Climate, Environment, Energy.

Bringezu, S. (2000a), 'Material Flow Analysis – History and Overview', paper presented to the 30th meeting of the OECD Working Group on the State of the Environment, Special Session on Material Flow Accounting', Room document – MFA 1, Agenda Item 2a, OECD, Paris, 24 October.

Bringezu, S. (2000b), 'Material Flow Analysis for Sustainable Resource Management in Germany and Europe', background paper for the SCOPE Workshop of the Project 'Material Flow Analysis for Sustainable Resource Management (MFAStoRM)', Wuppertal Institute, 23–4 November.

Bringezu, S. (2002), 'Industrial Ecology: analyses for sustainable resource and materials management in Germany and Europe', in R.U. Ayres and L. Ayres (eds), *Handbook of Industrial Ecology*, Cheltenham, UK and Northampton, MA: Edward Elgar, pp. 288–300.

Bringezu, S. and R. Kleinj (1997), 'Short review of the MFA work', in S. Bringezu *et al.*, *Regional and National Material Flow Accounting: From Practice to Paradigm of Sustainability*, proceedings of the ConAccount

Workshop 21–23 January, Leiden, Wuppertal: Wuppertal Institute, pp.306–8.
Bringezu, S. and H. Schütz (2000), 'Indicator Study: Total Material Requirement of the European Union', EEA Technical Report, Copenhagen: European Environment Agency.
Bringezu, S. and H. Schütz (2001a), 'Material use indicators for the European Union, 1980–1997', Eurostat working paper 2/2001/B/2, Luxembourg.
Bringezu, S. and H. Schütz (2001b), 'Total Material Resource Flows of the United Kingdom "DETR-MFA UK" ', final report for the Department of the Environment, Transport and the Regions (DETR), contract ref. no. EPG 1/8/62, Wuppertal Institute.
Bringezu, S. and Y. Moriguchi (2002), 'Material Flow Analysis', in R.U. Ayres and L. Ayres (eds), *Handbook of Industrial Ecology*, Cheltenham, UK and Northampton, MA: Edward Elgar, pp.79–90.
Bringezu, S., F. Hinterberger and H. Schütz (1994), *Integrating sustainability into the system of national accounts: The case of interregional material flows*, vol. II, proceedings of the International afcet (Association Française pour la Cybernétique Économique et Technique) Symposium 'Models of sustainable development', Paris, March, pp. 669–80.
Bringezu, S., H. Schütz and S. Moll (2002), 'Towards sustainable resource management in the European Union', Wuppertal Paper 121, Wuppertal: Wuppertal Institute.
BUND (2001), 'BUND-Marktanalyse', *Supermärkte durchschnittlich weniger als drei Prozent Bio*, Pressemitteilung 57 vom 2.7.2001.
Bunde, A. (2002), *The Science of Disasters, Climate Disruptions, Heart Attacks, and Market Crashes*, Berlin and Heidelberg: Springer Verlag.
Bundesministerium für Raumordnung, Bauwesen und Städtebau (BMRBS) (German Federal Ministry for Building) (ed.) (1997), *Haus und Wohnung im Spiegel der Statistik 1997/98* (House and Flat as reflected by Statistics 1997/98), 9th rev. edn, Bonn: BRMBS.
Bundesumweltministerium für Umwelt, Naturschutz und Reaktorsicherheit (BMU) (2001), 'Verordnung über die Erzeugung von Strom aus Biomasse', Bundesgesetzblatt, **1** (29), 1234.
Bundesverband Windenergie e.V. (2001), 'Windenergie 2001: Marktübersicht', Osnabrück: Bundesverband Windenergie.
Burgess, S.M. (1992), 'Personal Values and Consumer Research: A Historical Perspective', *International Journal of Research in Marketing*, **11**.
Carraro, C. and D. Siniscalco (eds) (1997), *New Directions in the Economic Theory of the Environment*, New York: Cambridge University Press.
Carroll, A.B. (1993), *Business and Society: Ethics and Stakeholder Management*, Cincinatti: South-Western.
Chen, X. and L Qiao, L. (2000), 'Material flow analysis of Chinese

economic–environmental system', *Journal of Natural Resources*, **15** (1), 17–23.

Clean Japan Center (2000), *Recycle-Oriented Society. Towards Sustainable Development*, Tokyo: Clean Japan Center.

Commission of the European Communities (CEC) (1993), 'White Paper on Growth, Competitiveness, and Employment', ch. 10, Thoughts on a New Development Model for the Community, COM (93) 700 final, Brussels.

Commission of the European Communities (CEC) (2000), 'Action Plan to Improve Energy Efficiency in the European Community' (COM(2000)247), Brussels: European Commission.

Commission of the European Communities (CEC) (2001), 'A Sustainable Europe for a Better World: A European Union Strategy for Sustainable Development' (Commission's proposal tothe Gothenberg Council), COM 264 final, May, Brussels.

Commission of the European Communities (CEC) (2001c), 'Environment 2010: Our Future, Our Choice – The Sixth Environment Action Programme', COM (2001) 31 final, Brussels, 24 January (http://europa.eu.int/comm/environment/newprg/index.htm).

Commission of the European Communities (CEC) (2001a), 'A Sustainable Europe for a Better World: A European Union Strategy for Sustainable Development' (Commission's proposal to the Gothenburg European Council), COM (2001)264 final, Brussels, 15 May (http://europa.eu.int/comm/environment/eussd/index.htm).

Commission of the European Communities (CEC) (2001b), 'DG Environment Management Plan 2001–2002', Brussels (http://europa.eu.int/comm/dgs/environment/mission_en.htm).

Commission of the European Communities (CEC) (2001d), 'European Climate Change Programme', report, June, Brussels.

Daly, H. (1991), *Steady State Economics*, 2nd edn, Washington: Island Press.

Daly, H. (1996), *Beyond growth. The Economics of Sustainable Development*, Boston: Beacon Press.

Daten- und Rechenmodell (2001), 'Schadstoffemissionen aus dem motorisierten Verkehr in Deutschland 1980–2020' (Data and Calculation Model: Emission of Pollutants from Motorized Transport in Germany 1980–2020), and 'TREMOD – Transport Emission Estimation Model', in Auftrag des Umweltbundesamtes, seit 1993, letzte Aktualisierung November 2001.

DEA (Danish Energy Agency)/Energy piano (2000), 'Workshop Report from Denmark', working paper for the Study on IRP in a Changing Market, Copenhagen.

De Marco, O., G. Lagioia and E. Pizzoli Mazzacane (1999), 'Material Flow Analysis of the Italian economy: Preliminary results', in: R. Kleijn, S. Bringezu, M. Fischer-Kowalski, and V. Palm (eds), *Proceedings of the*

ConAccount Workshop – Ecologizing Societal Metabolism, CML Report 148, Leiden: Leiden University, pp. 3–14.

De Moor, A. and P. Calamai (1997), *Subsidising Unsustainable Development. Undermining the Earth with Public Funds*, Toronto: Earth Council.

Department for Environment, Food and Rural Affairs (DEFRA) (2002), 'Resource use and efficiency of the UK economy', a report by the Wuppertal Institute for the Department for Environment, Food and Rural Affairs, London (http://www.defra.gov.uk/news/2002/020617a.htm).

Department of the Environment, Transport and the Regions (1999), 'A better quality of life: a strategy for sustainable development for the UK', www.sustainabledevelopment.gov.uk

DIN (2000), *DIN EN ISO 14031 – Environmental Management-Environmental Performance Evaluation Guidelines*, Berlin: Beuth Verlag (in German and English).

DIN German Institute for Standardisation (NAGUS) *et al.* (2001), 'Revision of the ISO 14001 – German Experiences and Recommendations', Berlin.

DIW (Deutsches Insitut für Wirtschaftsforschung/ German Institute for Economic Research)(1998), 'Indikatoren des Energieverbrauchs in Deutschland' (Indicators for the Energy Consumption in Germany), Wochenbericht (Weekly Report) 50/98.

Dixit, A.K. (2000), *The Making of Economic Policy. A Transaction-Cost Perspective*, Cambridge, MA: MIT Press.

Douglas, M and B. Isherwood (1978), *The World of Goods. Towards an Anthropology of Consumption*, New York: Basic Books.

Doutlik, K. (2000), after P. Henriques, 'The Role of Public Authorities in the Promotion and Development of Environmental Management Tools' in J. Peter, 'Business, Eco-Efficiency and Sustainable Development – The Role of Environmental Management Tools', an international workshop organised by INETI, Portuguese Directorate-General for Industry and the European Commission held in Lisbon, 1–3 March 2000, final report, Luxembourg: European Commission.

Doutlik, K. (2000), after UNEP, 'The Role of Public Authorities in the Promotion and Development of Environmental Management Tools' in J. Peter, 'Business, Eco-Efficiency and Sustainable Development – The Role of Environmental Management Tools', an international workshop organised by INETI, Portuguese Directorate-General for Industry and the European Commission held in Lisbon, 1–3 March 2000, final report, Luxembourg: European Commission.

Ecotec (2001), 'Economic and Environmental Implications of the Use of Environmental Taxes and Charges in the European Union and its Member States', Study on behalf of DG ENV (Contact Ref: 34-3040/99/

74628/MAR/B2), Brussels (http://europa.eu.int/comm/environment/enveco/taxation/environmental_taxes.htm).

EEA/Eurostat (1998), 'Europe's Environment: Statistical Compendium for the Second Assessment', Luxembourg: European Communities.

Eicke-Hennig, W. (1998), 'Niedrigenergiehäuser: Der Einfluß des Nutzerverhaltens' (The Influence of the User's Behaviour), BundesBauBlatt, 1998, 14–18, (http://www.impulsprogramm.de/neh/e_neh5.html, 8.3.1999).

ELFOR og Sjaellandssamarbejdet (1999), *Plan 2000*, Copenhagen: Fredericia.

EMNID (1991), *Kontiv 1989*, several vols, Bielefeld.

Empacher, C., K. Götz and I. Schultz (2000), 'Demonstrationsvorhaben zur Fundierung und Evaluierung nachhaltiger Konsummuster und Verhaltensstile', Institut für sozial-ökologische Forschung im Auftrag des UBA, Frankfurt.

Enquête-Kommission of the German Bundestag (1997) 'Protection of Humanity and the Environment – Objectives and General Conclusions of Sustainable Development' *The Concept of Sustainability – Prerequisites for Tomorrow*, Stuttgart: Metzler-Poeschel.

Enquête-Kommission 'Schutz des Menschen und der Umwelt' (ed.) (1993), Verantwortung für die Zukunft – Wege zum nachhaltigen Umgang mit Stoff- und Materialströmen, Bonn: Economica Verlag.

Enquête-Kommission 'Schutz des Menschen und der Umwelt' (ed.) (1994), *Die Industriegesellschaft gestalten – Perspektiven für einen nachhaltigen Umgang mit Stoff- und Materialströmen*, Bonn: Economica Verlag.

European Commission (1995), 'Small and Medium-Sized Enterprises: A Dynamic Source of Employment. Growth and Competitiveness in the European Union,' report presented by the European Commission for the Madrid European Council, CSE(95) 2087.

European Commission (2001a), 'Green Paper on Consumer Protection', Europe Information Service, Supplement to Europe Environment 597, October.

European Commission (2001b), 'Green Paper: Promoting a European Framework for Corporate Social Responsibility', COM (2001) 366 final, Brussels.

European Commission (2001c), 'Green Paper for Integrated Product Policy', Brussels.

European Commission (2001d), 'Measuring Environmental Performance of Industry' (MEPI), final report.

European Commission (2001e), 'Environment 2010: Our Future, Our Choice. The Sixth Environmental Action Programme', COM (2001) 31 final, Brussels.

European Community (2000), 'Richtlinie 2000/53/EC des Europäischen Parlaments und des Rates über Altfahrzeuge', Brussels.

European Environment Agency (EEA) (1999a), 'Making Sustainability Accountable: Eco-efficiency, Resource Productivity and Innovation', EEA Topic Report no. 11/1999, Copenhagen.

European Environment Agency (EEA) (1999b): Making Sustainability Accountable: Eco-efficiency, Resource Productivity and Innovation, EEA Topic Report no. 11/1999, EEA: Copenhagen.

European Environment Agency (EEA) (2000a), 'Environmental Taxes: Recent Developments in Tools for Integration', EEA Environmental Issue Series no. 18, Copenhagen (http://reports.eea.eu.int/Environmental_Issues_No_18).

European Environment Agency (EEA) (2000b), 'Environmental Signals 2000: European Environment Agency Regular Indicator Report', EEA Environmental Assessment Report no. 6, EEA, Copenhagen (http://reports.eea.eu.int/signals-2000/en).

European Environment Agency (EEA) (2000c), 'Total Material Requirement of the European Union', Technical Report no. 55, Copenhagen.

European Environment Agency (EEA) (2000d), 'Total Material Requirement of the European Union, The Technical Part,' Technical Report no. 56, Copenhagen.

European Environment Agency (EEA) (2001), 'Case Studies on Waste Minimisation Practices in Europe', Draft Topic Report, Copenhagen.

Eurostat (2000a), 'Environmental Taxes in the EU, Statistics in Focus – Economy and Finance Theme 2,' 20/2000, European Communities, Luxembourg (http://europa.eu.int/comm/eurostat/Public/datashop/print-catalogue/EN?catalogue=Eurostat&product=CA-NJ-00-020-__-I-EN).

Eurostat (2000b), *Statistical Yearbook 2000*, Luxembourg: Eurostat.

Eurostat (2001), 'Economy-Wide Material Flow Accounts and Derived Indicators – A Methodological Guide', Methods and Nomenclature Series, Luxembourg: Eurostat.

Federal Ministry for the Environment, Nature Conservation and Nuclear Safety, Germany (1998), Draft Programme for Priority Areas in Environmental Policy (Environment -Barometer)', BMU, Bonn.

Federal Ministry of Transport, Building and Housing (2001a), 'Guideline for Sustainable Building', Berlin.

Federal Ministry of Transport, Building and Housing (2001b), 'Towards Sustainable Human Settlements Development – National Report of the Federal Republic of Germany', revised by the Federal Agency for Building and Regional Planning, Berlin.

Federal Statistics Office (1999), *Datenreport 1999*, Wiesbaden.

Feldhaus, G. (2001), 'Beste verfügbare Techniken und Stand der Technik', *Neue Zeitschrift für 20. Jg.*, Heft 1, pp.1ff.

Figge, F., T. Hahn, S. Schaltegger and M. Wagner (2001), 'Sustainability Balanced Scorecard: Wertorientiertes Nachhaltigkeitsmanagement mit der

Balanced Scorecard, (Value oriented sustainability management with the balanced scorecard), Centre for Sustainability Management, University of Lueneburg.

Fischedick, M. and Lechtenböhmer, S. (1998), *Der Beitrag des Sektors Bauen und Wohnen zum Klimaschutz*, Endbericht, Wuppertal: Wuppertal Institute.

European Union (EU) (2000), 'Directive 2000/53/EC of the European Parliament and the Council of 18 September 2001 on end-of-life vehicles', Luxembourg: European Commission.

European Union (EU) (2001), 'Directive 2001/77/EC of the European Parliament and the Council of 27 September 2001 on the promotion of electricity produced from renewable energy sources in the internal electricity market', Luxembourg: European Commision.

Finanslov for finansåret (1999), www. oescs.dk/bevillingslove/docshelf?shelf=fl99.com

Fischedick, M., J. Nitsch and F. Staiß (2001), 'Politikstrategien für die Integration erneuerbarer Energien in Deutschland', Jahrestagung des Forschungsverbundes für Sonnenenergie, Potsdam.

Fraunhofer Institut für Systemtechnik und Innovationsforschung *et al.* (ed.) (1997), 'Interdisciplinary Analysis of the Possibilities for an Energy Conservation and Climate Protection Policy. Hindering and Promoting Conditions for an Efficient Energy Use in Private Households and their Associated Actors seen from an Economic and Social Psychological Perspective', final report at the End of the First Project Phase, Karlsruhe, Kiel, Wuppertal.

Freeman, R.E. (1984), *Strategic Management: A Stakeholder Approach*, Boston: Pitman.

Fried, W. and F. Scheucher (2000), 'Umweltorientierte Zusammenarbeit in der Automobilindustrie im Rahmen des Altfahrzeug-Recyclings', Umweltwirtschaftsforum, **2**, 31–35.

Furubotn, E. and R. Richter (1997), *Institutions and Economic Theory. An Introduction to and an Assessment of the New Institutional Economic*, Ann Arbor, Michigan: University of Michigan Press.

Gege, M. (ed.) (1997), Kosten senken durch Umweltmanagement, [Cost reduction through environmental management], Munich: Verlag Vahlen.

Georgescu-Roegen, N. (1971), *The Entropy Law and the Economic Process*, Cambridge, MA: Harvard University Press.

Gerhold, S. and B. Petrovic – Statistics Austria (2000), 'Material Balances and Indicators, Austria 1960–1997', Eurostat working paper no. 2/2000/B/6.

German Council for Sustainable Development (2001), online (www.dialog-nachhaltigkeit.de).

German Environmental Protection Agency (UBA) (2001), 'German

Environment Index' (Deutscher Umwelt Index DUX) (http://www.umweltbundesamt.de/dux-e/index.htm).

German Federal Statistical Office – Statistisches Bundesamt (2000a), 'Integrated Environmental and Economic Accounting – Material and Energy Flow Accounts', Fachserie 19, Reihe 5, Wiesbaden.

German Federal Statistical Office – Statistisches Bundesamt (2000b), 'Bericht des Statistischen Bundesamtes zu den Umweltökonomischen Gesamtrechnungen 2000' (Report of the German Federal Statistical Office on Integrated Environmental and Economic Accounting 2000), press conference of 17 October, Wiesbaden (http://www.destatis.de/download/ugr/bericht_engl.pdf).

German Federal Statistical Office (2000c), *Umweltökonomische Gesamtrechnungen 2000*, Wiesbaden.

German Federal Statistical Office – Statistisches Bundesamt (2001a), 'Integrated Environmental and Economic Accounting – Basic Data and Selected Results', Fachserie 19, Reihe 4, Wiesbaden.

German Federal Statistical Office – Statistisches Bundesamt (2001b), 'Report by the Federal Statistical Office on Integrated Environmental and Economic Accountings 2001' (Bericht des Statistischen Bundesamtes zu den Umweltökonomischen Gesamtrechnungen 2001), Federal Statistical Office, Wiesbaden.

German Federal Statistical Office – Statistisches Bundesamt (2001c), 'List of Tables of the German Environmental Economic Accounting' (http://www.destatis.de/basis/e/umw/ugrueb.htm).

German Wind Energy Association (2001), Comparative Analysis of Wind Energy Usage in Germany, USA and Japan. Osnabrück: BWE e. V.

Gesamttextil (1991/2000), 'Annual Report of the Textile Industry' (Jahrbuch der Textilindustrie) Frankfurt/M.

Global Reporting Initiative (2000), online (www.globalreporting.org).

Goldbach, M. (2001), 'Akteursbeziehungen in nachhaltigen Wertschöpfungsketten', EcoMTex-Diskussionspapier no. 03, Universität Oldenburg.

Graedel, T.E. and B. Allenby (1995): Industrial Ecology, Englewood Cliffs, NJ: Prentice-Hall.

Gravgaard Pedersen, O. (1999), 'Physical Input–Output Tables for Denmark', Statistics Denmark.

GRI (2000), 'Sustainability Reporting Guidelines on Economic, Environmental and Social Performance', Boston.

Gsänger, S. (2001), 'Das EEG goes global', *Neue Energie*, bk, 4, S. 94–6.

Hamm, U. (2000), 'Der Markt für Öko-Lebensmittel in Europa', in K. Zander and H. Waibel (eds), Ökonomie im Gartenbau, **83**, Institut für Gartenbauökonomie der Universität Hannover.

Hamm, U. and J. Michelsen (2000), 'Analysis of the Organic Food Market in Europe', in T. Alföldi, W. Lockeretz, U. Niggli (eds), *Proceedings of the 13th International IFOAM Scientific Conference*, Zurich: vdf Hochschulverlag (International Foundation for Organic Agriculture). pp.507–10.

Hamner B. and T. del Rosario (1997), 'Green Purchasing: A Global Channel for Improving the Environmental Performance of Small Enterprises', background paper No. 2, Workshop on Environmental Policy: 'Globalisation and the Environment: New Challenges for the Public and Private Sector', Paris, 13 and 14 November.

Hansen, U. and M. Bode (1999), *Marketing und Konsum. Theorie und Praxis von der Industrialisierung bis ins 21*, Jahrhundert, Munich: Verlag Vahlen.

Hansen, U. and U. Schrader (1997), 'A Modern Model of Consumption for a Sustainable Society', *Journal of Consumer Policy*, **20** (4), 443–68.

Hansen, U. and U. Schrader (2001), 'Nachhaltiger Konsum', *Campus Forschung*.

Hawken, P., A. Lovins and H. Lovins (2000), *Öko-Kapitalismus, die industrielle Revolution des 21. Jahrhunderts*, Munich: Riemann Verlag.

Hellberg, J. (2001), personal communication (fax, 28 May).

Hemmati, M. (2001), 'A Methodological Framework for Multi-Stakeholder Processes', a UNED Forum (Draft) Report, London.

Hill, C.W.L. (1995), 'National Institutional Structures, Transaction Cost Economizing and Competitive Advantage: The Case of Japan', *Organization Science*, **6** (1), 119–31.

Hillary, R. (ed.) (2000), *Small and Medium-Sized Enterprises and the Environment–Business Imperatives*, Sheffield: Greenleaf Publishing.

Hille, J. (1998), 'The Concept of Environmental Space: Implications for Policies, Environmental Reporting and Assessments', EEA's Experts Corner series, 1997/2, Copenhagen: European Environment Agency.

Hinterberger, F. and F. Schmidt-Bleek (1999), 'Dematerialization, MIPS and Factor 10 – Physical sustainability indicators as a social device', *Ecological Economics*, **29** (1), 53–6.

HM Customs and Excise Information Service (2001), 'Aggregates Levy', (http://www.hmce.gov.uk/bus/excise/).

Hoffmann, J., K. Ott and G. Scherhorn (2000), *Frankfurt-Hohenheimer Leitfaden*, Schriftenreihe zur ökologischen Kommunikation, bk 7, Munich: ökom Verlag.

Hoffrén, J. (1999), 'Measuring the Eco-Efficiency of the Finnish Economy', Statistics Finland Research Report 229, Helsinki.

Hook, R. (1998), *Summary of the Pravada 2 Project*, Frankfurt.

Hroch, N. and S. Schaltegger (2001), 'Berücksichtigt die betriebliche Umweltberichterstattung aktuelle umweltpolitische Themen?', *UmweltFocus*, **2**.

Hukkinen, J. (2001), 'Eco-Efficiency as Abandonment of Nature', *Ecological Economics*, **38**, 311–15.

IEA (International Energy Agency) (1997), *The Link between Energy & Human Activity*, Paris: IEA.

Imura, H. (1997), 'Japan', in M. Jänicke and H. Weidner (eds) (1997), *National Environmental Policies. A Comparative Study of Capacity-Building*, Berlin u.a.: Springer-Verlag, pp. 73–88.

Institut der deutschen Wirtschaft (Institute of German Industry) (eds) (1998), *Informationsdienst*, 42/1998, vol. 24/15.

Institute Wohnen und Umwelt (IWU) (1994), 'Wärmetechische Wohngebäude – Typologie für die alten und neuen Bundeständer', Endbericht für die 'Deutsche Bundestiftung Umwelt', Darmstadt.

Institut Wohnen und Umwelt (IWU) (2001), 'Guter Ansatz – schwache Standards: Stellungsnahme zum Referentenentwurf vom 29. November 2000 bzw,' Kabinettsbeschluss vom 7. März 2001, Darmstadt.

International Energy Agency/OECD (1999), *Energy Balances of OECD Countries 1996–97*, Paris: OECD.

Isacsson, A., K. Jonsson, I. Linder, V. Palm and A. Wadeskog, A. (2000), 'Material Flow Accounts – DMI and DMC for Sweden 1987–1997', Eurostat working paper 2/2000/B/2.

ISO (1999), 'ISO/TR 14032 Environmental Management – Examples of Environmental Performance Evaluation (EPE)', Geneva.

ISO (2001), 'The ISO Survey of ISO 9000 and ISO 14000 Certificates – Tenth Cycle', Geneva.

Jackson, T. and N. Marks (1999), 'Consumption, sustainable welfare and human needs – with reference to UK expenditure patterns between 1954 and 1994', *Ecological Economics*, **28** (3), 421– 41.

Jänicke, M. (1997), 'The Political System's Capacity for Environmental Policy', in M. Jänicke and H. Weidner (eds), *National Environmental Policies. A Comparative Study of Capacity-Building*, Berlin u.a.: Springer-Verlag, pp.1–24.

Japan Automobile Research Institute (JARI)/Japan International Cooperation Agency (JICA) (2000), 'Current Issues in the Recycling of Motor Vehicles in Japan: Training Course in Automobile Technology for the Improvement of Environmental Problems', unpublished paper, Tokyo: JARI/JICA.

Japan Automobile Research Institute (JARI) (2000), *JARI Research Journal*, April.

Japanese Environmental Agency (1992), 'Quality of the Environment in Japan 1992', Tokyo.

Japanese Environmental Agency (1998), 'Quality of the Environment in Japan 1998: To Realize Society for the 21st Century Keeping Sound Material Cycle and Harmonious Coexistence with Nature', Tokyo.

Japan Information Network (2000), www.jin.jcic.or.jp/stat/index.html

Japanese Statistics Bureau and Statistics Center (2000), 'Japan in Figures'.

Jungbluth, N. (2000), 'Umweltfolgen des Nahrungsmittelkonsums: Beurteilung von Produktmerkmalen auf Grundlage einer modularen Ökobilanz', dissertation de Verlag im Internet.

Juutinen, A. and I. Mäenpää (1999), 'Time Series for the Total Material Requirement of Finnish Economy – Summary', Eco-efficient Finland interim report, University of Oulu, Thule Institute (http://thule.oulu.fi/ecoef).

Kashima, S. and J. Koshi (1982), 'The Japanese Experiment with Mini-Cars', in K.-P. Hilber and K.O. Schallaböck (1985), *Reglementierungs- und Massnahmenansätze im Verkehrsbereich-Untersuchung*, Endbericht Phase II, **1**, Graz: Institut für Umweltforschung.

Kates, R.W., W.C. Clark *et al.* (2001), 'Sustainability Science', *Science Magazine*, 292, 641–2.

Keddie, A. (2000), 'The Contribution of Business to Sustainable Development', in J. Peter, 'Business, Eco-Efficiency and Sustainable Development – The Role of Environmental Management Tools', an international workshop organised by INETI, Portuguese Directorate-General for Industry and the European Commission held in Lisbon, 1–3 March 2000, final report, Luxembourg: EC.

Kerber, W. (1997), 'Wettbewerb als Hypothesentest: Eine evolutorische Konzeption wissenschaffenden Wettbewerbs', in K. v. Delhaes and U. Fehl (eds), *Dimensionen des Wettbewerbs. Schriften zu Ordnungsfragen der Wirtschaft 52*, Stuttgart: Lucius and Lucius Verlagsgesell-schaft, pp.29–78.

Klare, R. (2002), *Resource Wars: The New Landscape of Global Conflicts*, New York: Owe Books.

Klemisch, H. and H. Rohn (2002), 'Umweltmanagementsysteme in kleinen und mittleren Unternehmen (KMU) – Befunde bisheriger Umsetzung' (Environmental Management systems in small and medium-sized enterprises (SMEs) – Results of Implementations', KNI Papers 1/02, Cologne.

Klinkers, L., W. van der Kooy and H. Wijen (1999), Product-Oriented Environmental Management Provides New Opportunities and Directions for Speeding up Environmental Performance', *Greener Management Inter*.

Kloas, J., and U. Kunert (1993), Vergleichende Auswertungen von Haushaltsbefragungen zum Personenverkehr (KONTIV 1976, 1982, 1989), (Household Questionnaires on Passenger Transport in Comparison 1976, 1982, 1989). Berlin: Deutsches Institut für Wirtschaftsfor-schung (DIW).

Komiyama, H. (2002), 'Vision 2050' (unpublished paper).

Kuckartz, U. (2000), 'Umweltbewußtsein in Deutschland 2000. Ergebnisse einer repräsentativen Bevölkerungsumfrage', Auftrag des Umweltbundesamtes, Berlin.

Kuhndt, M. and B. Bilitewski (2000), *Towards Reduced Environmental*

Burden of Mobility: Improving the Automobile Life Cycle, in N. Wrisberg, A. Helias and U. de Haes (eds.) (2002), Analytical Tools for Environmental Design and Management in a Systems Perspective, Dordrecht: Kluwer Academic Publishers, 149–204.

Kuhndt, M. and C. Liedtke (1999), 'COMPASS – Companies' and Sectors' Path to Sustainability – The Methodology', Wuppertal paperWuppertal Institute.

Kuhndt, M. and C.T. van der Lugt (2000), *Der Kalender für effizientes Wirtschaften – Ein innovatives Instrument zur Verbesserung von Umweltleistungen in klein- und mittelständigen Unternehmen im globalen Maßstab* (The Efficient Entrepreneur Calendar – An Innovative Tool to Improve Environmental Performance in Small and Medium-Sized Enterprises World-Wide) Umweltwirtschaftforum, Berlin: Springer Verlag.

Kuhndt, M. and J. von Geibler and A. Eckermann (2002), 'Towards a Sustainable Aluminium Industry: Stakeholder Expectations and Core Indicators', Wuppertal: Wuppertal Institute.

KUNERT AG (2001), 'Umweltleistungsbericht 2000 nach DIN EN ISO 14031 – 10 Jahre Umweltberichterstattung', Immenstadt.

Langlois, R.N. and P.L. Robertson (1995), *Firms, Markets and Economic Change: A Dynamic Theory of Business Institutions*, London: Routledge.

Lazonick, W. (1999), 'The Japanese Economy and Corporate Reform: What Path to Sustainable Prosperity?', *Industrial and Corporate Change*, **8** (4), 607–33.

Liedtke, C. and E.U. von Weizsäcker (2000), *Unternehmen auf dem Weg zum Erfolg – die dreifache Gewinnstrategie machts möglich*, (Enterprises on the way to a success – possible through a triple-win strategy), in Bergische Wirtschaft, Zeitschrift der Industrie und Handelskammer Wuppertal – Solingen – Remscheid, April, pp. 8–11.

Liedtke, C., H. Rohn, M. Kuhndt M. and R. Nickel (1998), 'Applying Material Flow Accounting: Eco-Auditing and Resource Management at the Kambium Furniture Workshop', *Journal of Industrial Ecology*, 3 (1), Cambridge, MA: MIT Press.

Little, A.D. (2000), Renewable Energy Trends 2000, Boston (www.nrel.gov/ncpv/hotline/renewables_trends_2000.pdf).

Lorek, S. (2001), 'Household Energy and Water Consumption and Waste Generation', German case study, OECD Programme on Sustainable Consumption, Overath: Sustainable Europe Research Institute, p. 29.

Lorek, S. and R. Lucas (2003), 'Towards Sustainable Market Strategies: A Case Study on Eco-Textiles and Green Power', Wuppertal Institute No. 130, Wuppertal: Wuppertal Institute.

Lorek, S. and J.H. Spangenberg (2000), 'Changing Consumption and Production Patterns', Statement to the CSD 1995.

Lorek, S. and J.H. Spangenberg (2001a), 'Indicators for Environmentally Sustainable Household Consumption', *International Journal on Sustainable Development*, **4** (1), 101–19.

Lorek, S. and J. Spangenberg (2001b), 'Reichtum und Ökologie', in Jörg Stadlinger (eds), *Reichtum heute*, Münster: Dampfboot Verlag.

Lorek, S. and J. Spangenberg (2001c), 'Environmentally Sustainable Household Consumption: From Aggregate Environmental Pressures to Indicators for Priority Fields of Action', Wuppertal Paper No. 117, Wuppertal: Wuppertal Institute.

Lorek, S., J.H. Spangenberg and C. Felten (1999), 'Prioritäten, Tendenzen und Indikatoren umweltrelevanten Konsumverhaltens: Endbericht des UBA – Forschungsvorhabens', 209 01 216/03, Wuppertal Institute.

Lovins, A., L.H. Lovins and P. Hawken (1999), 'A Road Map to Natural Capitalism', *Harvard Business Review*, May/June, 145–58.

Lucas, R. (2001), *End-of-life vehicle regulation in Germany and Europe – problems and perspectives*, Wuppertal Paper 113, Wuppertal.

Lutzenhiser, L. (1992), 'A Cultural Model of Household Energy Consumption', Energy – The Internationl Journal, **17** (1), 47–60.

Lutzenhiser, L. (1997), 'Social and Behavioral Aspects of Energy Use', *Annual Review of Energy and Environment*.

Maddison, A. (1995), *Monitoring the World Economy 1820–1992*, Paris: OECD.

Mäenpää, I. (2000), 'Developing Methods of Physical Input–Output Accounting and Analysis in Finland', paper presented at the SCOPE Workshop, Material Flow Analysis for Sustainable Resource Management (MFAStoRM).

Manuskript für die Zeitschrift Umwelt Focus Juni (2000).

Matsuba, M. (2001), *The Contempory Japanese Economy*, Tokyo, Berlin, Heidelberg, New York: Springer-Verlag.

Matthews, E., C. Amann and S. Bringezu *et al*. (2000), 'The Weight of Nations – Material Outflows of Industrial Economies'. Washington, DC: World Resources Institute.

Matthias B., C. Pfeiffer, U. Schrader (2000), 'Strategies towards the Sustainable Household in Germany. Findings of an EU-Research Project on Clothing Care and Shelter', Universität Hannover.

Matzner, E. (1994), 'Instrument –Targeting or Context-Making? A New Look at the Theory of Economic Policy' *Journal of Economic Issues*, **28** (2), 461–76.

Meadows, D. (1972), *The Limits of Growth*, New York: Universe.

Metallgesellschaft A.G./World Bureau of Metal Statistics (1994), 'Metal Statistics 1983–93', Frankfurt.

Metcalfe, J.S. (1998), *Evolutionary Economics and Creative Destruction*, London: Routledge.

Metcalfe, J.S. (2001), 'Institutions and Progress', *Industrial and Corporate Change,* **10** (3), 561–86.
Meyer, A. and P. Hohmann (2000), *Other Thoughts; Other Results? Remei's bioRe Organic Cotton on its Way to the Mass Market*, Sheffield: Greenleaf Publishing.
Miljö and Energi Ministeriet (Danish Environmental Protection Agency) (2000), 'Green Accounting in Denmark – Experiences and the Future', Copenhagen, May.
Ministry of the Environment (1998), 'Key indicators for ecologically sustainable development: A proposal from the Swedish Environmental Advisory Council', Stockholm.
Ministry of the Environment (Finland) (1999), 'The Finnish Environment. Material Flow Accounting as a Measure of the Total Consumption of Natural Resources', Helsinki.
Ministry of the Environment (2000), 'The Swedish Environmental Objectives – Interim Targets and Action Strategies, Summary of Gov. Bill 2000/01:130' (http://www.miljo.regeringen.se/english/public.htm).
Ministry of the Environment (2000), 'Signs of Sustainability – Finland's indicators for sustainable development 2000', www.vyh.fi/eng/environ/sustdev/indicat/inds2000.htm
Ministry of Foreign Affairs (1998), 'National Environmental Policy Plan 3 – The Summary', The Hague, Netherlands.
Ministry of Housing, Spatial Planning and the Environment (1996), 'Dutch Bill Extending the Environmental Management Act to Provide for Environmental Reporting' (English trans.), The Hague.
Ministry of Housing, Spatial Planning and the Environment (no year), 'Environmental Reporting Decree', Explanatory Memorandum.
Minsch, J. (1996), 'Nachhaltige Entwicklung – Idee und Kernpostulate', in A.G. Absenger (ed.), *Zur ökolgischen Verantwortung; Natur und Geld*, Schriftenreihe zur Lehrerbildung im berufsbildenden Schulwesen, Heft 159, Pädagogisches Institut des Gundes, Vienna.
Mitchell, A. (1983), *The Nine American Lifestyles*, New York: Warner.
Moffatt, I. *et al.* (2001), 'Sustainable Prosperity: Measuring Resource Efficiency', Report to EC Department of the Environment, University of Stirling.
Monczka, J. and J. Morgan (1997), 'What's Wrong With Supply Chain Management?', *Purchasing*, January.
Montesquieu, Baron de (1748), *The Spirit of the Laws*, (reprinted 1989), Cambridge: Cambridge University Press.
Moriguchi, Y., S. Matsui and A. Saito (2000), '3-Dimensional Physical Input Output Tables for Environmental and Resources Analysis', 11th Conference Reports of Pan-Pacific Association of Input–Output Studies (PAPAIOS), 123–7, Sendai, 3–4 November (in Japanese).

Mündl, A., H. Schütz, W. Stodulski, J. Sleszynski and M.J. Welfens (1999), 'Sustainable Development by Dematerialization in Production and Consumption – Strategy for the new environmental policy in Poland', Report 3, Institute for Sustainable Development, Warsaw.

Muukkonen, J. (2000), 'TMR, DMI and Material Balances, Finland 1980–1997', Eurostat working paper no. 2/2000/B/1.

Nakata, T. and A. Lamont (2001), 'Analysis of the Impacts of Carbon Taxes on Energy Systems in Japan', *Energy Policy,* **29**, 159–66.

Natuur en Milieu and VNO-NCW (1997), 'The Public Environmental Report', a guidance document for drawing up public environmental reports as defined in the Act of 10 April 1997.

Neitzel, H., U. Landmann and M. Pohl (1994), *Das Unweltverhalten der Verbraucher: Daten und Tendenzen*, Berlin: UBA (The Federal Environmental Agency of Germany).

Nelson, R. (ed). (1993), *National Innovations Systems: A Comparative Analysis*, New York and Oxford: Oxford University Press.

North, D.C. (1990), 'A Transaction Cost Theory of Politics', *Journal of Theoretical Politics*, **2** (4), 355–67.

NRW decree (1998), 'Decree by the Minister for Construction and Living of Northrhine-Westphalia from 21.12.1998: Environmental Sound Construction of the State. Ministerial Gazette for the State Northrhine-Westphalia from 26. January 1999, no. 2, Duesseldorf' (Runderlass des Ministers für Bauen und Wohnen des Landes Nordrhein-Westfalen vom 21.12.1998: Umweltschonendes Bauen des Landes. Ministerialblatt fuer das Land Nordrhein-Westfalen vom 26. Januar 1999, Nr. 2, Duesseldorf).

Oates, W. (2001), 'Fiscal and Regulatory Competition: Theory and Evidence', paper prepared for the September 2001 Meeting of the Verein für Socialpolitik, Magdeburg.

OECD (1998), Policy Brief: 'Sustainable Development: A Renewed Effort by the OECD', 8, Paris: OECD.

OECD (2002), *Environmental Performance Review Japan: Conclusions and Recommendations*, Paris: OECD.

Ostrom, E. (2000), 'Collective Action and the Evolution of Social Norms', *Journal of Economic Perspectives*, **14** (3), 137–58.

Pacchi, C. (1998), 'Stakeholder enrolment and participation', paper at the Greening of Industry Network Conference, 15–18 November, Rome.

Pauli, G. (1998), 'Technology Forecasting and Assessment: The Case of Zero Emissions', *Technological Forecasting and Social Change*, **58**, 53–62.

Peters, T. (1996), 'Environmental Awareness in Car Design', in *Design for Environmentally Safe Automative Products and Processes*, Society of Automotive Engineers, USA.

Petersen, R. and H. Diaz-Bone (1998), *Das Drei-Liter-Auto*, (The Three-Litre-Car) Berlin, Basel, Boston: Birkhäuser Verlag.

Petersen, R. and K.O. Schallaböck (2001), 'Bedeutung der klimawirksamen Emissionen des PKW-Verkehrs und Bewertung von Minderungsstrategien', (Relevance of Climate-Influencing Emissions of Car Transport and Evaluation of Reduction Strategies), Wuppertal, on behalf of Porsche AG.

Pfeiffer, C. (2000), 'Shelter Germany – Project Report', SusHouse Project, University of Hannover, Lehrstuhl Markt und Konsum, Delft University of Technology, TBM Faculty, Delft.

Pischon, A. and D.G. Liesgang (1998), *Integrierte Managementsysteme für Qualität, Umweltschutz und Arbeitssicherheit*, Berlin: Springer.

Plante, M. (1999), 'SMILE – A Concept Car by Greenpeace', Graduation Report, Dfs Program, Faculty of Industrial Design Engineering, Delft University of Technology.

Poldy, F. and B. Foran (1999), 'Resource flows: the material basis of the Australian economy', Commonwealth Scientific and Industrial Research Organization (CSIRO) Canberra (unpublished manuscript).

Porter, M. and C.v.d. Linde (2001), 'Green and Competitive: Ending the Stalemate', in E.v.d. Wubben (ed.), *The Dynamics of the Eco-Efficient Economy*, Cheltenham, UK and Northampton, MA: Edward Elgar, pp. 33–55.

Powell, A. (2000), 'Greening the Supply Chain', in R. Hillary (ed.). *Small and Medium-Sized Enterprises and the Environment-Business Imperatives*, Sheffield: Greenleaf Publishing.

Prognos (1995), 'Die Energiemärkte Deutschlands im zusammenwachsenden Europa, Perspektiven bis zum Jahr 2020', in Auftrag des Bundesministeriums für Wirtschaft, Basle.

Prognos, EWI (1998), 'Die längerfristige Entwicklung der Energiemärkte im Zeichen von Wettbewerb und Umwelt. Trendskizze', Studie im Auftrag des BMWi, Basle, Cologne.

Prognos, EWI (1999), 'Die längerfristige Entwicklung der Energiemärkte im Zeichen von Wettbewerb und Umwelt', Studie im Auftrag des BMWi, Basle, Cologne.

Radermacher, W. (1998), 'Material Flow Accounting – Input into the Decision Process for Sustainable Development', in Bringezu *et al.* (eds), *Analysis for Action: Support for Policy towards Sustainability by Material Flow Accounting*, Wuppertal Special 6, Wuppertal Institute, pp.38–56.

Rat der Europäischen Union (2001), 'Richtlinie des Europäischen Parlamentes zur Förderung der Stromerzeugung aus erneuerbaren Energien im Elektrizitätsbinnenmarkt', Dokument 13100/00, Brüssels.

Ren, Y. (2000), 'Japanese Approaches to Environmental Management: Structural and Institutional Features', *International Review for Environmental Strategies*, **1** (1), 79–96.

Reusswig, F. (1994), *Lebensstile und Ökologie: gesellschaftliche Pluralisierung und alltagsökologische Entwicklung unter besonderer Berücksichtigung des Energiebereichs*, Frankfurt a.M.: Verlag für Interkulturelle Kommunikation.

Robért, K.-H., B. Schmidt-Bleek, J. Aloisi de Larderel, G. Basile, L. Jansen, R. Kuehr, P. Price Thomas and M. Suzuki (2002), 'Strategic Sustainable Development – Selection, Design and Synergies of Applied Tools', *Journal of Cleaner Production*, **10**, 197–214.

Ropke, Inge (1999), 'The dynamics of willingness to consume', *Ecological Economics*, **28**, 399–420.

Rosenkranz, B. and E. Castello (1992), *Leitfaden für gesunde Textilien*, Hamburg: Rowoht Verlag.

Rosenkranz, B., C. Becktepe, T. Strütt-Bringmann (eds) (1989), 'Der Stoff, aus dem die Kleider sind. Die Verbraucher-Initiative', Bonn.

Russel, T. (ed.) (1998), *Greener Purchasing: Opportunities and Innovations*, Sheffield: Greenleaf Publishing.

Sachs, W. (1999), *Planet Dialectics – Explorations in Environment and Development*, Halifax, Nova Scotia: Fernwood Publishing; Johannesburg: Witwatersrand University Press; London & New York: Zed Books.

Sachs, W., R. Loske, M. Linz *et. al.* (1998), *Greening the North*, New York: Zed Books.

Schafer, A. and D. Victor (2000), 'The Future Mobility of the World Population', *Transportation Research A*, **34** (3), 171–205.

Schalläböck, K.O. (1990), 'Limitierung des spezifischen Treibstoffverbrauchs der Neufahrzeuge' (Limitation of New Cars' Energy Intensity), in Enquête-Kommission 'Vorsorge zum Schutz der Erdatmosphäre' des Deutschen Bundestages (ed.), *Energie und Klima*, vol. 7, Konzeptionelle Fortentwicklung des Verkehrsbereichs, Bonn: Economica Verlag, pp. 679–776.

Schaltegger, S. and F. Figge (1997), *Umwelt und Shareholder-Value*, (Environment and Shareholder-Value), Basel: University Basel.

Scherhorn, G. and L. Reisch (1999), 'Sustainable Consumption', *Journal of Economic Literature*, D10–D12, D19.

Scherhorn, G., L. Reisch and S. Schrödl (1997), *Wege zu nachhaltigen Konsummustern: Überblick über den Stand der Forschung und vorrangige Forschungsthemen*, Marburg: Metropolis Verlag.

Schlegelmilch, Kai (ed.) (1999), *Green Budget Reform in Europe. Countries at the Forefront*, Berlin, Heidelberg and New York: Springer Verlag.

Schmidheiny, S. (ed.) (1992), *Changing Course. A Global Perspective on Development and the Environment*, Cambridge, MA: MIT Press.

Schmidt-Bleek, F. (1994), *Wieviel Umwelt braucht der Mensch? MIPS – Das Mass für ökologisches Wirtschaften*, Boston, Basle, Berlin: Birkhäuser Verlag.

Schmidt-Bleek, F. (2000), *Das MIPS Konzept: Weniger Naturverbrauch, mehr Lebensqualität durch Faktor Zehn*, Munich: Knaur Verlag.

Schmidt-Bleek, F. and U. Tischner (1995), 'Produktentwicklung: Nutzen gestalten – Natur schonen', Schriftenreihe des Wirtschaftsförderungs-institutes (270), Vienna.

Schneidewind, U. (1998), 'Möglichkeiten und Strategien des Stoffstrommanagements im Bereich Textilien sowie Grenzen des Stoffstrommanagements', in H. Friege, C. Engelhardt, K.O. Henseling (eds), *Das Management von Stoffströmen*, Berlin, New York: Springer, pp.115–24.

Scholl, G. and S. Zundel (1999), 'Neue Nutzungskozepte für Produkte: Entwicklungsperspektiven von Strategien zur Nutzungsdauerverlängerung und Nutzungsintensivierung', *Zeitschrift für angewandte Umweltforschung ZAU*, **12** (4), 517–31.

Seifert, E.K. (1998), 'Kennzahlen zur Umweltleistungsbewertung- Der internationale ISO-14031 Standard im Kontext einer zukunftsfähigen Umweltberichterstattung', in E. Seidel, J. Clausen and E.K. Seifert (eds), *Umweltkennzahlen. Planungs-, Steuerungs- und Kontrollgrößen für ein umweltorientiertes Management*, Munich: Verlag F. Vahlen, pp.71ff.

Seifert, E.K. (2001), 'Umweltleistungsbewertung nach der ISO 14031-Entwicklungsgeschichte, Konzeption, Anwendungserfahrungen', *Umweltwirtschaftsforum*, 9. Jg. H 4, December, Berlin: Springer Verlag.

Shipper, L. and L. Fulton (2001), 'Driving a Bargain? Using Indicators to Keep Score on the Transport–Environment–Greenhouse Gas Linkages', Washington, 75th Annual Transportation Research Board Meeting.

Sobel, M.E. (1981), *Lifestyle and Social Structure: Concepts, Definitions, Analyses*, New York: Academic Press.

Spangenberg, J.H. (1995), *Ein zukunftsfähiges Europa: Towards a Sustainable Europe*, Wuppertal Paper 42, Wuppertal: Wuppertal Institute.

Spangenberg, J.H. (ed.) (1996), *Towards Sustainable Europe: A Study from the Wuppertal Institute for Friends of the Earth Europe*, 2nd revised edition, Wuppertal: Wuppertal Institute, p. 12.

Spicer, A. *et al.* (1996), 'Disassembly Modelling Used to Assess Automotive Recycling Opportunities', in *Design for Environmentally Safe Automotive Products and Processes*, Society of Automotive Engineers (ed.), USA.

Stahmer, C., M. Kuhn and N. Braun (1998), 'Physical Input–Output Tables for Germany 1990', Eurostat working papers 2/1998/B/1, Luxembourg: Eurostat.

Staiß, F. (2001), *Jahrbuch Erneuerbare Energien 2001*, Radebeul: Bierbstein Verlag.

Starik, M., G. Throop and J. Doody *et al.* (1996), 'Growing an Environmental Strategy', *Business Strategy and the Environment*, **5**, 12–21.

Statistics Bureau – Management and Coordination Agency – Government of Japan (2000) *Japan Statistical Yearbook 2000*.

Statistisches Bundesamt (Federal Statistical Office Germany) (ed.) (1997), *Zahlen und Fakten über die Bundesrepublik Deutschland 1995/96* (Figures and Facts about the Federal Republic of Germany in 1995/96), Landsberg am Lech.

Stiftung Warentest (1998), 'Energiesparlampen' (Energy Saving Bulbs), test 8/1998, pp.70–74.

Strassert, G. (1993), 'Towards an Ecological Accounting of the Provision-Transformation-Restitution Cycle', in J.C. Dragan, E.K. Seifert and M.C. Demetrescu (eds), *Entropy and Bioeconomics*, Milano: Nagard, pp. 507–15.

Statsregnskab for finansåret (1998), www.oecs.dk/bevillingslove/docshelf?shelf=fl98.com

Takala, T. and P. Pallab (2000), 'Individual, Collective and Social Responsibility of the Firm', *Business Ethics: A European Review*, **9** (2), 109–18.

Tempelman, E. (1999), 'Sustainable Transport and Advanced Materials', PhD Thesis, Eburon Delft.

Teramoto, Y. and C. Benton (2000), 'New Development Model for a Post-Matured Japanese Industrial Sector', in F.-J. Richter (ed.) (2000), *The East Asian Development Model, Economic Growth, Institutional Failure and the Aftermath of the Crisis*, London: Macmillan Press, pp. 297–312.

Thomas, S., L. Carlos, A. Pierluigi and L. Pagliano (2000), 'The Possibilities for Policy Supporting IRP and DSM in the Liberalized Internal European Electricity and Gas Markets', in American Council for an Energy-Efficient Economy: Efficiency & Sustainability (ed.), *Proceedings of the ACEEE 2000 Summer Study on Energy Efficiency in Buildings*, Washington, DC: American Council for an Energy-Efficient Economy (ACEEE).

TREMOD (2001a), 'Daten- und Rechenmodell: Schadstoffemissionen aus dem motorisierten Verkehr in Deutschland 1980–2020' (Data and Calculation Model: emission of pollutants from motorised transport in Germany 1980–2020).

TREMOD (2001b), Transport Emission Estimation Model', on behalf of the Umweltbundesamt; from 1993, latest update November 2001.

UBA (Umweltbundesamt) (1997), *Nachhaltiges Deutschland. Wege zu einer dauerhaft umweltgerechten Entwicklung*, Berlin: Erich Schmidt Verlag.

UBA (Umweltbundesamt) (2000), *Umweltbewusstsein in Deutschland – Ergebnisse einer repräsentativen Bevölkerungsumfrage*, Berlin: Bundesministerium für Umwelt, Naturschutz und Reaktorsicherheit.

Ueta, K. (1997), 'An Economic Analysis for Designing Environmental Tax System', *Keizai Bunseki* (Economic Analysis) no. 153.

UK Roundtable on Sustainable Development (1998), 'A Stakeholder Approach to Sustainable Business', London.

Umweltbundesamt (2000), 'EMAS in Germany – Report on Experience 1995 to 1998', Berlin (German version 1999).

Underhill, P. (1999), *Why We Buy. The Science of Shopping*, New York, Simon and Schuster.

UNDP (1997), Human Development Report 1997, Oxford: Oxford University Press.

UNDP (1998), Human Development Report 1998, Oxford: Oxford University Press.

UN-EMA Group (2001), *Environmental Management Accounting Procedures and Principles*, ed. UNDSD, New York.

UNEP (1995), 'Environmental management tools', *Industry and Environment*, **18** (2–3), 1–10.

UNEP Division of Technology, Industry and Economics (1997), 'Developing better systems for communicating environmental best practice in business', final report, Paris.

United Nations (1993), *Integrated Environmental and Economic Accounting*, New York: United Nations.

United Nations (1994), *Industrial Commodity Statistics Yearbook: Production and Consumption Statistics*, New York: UN, p.931.

United Nations (1997), 'Special Session of the UN General Assembly (the 19th UNGASS)', June, New York.

United Nations (1999), 'The Global Compact and the Environment' (http://www.unglobalcompact.org).

Update (2000), 'DaimlerChrysler Mandates ISO 14001 to Entire Supply Chain', *Update News and Information on ISO and the Environment*, **7** (11), November.

Volkswagen AG (2000), *Political News*, **2000** (4), 7.

Wallace, D. (1995), 'Japan', *Environmental Policy and Industrial Innovation. Strategies in Europe, the US and Japan*, London: Earthscan Publications, pp. 93–110.

Wallau, F. (2000), 'Systematisierung von Finanzierungsmodellen für eine kostenlose Rücknahme von Altprodukten dargestellt am Beispiel der Altautoentsorgung', in *Müll und Abfall*, **2**, 89–94.

Wallbaum, H. *et al.* (1999), 'The Renovation of a Building – A Chance for Climate Protection and the Labour Market', Wuppertal Institute for

Climate, Environment and Energy study on behalf of the trade union for building, agriculture, forestry and the environment and Greenpeace.

Watanabe, C. (1999), 'Systems Option for Sustainable Development-Effect and Limit of the Ministry of International Trade and Industry's Efforts to Substitute Technology for Energy', Research Policy, **28**, 719–49.

Weaver, P. *et al.* (2000), *Sustainable Technology Development*, Sheffield: Greenleaf Publishing.

Weizsäcker, E.U. von, A. Lovins and H. Lovins (1997), *Factor Four: Doubling Wealth – Halving Resource Use*, London: Earthscan.

Wilhite, H., H. Nakagami and C. Murakoshi (1996), 'The dynamics of changing Japanese energy consumption patterns and their implications for sustainable consumption', *Proceedings from the ACEEE 1996 Summer Study on Energy Efficiency in Buildings,* Washington, DC: American Council for an Energy Efficient Economy.

Wilhite, H., E. Shove, L. Lutzenhiser and W. Kempton (2000), 'The legacy of twenty years of demandside management: we know more about individual behaviour but next to nothing about demand', in E. Jochem, J. Stathaye and D. Bouilee (eds), *Society, Behaviour and Climate Change Mitigation*, Dordrecht: Kluwer Academic Press.

Wohlfahrt, W. (1999), *Der Weg zum Umweltmanagementsystem. Gegenüberstellung von Öko-Auditverordnung und DIN EN ISO 14001*, Berlin, Vienna, Zurich: Beuth Verlag.

Woods, J. (2000), 'Equity Finance of Residential Real Estate: A Potential Market Transformation Program'. American Council for an Energy Efficient Economy (ed.), *Proceedings 2, Residential Buildings: Program Design, Implementation and Evaluation*, Washington, DC.

World Bank (2000), *The World Bank Approach to the Environment*, Washington DC: World Bank.

World Business Council for Sustainable Development (WBCSD) (1998), 'Eco-efficiency Metrics and Reporting', Eco-efficiency brief no. 1, Geneva, June.

World Business Council for Sustainable Development (WBCSD) (2000), 'Eco-Efficiency Indicators and Reporting' http:wbcsd.org, Geneva.

World Commission on Environment and Development (WCED) (1987), *Our Common Future*: The Brundtland Report on Environment and Development, Oxford: Oxford University Press.

Wuppertal Institute *et al.* (2000), 'Completing the Market for Least-Cost Energy Services: Strengthening Energy Efficiency in the Changing European Electricity and Gas Markets', A study co-funded by the European Commission (DGXVII, SAVE programme). Project Final Report, Wuppertal.

Wuppertal Institute (2001), 'Application of European-Based Policies on Resource Flows and Energy to Japanese Sustainable Development Policies', Interim Report, part of Collaboration Projects under the trust of the Economic

Planning Agency of Japan and Mitsubishi Research Institute, Wuppertal: Wuppertal Institute.
Wuppertal Institut/Öko-Institut (1998), 'Der Beitrag des Sektors Bauen und Wohnen für den Klimaschutz', Gutachten im Auftrag des Bauministeriums NRW, Wuppertal.
Wuppertal Institut/Öko-Institut (2000), 'Bewertung eines Ausstiegs aus der Kernenergie aus klimapolitischer und volkswirtschaftlicher Sicht', Endbericht im Auftrag des Bundesministeriums für Umwelt, Naturschutz und Reaktorsicherheit, Wuppertal.
Wüstenhagen, R., A. Villiger and A. Meyer (1999), 'Die Landkarte des ökologischen Massenmarktes: Eine Orientierungshilfe in Sachen Ökologisierung des Einzelhandels', in IÖW/VÖW (eds), *Ökologisches Wirtschaften*, **1**, 27–9.
Wüstenhagen, R., A. Meyer and A. Villinger (2000), *Jenseits der Öko-Nische*, Basel: Birkhäuser Verlag.
Wüstenhagen, R., A. Meyer and A. Villiger (2003), 'The Sustainability Roadmap: A Tool to Analyse the Transition from Eco-Niche to Mass Market', Paper presented at the Greening of Industry Network Conference, San Francisco, CA, 12–15 October.
Yamamoto, R. (2001), *Sustainable Company. Successful Business Models and Eco-Services in the Century of the Environment* (in Japanese), Tokyo: Tokyo University.
ZMP, Arbeitsgemeinschaft Ökologischer Landbau, Stiftung Ökologie und Landbau (1999), 'Zentrale Markt- und Preisberichtstelle für Erzeugnisse der Land-, Forst- und Ernährungswirtschaft GmbH', Customer Services Department, Bonn.
ZMP, Arbeitsgemeinschaft Ökologischer Landbau, Stiftung Ökologie und Landbau (2003), 'Zentrale Markt – und Preisberichtstelle für Erzeugnisse der Land-, Forst-und Ernährungswirtschaft GmbH', Bonn.

INTERNET SOURCES

http://www.bmvbw.de/Leitfaden-nachhaltiges-Bauen-.565.htm
http://www.detnaturligasteget.se
http://www.idis2.com
http://www.kompetenzzentrum-iemb.de
http://www.press.detr.gov.uk/0101/0028.htm
http://www.sozialestadt.de
http://www.sustainable-devleopment.gov.uk/indicators/headline/index.htm
http://www.unglobalcompact.org/Portal/Default.asp
http://www.zeri.org

Index